Praise for
Better Teams

"*Build Better Teams* is an insightful book offering leaders a compelling and practical team building 'code' to optimize team performance. Starting with a riveting extreme case study of a team that hiked the entire Amazon, the book is refreshingly grounded in the academic research on what makes teams effective. The book illuminates the challenging relational work that drives great teamwork and provides a well-constructed way forward through this complexity."

—PROFESSOR AMY C. EDMONDSON, Harvard Business School, and author of *The Fearless Organization: Creating Psychological Safety in the Workplace for Learning, Innovation, and Growth*

"As a fast-growing SME scaling organically over the past few years, I found myself reaching out to George and his team to better understand how to grow, gel, and retain my growing and diverse team. The code he gave us, with a simple method and the clear scientific base, immediately made sense. We soon found we were able to galvanize our team and even improve our recruitment model. The results are clear: under lockdown, we increased our team by 30 percent, doubled sales, and won a Queens Award for Enterprise. Implementing the code in this book has had a significant impact on this positive growth."

—ADRIAN THOMPSON, CEO and Founder, image HOLDERS Ltd

"In an age where the solving of vital problems depends more than ever on teams of teams, we have in this a serious book that brings the field of group dynamics into the present. Not only does the book review other models of teamwork, but it builds effectively on them to provide a model that is ready to deal with the ever-growing complexity that organizations will face. Adaptive behavior will not come through great individual heroes but though effectively managed fluid systems of teams. This book is an important addition to the group dynamics literature."

—EDGAR H. SCHEIN, Professor Emeritus MIT Sloan School of Management, and coauthor with Peter Schein of *Organizational Culture and Leadership*, 5th Ed. (2017), *Humble* Leadership (2018), and *Humble Inquiry*, Revised Ed. (2021)

"Build Better Teams is a hugely refreshing and inspirational addition to the practice of team-building, being strongly grounded in academic research, accessible, and fun. My personal engagement with the Code was seriously transformational, enabling me to mainstream the values that mattered to me and my team, and to capture and promote the diversity, the individual egos, and talents and create a thriving, single-acting team for which anything seemed possible. This complex and turbulent 20-first century is an age for inclusion and collaboration, and this new work is a powerful tool. I recommend it to all teams and team-builders. It's a book that will remain on my desk, not on my bookshelf!"

—PROFESSOR MIKE HARDY MBE, Chair of the International Leadership Association and a visiting scholar at Yale University's International Leadership Center

"I absolutely loved reading *Build Better Teams*. It all made perfect sense to me as George Karseras and I have been very successfully using the code described in the book for a long time now. Karseras rightfully emphasizes in his book the importance of understanding shared goals and the importance of sub-teaming. In starting here with Get Set rather than initially focusing on the relationship stuff, he really does set up teams to succeed from the word 'go.' The speed of technology transformation and change now means we simply have to work more autonomously in sub-units, and the emphasis and help Get Better Teams provides here is notable. I recommend his book wholeheartedly."

—JACKIE LEIPER, MD of Pensions, Stockbroking and Distribution, Scottish Widows (Lloyds Banking Group plc FTSE 100)

"*Build Better Teams* is an incredibly helpful book for leaders of small businesses who, like us, want their teams to win against the competition. The book provides an uncomplicated, entertaining, step by step approach to building the high-performing team. We know first-hand the code George provides really does work, and so we heartily recommend this book as a must-read for any ambitious small business owner."

—WILL LEWIS AND DOM HORRIDGE, Directors of Obi Property Agency, Niche Agency Team of the Year Property Awards 2019

"I've used 'the code' within *Build Better Teams* with my teams and can confirm this highly readable book does exactly what it says on the tin—it helps build better teams to generate impressive commercial success. *Build Better Teams* offers a simple and effective way to avoid so many of the bear traps that executive level teams can fall into. I heartily recommend it to any leader of any team."

—ADRIAN GRACE, former CEO AEGON UK (AEGON NV Fortune 500)

"There are over 5.2 million research papers looking at every aspect of team performance, leadership/management, and development. Sadly, many people don't know what this invaluable research evidence says, all too often falling back on 'gut' feel, opinion, and consultants who engage in 'creative' hyperbole. What sets *Build Better Teams* apart is that it pulls together some of the most recent research evidence and presents it in an easy-to-digest, practical, and knowledgeable way. This book will help anyone who wants to use a more intelligent and evidence-based approach to developing better teams."

—DR. DAVID WILKINSON, Editor-in-Chief, *The Oxford Review*

"As a coach, George is engaging, insightful, honest, eloquent, driven, and motivational. All these qualities come across in this gripping quest for a simple, memorable, and actionable code to give a team the greatest chances for success."

—ROGER GRAY, former CEO, USS Investment Management; CEO, UBS Asset Management Switzerland, CIO Rothschild Asset Management

"In his book, *Build Better Teams*, George Karseras has impressively taken the dark art of building teams and simplified it into a proven scientific code. Having successfully worked with George for a number of years now, I can readily vouch for the order in which he builds teams, and especially the importance of Getting the team Set and building swift trust as the starting point. This book really is must-read leadership text for any actual or aspiring leader."

—MARK TILL, CEO and Executive Vice President, Unum International (Unum Group Fortune 500)

"It's rare to see an effective blend of hard scientific data and pragmatic relevance for leaders on the ground. *Build Better Teams* pulls off this impressive feat and provides a scientifically validated, data-driven team development plan that any leader can easily adapt to their needs. I'll be encouraging my clients to get a copy of this groundbreaking book. If you care about the effectiveness of your team, you should get a copy of the book for yourself and for other leaders in your organization."

—DR. GLEB TSIPURSKY, author of the bestsellers *Never Go with Your Gut: How Pioneering Leaders Make the Best Decisions and Avoid Business Disasters* (Career Press, 2019) and *The Blindspots Between Us: How to Overcome Unconscious Cognitive Bias and Build Better Relationships* (New Harbinger, 2020)

"George Karseras accurately identifies the key challenges faced by modern leaders in the new digital world and relates his methodology expertly to relevant anecdotes. This whole subject—made even more complex by the global COVID-19 pandemic with virtual meetings and the lack of face-to-face engagement—has exacerbated these challenges, put pressure on relationships like nothing else, and magnified the complexities associated with this form of leadership. Leading successful teams in this landscape requires an approach with clear methodology. In his book, *Build Better Teams*, Karseras proposes a novel approach which is logical, clear, and well-articulated. I commend this book to the modern-day leader as relevant and thought provoking, a must-read."

—CORIN PALMER, Performance Director, Ospreys Rugby

Build
Better
Teams

GEORGE KARSERAS

Build Better Teams

Creating Winning Teams in the Digital Age

FIU | Business Press
FLORIDA INTERNATIONAL UNIVERSITY

CORAL GABLES

Cover Design: Jermaine Lau
Layout & Design: Megan Werner
Author Photo: Emma Lewis

For permission requests, please contact the publisher at:
Mango Publishing Group
2850 S Douglas Road, 4th Floor
Coral Gables, FL 33134 USA
info@mango.bz

For special orders, quantity sales, course adoptions and corporate
sales, please email the publisher at sales@mango.bz. For trade
and wholesale sales, please contact Ingram Publisher Services at
customer.service@ingramcontent.com or +1.800.509.4887.

Build Better Teams: Creating Winning Teams in the Digital Age

Library of Congress Cataloging-in-Publication number is available
upon request
ISBN: (print) 978-1-64250-692-1, (ebook) 978-1-64250-693-8
BISAC category code BUS096000, BUSINESS &
ECONOMICS / Office Management

Printed in the United States of America

Dedicated to my most treasured team of all, Caro, Emily, Sophie and Alexander and to Dad

Table of Contents

Foreword   15

Introduction
Teams that Walk the Amazon   17

PART 1
Extreme Teaming   **24**

Chapter 1
Extreme Times for Extreme Teams   25

Chapter 2
In Search of the Holy Grail   39

PART 2
A Code for Extreme Teams   **50**

Chapter 3
Building Swift Trust   51

Chapter 4
The Code   66

Chapter 5
The Code in the Amazon   80

PART 3

Real Teaming in the Digital Age 91

Chapter 6
Digitalization and the Code 92

Chapter 7
Virtual Teaming and the Code 121

PART 4

How to Use the Code 143

Chapter 8
How to Get Set 144

Chapter 9
How to Get Safe 171

Chapter 10
How to Get Strong 196

PART 5

Teaming and The Future 222

Chapter 11
The Third Rail 223

Chapter 12
It's Our Destiny 231

Acknowledgments 240
About the Author 243
References 244

Foreword

When George asked if he could interview me for a book he was writing on teams, I visibly cringed. I've always struggled a bit when it comes to corporate leadership and team building, with all its jargon and template way of doing things. I guess I felt that it was a world that I didn't know and didn't really want to be a part of. In my mind, it went hand in hand with having to wear a suit, have a shave, and commute to work every morning—none of which have ever been very high on my bucket list.

But, having delivered "Walking the Amazon" as a motivational talk to companies all over the world about one hundred and fifty times now, focusing on things far more in my comfort zone (like enduring hardship and overcoming obstacles), there was a part of me that suspected that there might be more lessons to be wrung out of my little jaunt than the self-deprecating pub story I was currently regurgitating.

So I said, "Yes," partly out of intrigue into what things George would focus on. For my part, it's often been hard to step outside of my own story and see it with perspective in order to learn from it. Indeed, doing so might even stop me from making the same blunders on future expeditions or in other areas of work life.

The interview didn't disappoint. As someone who's always made things up as I've gone along, suddenly there appeared to be a logical framework that explained clearly and simply where I'd gone wrong with my first expedition partner Luke, and (unbeknownst to us) how my second walking partner Cho and I absolutely got it right and smashed the final two years of the expedition together, becoming such a close-knit team that I would have died for him.

It might seem that expeditions are a million miles from the workplace, but I have found that in fact, expeditions are an extraordinary training ground for life. To be able to deal with unknown challenges that you undoubtedly don't have all the answers for cannot fail to make you grow as a person, enriching your experience and capacity to deal with whatever work or life throws at you.

In *Build Better Teams*, George has tapped into a very simple and usable code to harness all the lessons of yesterday in order to prepare you to build the very best teams of tomorrow. George has cleverly brought this code to life with his stories and examples. He presents a modern-day code that parallels a societal trend toward increased vulnerability, honesty, and compassion. As I have grown to know George, I can tell you it's also written by someone with these very same characteristics; as a result, it's a book that has both depth and integrity.

The code in this book really will help anyone who works in a team environment and I suspect will prevent them from falling into the same pitfalls that I plunged into time and time again in the jungle. I wish all the leaders and future leaders out there the very best of luck!

—ED STAFFORD, LEICESTERSHIRE, ENGLAND, 2021

Teams that Walk the Amazon

On April 2nd, 2008, two friends, Ed Stafford and Luke Collier, set out to complete one of the most audacious expeditions ever undertaken.[1] They intended to walk the entire 4,000-mile length of the Amazon River, and to be the first humans ever to have completed such a journey. To gain a Guinness World Record, they had to complete the entire journey by foot and avoid making any progress by any other means. Nobody thought it was possible. The expedition community felt it was just too long and the terrain too challenging. They wouldn't be able to carry the necessary food and be sufficiently safe from injury, attack, malnutrition, or disease. There was danger everywhere—caiman, killer bees, bogs, jaguars, bullet ants, scorpions, spiders, anacondas, and poisonous snakes. If these didn't get them, there were aggressive tribes and armed drug runners, neither of which would think twice about killing them on the spot. The National Geographical Society refused to sponsor them, saying the trip was "impossible." Fixers in Brazil believed the trip too dangerous and that the trekkers, although both experienced, would probably die. They refused to have anything to do with them.

Despite all the doubters, Ed and Luke believed, secured the necessary sponsorship, and set off with guides from the Peruvian coastal town of Camaná to start their adventure of a lifetime. They had forecast a year-long trek through Peru, Colombia, and Brazil. But after only three months, their relationship became so fractured, that Luke decided he didn't want to continue and returned home, leaving Ed to carry on without him.

Many guides came and went as Ed progressed until he met Gadiel "Cho" Sanchez Rivera Cho, a local Peruvian forestry worker. Cho agreed to guide Ed for five days but ended up walking with him for two years. They hacked through jungle, swam and paddled across rivers (always back tracking so they didn't gain meters), survived several near-death experiences until, on August 9, 2010, they finally arrived at the Amazon's mouth at the Atlantic coastal town of Marudá, Brazil. The walk had taken Ed 859 days and he had clocked over 6,000 miles.

Sir Ranulph Fiennes described the trip as *"truly extraordinary...in the top league of expeditions past and present."*[2] Stafford was announced as one of National Geographic Adventurers of the Year, 2010 and European Adventurer of the Year, 2011.[3;4] Soon after he was awarded the MBE. He has since written several books and has starred in several expedition and survival series on the Discovery Channel.

This is a story of incredible bravery, persistence, self-belief, and resilience. It's no wonder that Ed is a popular speaker on the corporate conference circuit. He's got one hell of a story to tell, and he tells it extremely well—with humility, charisma, and candor.

More quiet and unassuming compared to other well-known media stars in the survival field, Ed has proven he is the real deal. I wanted to speak to him for different reasons, though. It wasn't his heroics that really interested me, impressive and awe-inspiring as they were. It was the story of team-working that most fascinated me. The team he formed with Luke, one of his closest friends, crashed and burned spectacularly after only three months, yet the team he formed with Cho, whom he'd only just met, worked so well it continued for two years right up to the end. Why was that? What can we learn from what went so dramatically wrong that then went so dramatically right? I wanted to speak to Ed and find out more.

I felt any learning I could extract from Ed's story would be highly relevant to today's teams because the circumstances that he and his respective teams faced, were very similar to those that teams face today. In the first instance, even though on face value, the team only amounted to two core permanent members, Ed and Luke, and then Ed and Cho, both teams resembled today's project and cross-functional teams, where additional members come and go through the lifespan of the team. They hired hundreds of guides and translators, without whom the trip would simply not have succeeded. The diversity of these teams was obvious. Ed and Luke were white Anglo Saxon, the guides were indigenous, and Cho looked quite different, being of Afro-Peruvian descent, and was considered very much mixed race. Ed was referred to as "Gringo" and Cho as "Negro."

Like most workplace teams, they had to manage stakeholders, all outside of the jungle, in the form of sponsors, press, and the general public, whom they had to rely on to fund the walk. These relationships were virtual. Laptops and phones were their only means of communication.

They were also operating in the most VUCA of environments, characterized by Volatility, Uncertainty, Complexity, and Ambiguity. They had a plan, but it was highly unstable, and they actually had no idea how long the walk would take them. They had guessed about a year. It took over two. They thought they'd walk not that much more than the 4,000 miles of river; in fact, they walked 6,000. They had several known unknowns and a multitude of unknown unknowns to deal with. They had no way of predicting the reactions they would receive from tribes, drug runners, village guides, the thickness of the jungle, nor the weather conditions, especially water levels. On one occasion they called ahead by radio to give advance warning to a tribe that they were arriving and who meant to harm them. They were told if a white person comes through, they would be killed immediately. So they tried to circumnavigate the community using their rafts but were chased by five or six boats full of indigenous people who caught up with them on a sandbank.

"They ran towards us at high speed in a state of panic and aggression, pointing shotguns, waving machetes, and aiming loaded bows and arrows in our direction. If we had acted aggressively, I have no doubt they would have killed us."

—ED STAFFORD

Ed and Cho were escorted at gun and arrow point back to the village, and only allowed to leave after hours of explaining their electronic equipment to the tribe. As part of their release, they also had to give up their only machete and agree to hire the tribe's chief and his brother as guides.

On other occasions, Ed was arrested for both drug smuggling and murder—the latter occurring when the team had coincidentally arrived at an isolated settlement the same day as a community member had gone missing. He was locked in a wooden hut for eight hours before being allowed to continue his journey.

Expedition success was determined by managing multiple interdependencies. The terrain would determine their route, which would determine their food supplies, which would determine where and when they had to restock and the guides they could afford to feed. They would sometimes navigate to places to restock supplies only to find the entire area and communities within cleared by deforestation. On one occasion in Brazil, this set them back 11 days, forcing them to live off the land, foraging for palm hearts and fishing. The duration of their journey would determine when they ran out of money and their location would determine whether they were in a position connect to Wi-Fi or make calls to raise more funds. For many corporate teams, this will all sound very similar—not knowing how long the "project" will actually take, having to work to a budget that quickly becomes unrealistic, not knowing what will be discovered from the tech until it is discovered, not knowing how the work will be received by various stakeholder groups. Having to exploit the resources available at the same time as finding ways to create new resources. Always having to move and adapt without knowing what this adaption will actually look like. Dealing with fatigue. The list goes on.

As well as sharing the challenge of working in VUCA-type environments, Ed's team were also subjected to relentless "compliance" checks. They didn't just have a mountain of bureaucracy to complete before they started, they had it throughout their journey, sometimes when they expected it while crossing borders or entering new districts, but sometimes unexpectedly when they entered villages where they were made to wait for hours while the elders checked out what they were carrying and confirmed they were safe to pass through. As Ed commented to me:

> "At one point we were stopped and held because the Queen had not personally signed my passport!"

They were held in a hut for twenty-four hours before eventually being freed. And we think compliance is too strict in our organizations?!

Just like today's teams, they also had to manage their mental health in the most pressing of circumstances. Being bitten to shit by mosquitos, lost in their own thoughts for days and days, coming up against hurdle after hurdle, and dealing with physical exhaustion, sleep deprivation, and financial pressures all took their toll.

> "For days and days, I felt lost in my thoughts, extremely negative, alone and utterly miserable. I was unquestionably depressed."
>
> **—ED STAFFORD**

Ed's Amazon walk struck me as a wonderful metaphor for something I've come to realize in my twenty-five year consulting career: that team working is no walk in the park. Ed and Luke were young, fit, motivated, and good mates, so why did they fail? And what explains the success of Ed and Cho as a team? While it's unlikely "teaming intelligence" explained Ed and Cho's success, it was almost certainly a lack of it that explained why Ed and Luke bombed out so spectacularly. We'll see over the course of the first section of the book that they probably should have never set off together in the first place.

The purpose of this book is to help today's leader, regardless of level, industry, or type of organization, build any team, at any stage in its existence into a more successful entity. It's a book for both the seasoned leader and the aspiring leader. It's been written to stimulate thinking, to be an enjoyable read but more than anything else, to be of help to the Ed's of this world. It's written for good people who lead or will lead good people who are looking to create something amazing—a tight, highly-functional, caring, and successful team.

The two chapters in Part One describe the six extreme conditions of our time and what's now needed for teams to thrive in this environment, given these and a poor track record in team working.

Part Two is all about a solution to the challenges presented in Part One. Chapter Three explores the critical component of modern team-working— the acquisition of Swift Trust—while Chapter Four introduces the first ever science-based team building code that delivers swift trust and describes how it meets all the requirements a code has to satisfy. Chapter Five then applies the code, to explain, almost perfectly, what happened to Ed and Luke and then Ed and Cho in the Amazon.

Part Three contains Chapters Six and Seven, exploring the effects of digitalization and virtual working on teams and what we can expect to happen that will affect how teams will work in the future. They will highlight which parts of the code are most important to focus on in both environments.

In Part Four we delve into each of the three main component parts of the code, Chapter Eight helps you get your team "set," Chapter Nine helps you get it "safe" and Chapter Ten, how to get it "strong."

Finally, we turn to the future in Part Five where we challenge two outdated but commonly held assumptions about teambuilding in Chapter 11 before offering hope and optimism that despite scary times, we'll all be OK in the end.

While most of us are not confronted by flesh-eating piranhas at our places of work—even though some of us could probably point to a few colleagues who would qualify—the next chapter will illustrate in more detail how we also face hostile conditions like those faced by our Amazon walkers. Building our teaming intelligence starts here, understanding the terrain we are walking through.

PART 1

Extreme Teaming

Chapter 1

Extreme Times for Extreme Teams

The teams Ed formed with Luke and then Cho, qualified for "extreme team" status as lives were at stake. Not many of us would have put our hands up and volunteered to join this type of team. Yet so many of us, in our own way, belong to extreme teams. Even though we may not be risking our lives, many of the conditions faced in the Amazon in 2008 are very similar to those we now endure. Much of Ed's success revolved around his team's perseverance, mental strength, resourcefulness, and talent to make their expedition a success. We require a bit more than these qualities to succeed. The pressures of today conspire to make teaming in our places of work so exceptionally difficult, unquestionably more so than any of us have ever experienced before. Understanding these current day dynamics will help us to equip ourselves to better deal with them.

The Digitally Transforming VUCA World

Ed and his two teams faced unknown after unknown after unknown. In our places of work, we are enduring digital transformation after digital transformation after digital transformation, each one taking us into unknown territories. Agile working, robotics, automation, and AI are all producing huge disruption as we are forced to innovate, migrate expensive architecture and shed thousands of jobs. Many organizations are now grappling with the cloud and how to best leverage it. Most teams, no matter where they sit in the value chain, are smack bang middle in the world of VUCA. The uncertainty and pace of change is so fierce, for some of us we might as well be in the jungle surrounded by flesh eating piranhas and jaguar.

Apparently, the aim of digitalizing our places of work is to leverage advances in our tech to simplify and make life easier for our customers. Most leaders of the teams I work with would say that right now, it is achieving the polar opposite. You might also point to stress, pressure, anxiety, and fatigue. As one board member of a major UK institution told me recently:

> *"It's been a relentless slog."*

For many reading this, digitalization and all that it brings means you have to move at the speed of light, rapidly learn, innovate, pivot, collaborate across boundaries and influence without positional power. Pivoting is not simply unilaterally making a change in direction and hoping that everyone else follows suit, and learning is no longer achieved simply by going on courses, taking notes, and accruing personal know-how. Both are team sports. We all have to become far more intelligent in how to team these days. We have to understand, at a far more pronounced level, how to create the conditions that *produce* team outcomes rather than individual outcomes. Ed couldn't just change direction in the jungle; he had to synchronize with the rest of the team. It'll be the same for you.

Many are of the opinion that thanks to the pace of tech, we'll never ever actually return to a steady state. That these transformations are not going away any time soon. Indeed, only last year, the 2020 Gartner Digital Enterprise Survey found that 67 percent of business leaders agreed that if their company did not become significantly more digitalized, their organizations would no longer be competitive. Most of these global senior managers were already experiencing some sort of digital transformation before they even took part in this survey. It's a miracle they had the time to complete the survey.[1]

Virtual Working

One of the consequences of tech advancement has been the adoption of virtual working. The reality is COVID-19 simply turbo boosted an already existing trend. As we all know by now, it is much tougher to lead and participate in the virtual team, or partially virtual team than a non-virtual one. It's not just a question of making sure we are presentable and sharp on screen. As we'll discover in Chapter Eight, ensuring the team is on the same page, well-coordinated, with minimum interpersonal conflict are the main challenges we face. Not so long ago I coached the executive risk team in a well-known UK financial institution and, at the same time, the CIO and his team at a well-known global software business whose clients happened to include the very same financial institution. It was ironic that in both teams, there was conflict which centered on a team member working in a certain city in Scotland. At one point I wondered if it was the same person. It turned out it wasn't someone pocketing two salaries, but the only person in both teams who was working totally remotely.

Complexity from Diversity

We all know that diversity is a good thing from a moral and ethical standpoint, but did you know that diverse teams, if well led, perform better than the more homogenous?[2-6] More diversity means more complexity, though, and more complexity, as you may have found out, usually equates to more stress. These days, you have to deal with diversity in diversity.

Age Diversity

Globally, we have seen retirement ages rise from an average of sixty to sixty-five with some forecasting it will go up to seventy-five within the next ten to fifteen years. Coupled with falling birth rates, particularly in developed countries, this means that we can expect to see the proportion of older workers, our Baby Boomers (born between 1946 and 1964) increasing.[7]

Meanwhile it has been estimated that by 2025, the younger Millennial generation (born 1980–2000), will make up 75 percent of the global workforce.[8] And let's not forget the Silent generation (born pre-1946). Mick Gibson, a postman in Derbyshire UK is still going strong at eighty! Good on him, I say. However, managers are now leading teams composed of all these generations plus Gen X (1965–1980) and Gen Zs (1995–2010) all at the same time. The inclusion of an unprecedented four different generations in the workplace, with a fifth on the way, is expected to create more complexity and ultimately more conflict to manage in the team. [9; 10]

Telling stories and anecdotes and using language that connects with all ages can't be easy, nor can employing a leadership style that works for all. Baby Boomers are generally more comfortable working alone under a chain of command and are less comfortable collaborating[11] while their Millennial team members prefer their bosses to be less paternalistic and more socially responsible.[12; 13]

Diversity of Tenure

Ed and his team saw a high turnover of guides, continually hiring new ones as they progressed along the Amazon. This was because their guides were only able to guide in the territories they knew. In our places of work, Millennials are less tolerant of role uncertainty than their older colleagues and as a result, just like Ed's guides, they move around more. They are also in a better position to move jobs as they are more likely to be single—three times more in fact than "Silents" were at comparable ages. Additionally they are far better educated and much more likely to be living in cities than their predecessors,[14] both of which provide them with even more mobility. All the above explain why they are more likely to move jobs and take on more jobs over their careers than Gen Xers, and spend less time in each job than Boomers.[15] In Western organizations, Millennials are also more ambitious, valuing faster and better career advancement[16] than Gen X who themselves value promotions more than Boomers. It seems that generations are getting more and more ambitious. Ambition is great, but it needs to be thoughtfully managed.

Unsurprisingly, employee resignations have been increasing steadily since 2012, when it was only 10.6 percent, to a five-year high of 15.5 percent. The median tenure for workers aged 25 to 34 is only 3.2 years[17] whereas for those aged sixty-five and over is over three times longer at 10.3 years. As Ed found in the Amazon, teams are now less stable and membership changes more readily.

Job Diversity

Leading a team of "full-timers" is going to be more simple and less complex than leading a team composed of workers with "portfolio careers," who hold multiple jobs. In July 2017, the number of Americans holding multiple jobs increased by 2 percent to highs not seen in 20 years.[18] Portfolio working has also increased in the UK, with one in five UK working Millennials now having two or more jobs, more than at any other time. Thanks to new technology and the flexibility created, the Gig Economy is growing exponentially.[19] One study found that 4.4 percent of British population, roughly 2.8 million workers, have worked in the gig economy in the last year.[20]

Gender Diversity

There's good news and bad news here. The good news is that we are seeing more equality, and thanks to the #MeToo movement, far more social awareness of gender equality than at any other time in our working lives. The bad news is that we are nowhere near where we need to be, and gender bias remains very alive and kicking, especially at the top of our organizations. More women than ever before are now working, over 70 percent of those aged sixteen to sixty-four are now employed at work in the UK.[21] This represents a sizeable increase from the 53 percent recorded in 1971, yet the percentage of women in senior leadership roles is meager, at only 22 percent.[22] As the head of a UK Workplace Pensions team I was working with recently confessed to me:

"The team is going well, but we have a serious diversity issue. I'm embarrassed to say I employ a team where literally every one of them is white, male and over forty-five, apart from one, who is white, male and over forty."

He would never have said this two years ago. Then again, he didn't have a female boss two years ago. Nor did he have an equality target to hit like he does now. Leading a bunch of pale, male, and stale forty-somethings may not be ethical, but it's far simpler and less complex than leading a team composed of purely male, female, gender neutral, and gender-fluid individuals—or even robots. That is not to condone homogeneity, it's just to recognize, that in one way, homogeneity makes for a far simpler life. Ignorance, as they say, can be bliss.

The truth is that despite what others may claim to the contrary, men and women are different. We differ in what we want from our leaders and in our personalities and value sets: 66 percent of women prioritize compassion as a leadership quality compared to only 47 percent of men; 61 percent of women see innovation as crucial, compared to only 51 percent of men; while 57 percent of women see ambition as an essential trait for a leader, yet only 48 percent of men regard it as essential.[23]

What is consistent, according to various global studies of tens of thousands of people is that women are more conscientious, more agreeable with others, and more anxious than men.[24] Higher scores on the *conscientiousness* continuum suggest they are more likely than men to enjoy spending time preparing, finishing important tasks straight away, paying attention to detail, and scheduling.[25] Higher scores on *agreeableness* suggest women take more of an interest in other people, care about others, feel empathy and concern for other people and enjoy helping and contributing to the happiness of other people.[25] Writing this, I realized I've just described my wife, Caro. Higher scores on neuroticism suggest women experience more stress, worry more, get upset more easily, and experience more mood shifts. Writing this I realize I'm still describing my wife, Caro.

Racial and Ethnic Diversity

Ed, Cho, and their guides were very much the ethnically diverse team. However, despite moving the dials in recent years, we are miles away from achieving the same balance in our organizations.

+ Only eighty-five of 1,050 director positions in the FTSE 100 are held by people from ethnic minorities.[26]

+ Although 14.4 percent of the working population in the UK are BAME (Black, Asian, Minority Ethnic), only 12.5 percent of employees are BAME and only six percent of management positions are held by BAME individuals.[27]

It is expected that the UK working population made up of BAME will grow over the next few years from its current level of 12.5 percent to closer to 20 percent.[27] More recently, the Black Lives Matter movement has helped put racism squarely onto board room tables.

Attending inclusion and diversity training courses is all very well, but sociologists believe that it is only really by actively encouraging interaction of diverse ethnicities in our workplaces that we will be able to build greater trust.[27]

However, they also point out that although the social trust rewards are there to be gained, bad management could also point to disaster.[28] What actually determines levels of social trust is the real-life experiences that people of diverse ethnic origin have of working with each other. If these are positive, then social cohesion and trust are high, even higher than they would be amongst more homogenous groups. However, if these are negative, then both social cohesion and trust fall even lower than they would if we didn't have ethnic diversity in our teams. The stakes are higher then. As the leader of the Commonwealth, grandmother to Prince Harry and Meghan Markel, and Queen of the United Kingdom will testify, if you're a leader of an ethnically diverse team, then you will be aware that there is much at stake in ensuring positive social experiences are had by all.

Multi-Team Diversity

If you work in a large organization then the chances are your team is now probably composed of members who also belong to other teams. Your team members are not solely "yours," yet you want them to be loyal and committed to you. The reality is they also have to be loyal and committed to other teams, too. They have to divide their attention, adapt to different leadership styles, adopt different team norms and deal with conflicting demands. In one recent study, 95 percent of team members were found to be members of more than one team and two thirds of these teams were geographically spread around the world.[29] A staggering 20 percent of employees in another study reported to be or having being members of four teams at once.[30]

Flattening structures also mean many leaders now lead larger team than they would like. Last year I worked with a very senior team in a UK financial institution of fifteen people. The ideal number for a team is between four and six. Many commentators report dysfunction when numbers exceed ten to twelve. This is because bigger teams are tougher to galvanize. In a team of fifteen, there are one-hundred-and-five relationships impacting the team's performance. The complexity of that team meant I aged five years working with them and I was only with them for two days!

Growing Societal Individualism

You may have realized this already, but we now live in a more individualistic world with less of a "team comes first" mentality and more of a "what's in it for me" mind-set. It has been calculated that individualism has increased by about 12 percent worldwide since 1960.[31] We are moving from a "We" society toward an "I" society. For many the compassion shown in the COVID-19 epidemic has been a breath of fresh air. But will it last?

Sociologists use a number of parameters including what we value and how we name our children to measure levels of individualism. In recent years, fame has been portrayed as an important and achievable value by popular tween TV shows, and ranked the highest of tweens' goals, when not long ago it was ranked only fifteenth.[32] Americans and Brits are now using more individual names to name their children.[33] There are less Arnolds and Barbaras[34] and more children named Genesis and Brixton. In the UK, we are seeing common names moving toward extinction. In 2017 there were 1,202 baby girls called Kirsty, while in 2019 there were only 11, a whopping 99.1 percent decrease.[35] Even in Japan, famously one of the more collectivist societies, the number of popular letters in names has gone up from 2004 to 2013, but the number of popular ways of pronouncing those letters has gone down, meaning that people are coming up with new ways of pronouncing common letters to form unique names.

While our societies are becoming increasingly better educated and increasingly wealthier,[37; 38] sociologists believe we are correspondingly becoming more and more selfish.[39; 40] Most countries are witnessing community spirit diminishing and compassion being replaced by personal ambition. As I was only saying to Prince Charles and Beyoncé the other evening, more and more of us are now characterized by self-promotion, whatever the cost to others.[41]

Meanwhile, at the more extremes, the "dark side" of personality is getting darker. Narcissists, psychopaths, and Machiavellians are not just selfish, unpleasant people, they can cause serious damage around them. Narcissists are like peacocks, believing they are special and possessing an extreme, grandiose view of their own talents and a craving for being admired by others. They tend to be arrogant, domineering, and utterly preoccupied with success and power. They are envious of others and arrogant, thinking of themselves as exceptionally talented, remarkable, and successful. Donald Trump ticks all of these boxes. Remember, he believed he should have won the Nobel Peace prize. Narcissists believe they are unique and possess an unhealthy high sense of entitlement that drives exploitative and manipulative behaviors. For some, narcissism is more than the "dark side" of individualism—it is the "extreme dark side." Think Bernie Madoff, Jeffrey Epstein, and Max Clifford for the lowest of the low. Think Lance Armstrong, Steve Jobs, and Simon Cowell for the more tainted geniuses who are also likely narcissists.

All the evidence suggests that narcissists are increasing in numbers in the workplace. A meta-analysis of data shows a near steady increase in scores on the Narcissistic Personality Inventory from 1985 to 2008.[42; 43] Twenge, one of the most prominent researchers in the field, believes the evidence that narcissism is increasing from generation to generation is overwhelming, citing results spanning 11 studies from three different countries.[44; 45]

Machiavellians meanwhile have been busy ingratiating themselves, building their power bases, exiting those who get in their way, undermining the competition, taking credit for others' work, and putting on shows of altruism in order to look compassionate. Machiavellianism also appears to be on the increase,[46; 47] and it also seems younger folk are more prone to it than the older generation.[48; 49; 50] Expect to see more of it going forward.

Finally (thank God), we have psychopaths. They are an unappetizing cocktail of narcissism and Machiavellianism, at worst, ingeniously combining cruelty and impulsivity with an urge to manipulate. If you want a bona fide pain in the backside in your team, these provide the best bang for your buck.

Unfortunately, as they are highly socially skilled and make very good first impressions, they are very adept at getting selected for senior executive roles. Equipped with plenty of charisma, smart strategic thinking and buckets of energy and self-confidence, they make for highly desirable leaders who can fake their interviews.[51] Their thick skin means they appear very much in control and are adept at showing off their strengths to others without appearing too big headed. These "faux" leaders operate often without a moral compass nor the empathy to use it. Watch out for them. They tend to be attracted to organizations in transformations as they can easily withstand conflict and stress. They possess little or no empathy, and often expect others to be equally resilient and work the same ridiculous hours as they do. In one global software organization I consult to, a recent CEO left and his staff were literally dancing on their desks.

Businesses attract them; proportionally, there are more of them here than the 1 percent found in the general population.[52] Amounts tend to vary, with one study finding 3 to 4 percent occupying the more senior business positions, while another one in Australia found 5.76 percent in white-collar management roles.[53; 54; 55] The same study also claimed that 10.42 percent of other Australian white-collar managers could also quite easily being described as not quite certifiable "psychopaths" but still "dysfunctional with psychopathic tendencies."[54] When we get to CEO land, the figures are even more staggering. It has been estimated that 20 percent of CEOs are psychopathic.[56]

As if it couldn't get any more worrying, psychopaths breed psychopathic tendencies in those who follow them—specifically bullying tendencies.[57] They are like aliens laying their eggs on Ridley Scott's space craft. They breed other ugly, toxic, fear mongering, blood curdling little monsters and increasingly competitive workplaces in our more complex, digital, and fast-paced world will surely help them prosper even more.

So in the vortex of the digitally transforming, virtual, diverse world we now live in, leaders have to build a collective spirit out of increasingly individualistic component parts, with a growing risk that some of them will prove to be largely unmanageable.

The Mental Health Challenge

As Ed and almost certainly Luke found, mental health is not easy to maintain when working in extreme environments. It's sad but true that as a species we are getting more and more depressed. We know this not just because sales of antidepressants are going through the roof but from a plethora of studies conducted in the area. Some of the data originates from the US where the prevalence of depression increased significantly between 2005 and 2017.[58; 59] In the UK, mental ill health is amongst the most common causes of long-term absence at work along with musculoskeletal injuries, stress, and acute medical conditions. In 2019, more organizations than ever listed mental ill health as a cause for both short- and long-term absence.[60] Fifty-nine percent of respondents reported mental ill health as their single greatest cause of long-term absence.[60] An astounding 79 percent of British adults in employment during 2020 experienced work-related stress, making it the most common form of stress in the UK.[61]

COVID-19 has made things worse, not better.[62] And we haven't even started to cope with the economic impact of the virus. We can expect more, not fewer mental health issues going forward. The impact on leaders? Well, put simply, leaders have to be fluent in the domain. They have to be able to do more to prevent it, do more to spot it, and do more to deal with it when it happens, not by acting as therapists, but certainly knowing when it might be occurring, how to recognize the signs, where to point people and by showing empathy and compassion.

So, we can add coping with mental health to the digital age storm, and further pressure team leaders to be able to build high levels of psychological safety to minimize mental health issues.

Regulatory Pressure

We may not have to prove the Queen signed our passports like Ed had to, but we are living in an increasingly regulated world. We have many people to thank for this: avaricious and callous sales people who miss-sold us PPI (Payment Protection Insurance); opportunists who silently sold our personal data; greedy executives who, before instructing the administrators, took bonuses instead of protecting the pensions of loyal workers; unscrupulous boards with "win at all costs" mentalities and no real regard for environmental consequence; or cyber low-life leeches who stole, by stealth, the identities and life savings of the most vulnerable.

I won't sit on the fence here; I regard anyone who gains benefit from subjecting others to pain as irreprehensible. As a psychologist, I suppose I could be a little more understanding and empathic—after all, it is quite possible that the perpetrators of these corporate crimes are simply victims of a disadvantaged past, who deserve at least some compassion and understanding. *I'm out of compassion though—my life is now so much more complicated because of all the resulting regulations. And although they are there to safeguard me—sadly it doesn't feel like it.*

A think tank recently calculated that in 2015 alone over 50,000 regulations were published in the G20 countries, the same number that were published in all four years together between 2009 and 2012.[63] A 2018 report from the RegTech Council (RTC) estimated that each week there are forty-five new regulatory related documents being issued and that the extreme regulatory growth rate they were witnessing was indeed "the new normal."[63] The number of federal regulations in the US has nearly doubled since 1975.[64] It's the same all over the globe. We work in ever more regulated organizations. The impact on our places of work is that we have to put in bureaucracy, governance, and controls to manage risks, while simultaneously having to be nimble enough to quickly pivot and adapt to the changes we are forced to make—from regulatory change or from our ever-increasing digitalized workplaces, or both. This additional pressure, stress, and complexity requires even more intelligent responses from the leaders of our teams.

These are the conditions of our time. Make no doubt about it, leaders of teams really are in the vortex of a rather perfect storm. The irony is that not only do these make it much tougher to team, but they also *require* us to be better at team working. And they demand that our teams are more curious, more open-minded, and better collaborators with other teams, to be part of a team of teams at a time when, given all of these threats, the more natural reaction might be for a team to seek refuge, play it safe, and avoid the kind of interactions and experiments it most needs to excel.

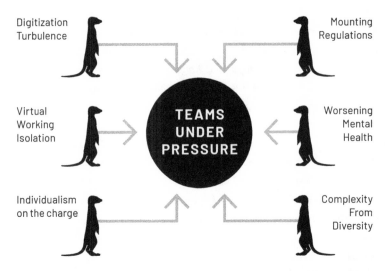

The Paradox of Pressure: Today's perfect storm paradoxically demands more open-minded, curious, and collaborative teaming.

Undoubtedly, team working has never been so important and never been so complex. If you're feeling more under pressure to get the most out of your team than you have at any time in your career, then perhaps you can now understand why. As Ed and Luke found out, help is desperately needed.

TAKEAWAYS

1. There has never been a tougher time to lead a team.

2. Challenges arising from accelerating digitalization, increased virtual working, growing diversity, societal individualism, worsening mental health, and more regulation are all conspiring to make the team leader's job far more complex, challenging, and stressful.

Chapter 2

In Search of the Holy Grail

As Ed and Luke illustrated, the track record of leaders being able to build "high performing" teams really is rather sketchy. It seems our senior leaders, in particular, have not been covering themselves in glory. Far from it, studies reveal that 79 percent of top teams have been found to be mediocre at best[1] and 60 percent of all teams fail to achieve their goals.[2] Even leaders themselves admit that only 10 percent of organizational teams are high performing.[3] In a detailed study of ninety-five teams in twenty-five leading corporations, chosen by an independent panel of academics and experts, Tabrizi, a lecturer of transformational leadership at Stanford University, found that nearly 75 percent of cross-functional teams could be described as "dysfunctional."[4] Take it from me, being given the label of being dysfunctional is not something to be proud of. Elsewhere, numerous other studies have shown that only one in five teams are considered high performing.[4] Bear in mind that all these studies were conducted before we entered this mad digitalized world. God knows what the data would tell us now. You be the judge.

So not only do our teams not function properly, but they also don't appear to be connecting with other teams that well either. This was less of an issue fifty or sixty years ago, when environments were much more predictable and orderly, and teams were by nature organized in hierarchies and functional departments. Nor was it important for Ed either. He didn't need to connect his team with other teams in the jungle. He was saved this additional complexity. But in the corporate world, building ecosystems of interconnected teams is a vital part of our everyday existence. In his book *Teams of Teams*, General Stanley McChrystal, Head of the US Joint Special Operations Task Force in 2004, shared the extent of the connectivity and coordination challenges he faced. Believing them to be sufficiently significant to be compromising mission success, he set about transforming the task force culture to become his famous "team of teams." He credited the adaptability this inter-connectivity created, as the principal reason he was able to eliminate Abu Musab al Zarqawi and to finally start winning the fight against Al Qaeda in Iraq. The reality is that these days, as McChrystal discovered, most employees neither cooperate with each other nor share their knowledge well with other departments.[5]

So if we don't have a great track record of building great teams or being part of a teams of teams, even in the most placid of times, realistically, what hope do we have that our teams can work well in today's much more challenging Amazon-like conditions? Many of leaders simply don't have the time to wait to discover the secrets of teaming. Their jobs are on the line. Their mental health is at stake.

If you are a leader, you could probably do with a bit of help. Maybe a practical tool you could rely on to guide you through this most hostile of terrains would be of some use. Perhaps even a code that you could apply to help you get the most out of your team. The type of code, if Ed and Luke had it at their disposal, would also have given them a fighting chance of succeeding together.

The Holy Grail

So where do you turn to get this code? Writers, gurus, and academics, past and present, have contributed much to the field of leadership and team building. We've got Simon Sinek's emphasis on getting in tune with our team's purpose;[6] Edgar Schein coined the phrase "psychological safety,"[7] which has more recently been researched in teams by Amy Edmondson;[8]

Brené Brown has focused our attention on vulnerability;[9] Adam Kahane writes on conflict resolution;[10] Daniel Goleman is your go-to authority on emotional intelligence in leaders;[11] Syer and Connolly[12] told us how to build a "team identity;" Roger Fisher and William Ury know how to help us collaborate;[13] Edgar Schein[14] has helped us understand the importance of challenging assumptions, and more recently with his son, Peter Schein, has emphasized the importance of humility in effective team leadership;[15] Nassim Taleb has championed getting skin in the game;[16] Fred Kofman knows about commitment-making while Peter Senge taught us all about learning;[17; 18] Jon Katzenbach and Douglas Smith introduced to us the importance of galvanizing around shared goals;[19] Peter Hawkins[20] has shone the light on "outside in" thinking; David Clutterbuck emphasizes the importance of a team development plan; Debora Meyerson[21] educated us on Swift Trust; and Robert Bruce Shaw has written about teaming in extreme conditions.[22] All of these writers, their models, and their work have been studied in detail and have informed the writing of this book.

Hundreds and hundreds of other gifted and erudite writers have also provided superb contributions in the fields of resilience, trust, strategy, communications, innovation, and an array of "hard" and "soft" skills. We're spoilt for choice! But are we? They are all brilliant contributions to the field of leadership and some of them in the field of team dynamics. But I have found no compelling way of joining all these approaches up into one kind of catch-all approach that any team leader of any team, in any organization can adopt. Up until now, there has been no sequential team building code available anywhere to help our leaders.

William Gibb Dyer, Jeffry Dyer, and William Dyer came close. They devised their Four C's Team Building Model, in which they recommend teams work through: Context, Composition, Competence, and Change Management. Their book, *Team Building*,[23] is as good a book I've read on team building. It was initially written by the late William Dyer, a colleague of Edgar Schein back in the 1960s, and a highly regarded group process academic and practitioner. It has since been refined several times over and is now in its fourth edition. Gibb and Jeffry Dyer are respected academics and consultants in the team development field, who have collaborated closely as siblings, and formerly with their father, William, to work and refine his original text. It's a wonderfully written book, full of ideas and generous practical exercises to develop corporate teams written by a tight family team. For all these reasons, their book provides a rare combination of substance and soul. It leans toward team development at the most senior levels though, as two of their four Cs are about what happens either before the team is formed or relates to the influence of the wider organizational culture on a team. All excellent and relevant stuff, yet the vast majority of team leaders don't actually sit in the C-Suite. What many of these teams most want is a tool they can use without paying consultants like me or the Dyers to guide them through their journey.

The codification of effective team working is not a new endeavor. One of the earliest models was devised by Ed Schein, who's four-stage model of team development was constructed in 1965, heavily influenced by the work of the social psychologist, Bion.[24] Extending Bion's work, Schein believed that all teams have both a social agenda, where team members want to form rewarding relationships to help task completion, and a technical agenda in which they want to complete their tasks. He believed that all relationships encapsulated both agendas and described how the team moves through four socio-technic stages:

1. **Group Formation:** characterized by a dependency on the leader to know everything and where the teams start the process of unconscious norm forming.

2. **Group Building:** characterized by what he termed "fusion assumption" where the team is consumed by efforts to show that "we like each other."

3. **Group Working and Functionality:** where these fusion assumptions become replaced by a more mature mutual acceptance of similarities and differences, and where norms begin to form as the group starts to do real work together.

4. **Group Maturity:** where the norms begin to be established as the team experiences successes, strong shared emotions, and moments of inevitable tension between maintaining comfort levels and stretching out to change and adapt.

Tuckman[25] followed Schein with his famous Forming, Norming, Storming, and Performing model. It is memorable and descriptive and still very much in use today, but it doesn't really delve into "how" leaders can excel in any of these stages, nor does it carry the same depth as Schein's maturity model. Additionally, both were devised for very different types of teams than exist today—teams that operate in more predictable, less inter-connected, fast-paced environments. They are also mainly applicable to teams that are at the forming stage. Today's team leaders require help mid-way through their team life cycles, not just at their beginning. Overall, then, these models, along with other maturity models created since, strike me as being more descriptive and interesting rather than instructive and helpful.

More recently, the charismatic Patrick Lencioni constructed his simple Five Dysfunctions approach.[26] Although popular, when we subject it to scrutiny, we will see it doesn't really hold up as a reliable code at all.

Many other comprehensive and excellent models of team working, such as David Clutterbuck's PERILL model[27] and Peter Hawkins five Cs[20] approach, allocate the component parts of "good team working" into various component parts for leaders and especially team coaches to address. Although these models are comprehensive summaries of what drives team performance, they do not actually arm leaders with a repeatable pathway through their model and they too strike me as being designed for the most senior of teams.

I believe there is much more we can do for our leaders. Team leaders these days need more than a bunch of buckets to work with; they need help to know which buckets to pick up first and what bucket to go to next. Academics have constructed detailed models that attempt to do this, but these are just far too complex to be practical, and from what I've seen, they miss a few important elements, too. I came across one team diagnostic recently that required team members to answer seventy-five questions. I came across another in flow chart mode, with so many boxes and multidirectional arrows it scared the life out of me.

So in today's rather extreme environment, it's high time we provided our leaders, whether they be expedition leaders like Ed, CEO's who run multinational companies, research heads whose teams bring drugs through clinical trials, or Mr. and Mrs. Clark who run the village shop, a set of guidelines or a code to follow that gives them the best chances of building truly amazing teams, a code that is relevant for today's crazy world. To be fit for purpose though, such a code would have to satisfy strict criteria. A bit like the search for the Holy Grail, up until now, there has simply never been a code we can turn to that satisfies these criteria.

1. Simplicity

Attention spans are shrinking. Guidelines to build an effective team have to be simple and they have to be memorable. Leaders have to be able to remember what to do in the heat of the battle. Tuckman and Lencioni unquestionably ticked this box.

2. Comprehensive and Measurable

In the UK, all cars over three years old have to pass an annual Ministry of Transport road safety test called an MOT, and when they pass, we receive back a piece of paper with a bunch of boxes that are either ticked or crossed depending on whether the car has hit one of the specified standards. If the authorized mechanic gives your car a cross, no problem, you get it fixed so that it then passes the test. Your car is then officially safe to drive. Our teams need to satisfy a test like this. Many, but not all the team development models constructed by academics contain all the right boxes and pass this test with flying colors; Tuckman and Lencioni, however, palpably fail. Their models simply don't include the right boxes that require ticking.

3. Actionable

Now we're getting into trickier waters. Rather than being nicely descriptive, the code also has to tell leaders at all levels the practical steps they can take to move their teams forward. Specifically, the code has to be designed for team leaders to use rather than the consultants and coaches to use with the more senior teams. This is where the vast majority of respected, science-rich team development models fall short.

Richard Hackman and Ruth Wageman, both hugely respected in the team development field, identified six conditions that they found determined team success. They further divided these into groups of three and entitled these groups "essentials" and "enablers."[1; 28] However, their model was based on research that was only conducted with the most senior teams and at least one of their conditions, organizational support, simply cannot be actioned by any teams other than the most senior of teams.

Furthermore, while collecting and unpicking cultural information is always relevant, and addressing root causes is never to be sniffed at, believe me, top line executive teams don't need an excuse to be sidetracked from looking at themselves in a mirror. And in any case, most organizations these days capture cultural data elsewhere.

4. Sequenced

"I'm playing all the right notes. Just not necessarily in the right order."

The late, great UK comedian Eric Morecambe[29] uttered these words to Andre Previn, the world-famous conductor, who told him in sketch that his piano playing wasn't good enough. Getting the notes in the right order is also where team development models really struggle. Lencioni went out on a limb and advised a sequence, but one drawn only from his own personal experience with absolutely no empirical support behind it. Its main strength has been its simplicity. In the complex world of teaming, this has been no bad thing, with little else simple on offer in the team development field, apart from good ole Tuckman, and because of his flair on the podiums, his approach has been lapped up. Yet while it contains several well-known drivers of team success, it leaves a hell of a lot out. Moreover, the science tells us we don't build teams, especially today's more extreme teams, by following his advice and first building vulnerability-based trust or first attending, as he suggests, to the relationships in the team. Rather we start the team development journey by getting the team on the same page from the get-go and agreeing what's most important for the team to achieve and we build relationships while we do this, not before we do this. A bit like a Big Mac, the Five Dysfunctions model is memorable, simple, and easily consumed, but at the same time it is lacking in important vitamins and minerals to be considered a healthy enough square meal to be consumed with confidence.[e.g., 27]

Constructing a sequence for a team to confidently follow is a bloody difficult task. It's occupied my thinking for the twenty-five years I've been working with teams. I've made my living analyzing, designing, and facilitating bespoke team development solutions for teams at all levels of the organization, most commonly though, the top teams. I've found that all these teams are complex emergent systems, composed of people like Jack and Jane who are fallible, political, emotional, and frequently illogical. They are real people, and this really happened.

Jack and Jane work in the same team, but Jack doesn't trust Jane. As a result, Jack doesn't really engage with Jane in the same smiley and positive way he does with everyone else in the team. Jane's no idiot, and she sees this. She feels ostracized, rejected, and upset. Jane also requires Jack's collaboration on a piece of work and so she makes a point of engaging with Jack at team meetings and drawing him into conversations in order to build her relationship with him. She does this a bit more clumsily than she would normally do as she's feeling low on confidence because of her anxiety. Jack doesn't know Jane is having a crisis of confidence and because he isn't impressed by Jane's lack of eloquence and subtlety, he trusts Jane even less. But Jane is no quitter, she may not have guile, but she's got persistence, so she tries even harder. But Jack knows what good influencing looks like and this is not it. His trust diminishes further, he disengages even more, and the vicious cycle continues.

Teams often only see the symptom, not the causes, so it's a dangerous and a shortsighted game to apply linear cause and effect thinking by pointing the finger at one person, as several in this team actually did. Team members and their relationships are interconnected, each one invariably affecting another. It turned out Jack and Jane had different interpretations of Jane's role in the team. The team leader had inadvertently created two different understandings of her role. Yet more complexity to work with. Additionally, there were also outside influences that were putting pressure on Jack: market conditions; access to resources and the quality of help he was getting from other teams across the organization which he felt were unappreciated by Jane and others in the team. When we look into the myriad of relationships in a team, we invariably layer on yet more complexity through which we then have to wade.

Any team development code has to accommodate all of this complexity. That is why all the models out there are based on the assumption that these component parts are so interconnected that finding a pathway through such a complex system can only really be done well by a skilled coach and that providing any "prescriptive" order is simply foolhardy. It's an understandable assumption, but as we will see, it is not actually correct.

5. Scientific

Academics are our friends. They can sometimes be accused of being impractical or not pragmatic enough, but it's not their job to be practical. It is their job to stand behind good science and to tell us the truth. What I particularly like about the academics is their preference for function over form and substance over style, which is how my wife describes me, my haircut, and my dress sense. The conclusions and recommendations we get from academics are without the usual commercial self-interest or shiny wrapping that we see elsewhere. They are the proper experts, and a code has to stand up to their scientific scrutiny by satisfying three conditions:

1. It has to contain the factors that science tells us predict performance
    (it has content validity);

2. It must include not just some, but all the known factors that
    determine team performance (it has content validity and covers the
    ground); and

3. Each stage of the code has to predict performance in the next stage of
    the code, and the final stage of the code has to predict overall team
    performance (concurrent and predictive validity).

6. Builds Swift Trust

Today's teams have to be able to pivot and adapt at lightning-fast speeds.
When Tuckman wrote his phases in 1965, the environment was quite
different. His approach was built for his time. We now want a code that is
built for our time. The necessity to build lots of trust and quickly is an
obvious requirement in this new world. Swift trust results in faster team
working which equates to faster results. And if there's one thing that defines
the future, it's speedy team working. The next chapter delves deeper into
how we build swift trust and reveals new research that challenges the more
traditional thinking of how we best go about accruing it. It seems that being
vulnerable and building psychological safety is not the quickest route for us.

TAKEAWAYS

1. The vast majority of teams are not high performing at all—they are, at best, mediocre.

2. Team leaders now, more than at any other time in their careers, desperately require help to build the highly functional team that can exist in a system of highly functional teams.

3. This help could come in the shape of a team building code or sequence that leaders could easily follow.

4. To work well, this code would have to be simple, comprehensive, actionable, measurable, sequenced, scientific, and be able to generate swift trust.

5. Until now, no such code has ever existed

PART 2

A Code for Extreme Teams

Chapter 3

Building Swift Trust

Two Different Types of Trust

At team building off-sites, when I ask the team to name their most important outcome from our time together, "building trust" is second only to having nice big juicy prawn sandwiches for lunch. I know for some this might come as a bit of a shock, but trust, although less tasty, is actually far more useful to a team than a prawn sandwich. Despite what the sandwich seller might say, prawns don't help teams to cooperate more, take more balanced risks, share their opinions and knowledge, communicate, and collaborate better. Trust in a team creates all of the above.[1-3] As we all know, teaming is so much easier when the team trusts each other. However, as Ed and Luke discovered, the reverse is also true, low trust can be an absolute killer. Without trust, teams experience unresolved conflict, suspicion, and backside covering, all of which combine to form a vicious cycle of dysfunction.[4; 5]

Any code that promises to optimize the chances of team success unquestionably has to demonstrate it will not only build trust but accelerate its construction. New research shines some fascinating light on trust that any leader, serious about leading the most effective teams, would do well to understand.

Trust is defined as:

> *"Our willingness to be vulnerable to the actions of another person."*

> —ROGER C. MAYER, JAMES H. DAVIS,
> AND F. DAVID SCHOORMAN[6]

We form two different, but connected forms of trust: cognitive-based trust and affective-based trust. They combine together in rather complex ways to form trust, which is also commonly referred to as "inter-personal trust."[7-11] For the sake of simplicity, I'm going to treat these forms of trust as separate from each other.

Cognitive-Based Trust

We build cognitive-based trust if we believe someone is reliable, competent, and dependable.[4; 12] It's the trust we form on what we *imagine* about someone's *ability* and someone's *character*. We cognitively trust someone if we believe they possess both *expertise* and *integrity*. I would trust a consultant heart surgeon with twenty-five years of experience, who I've never met before, to fix my heart, simply because she is a consultant heart surgeon with twenty-five years of experience. We therefore form cognitive-based trust on the basis of someone's CV's, reputation, or who they've worked with previously. Why do you think some people drop names? I once observed the Executive Committee of a UK insurance firm where a speaker dropped so many names he came across as a borderline stalker. Obviously, it has worked for him, though; he's trusted and respected and had been invited to speak to a team of people who ran one of the most important arms of a massive global operation. He clearly generated cognitive-based trust, even though, to me at least, his self-promotion didn't work so well. There is no doubt that Ed and Luke started their trip with very high levels of cognitive based trust. Experienced trekkers, climbers, and guides, they respected each other's skill sets and their pedigree. They also trusted each other's integrity.

Emotion-Based Trust

Emotion-based trust is different, though. We build this type of trust more on the degree of *emotional connection* we feel toward others. These emotions are based, not on the expectations we have of their competence but the feelings we experience due to the quality of the relationship we actually have with that person.[13;14] When I've met my heart surgeon, did I connect with her, did I like her, did I think she would look after me and care for me after my operation?

The levels of emotion-based, affective trust between Ed and Luke would have been very high from the outset. Luke had even asked Ed to be best man at his wedding. Just like when Ed and Luke first met, we build emotion-based trust with someone when we experience kind, caring, and respectful interactions with them. It is not based on what we imagine, like cognitive-based trust, rather it is based on how we experience them.[15-17]

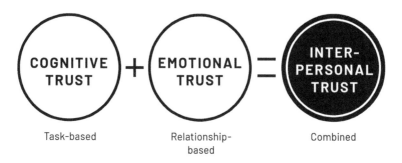

| COGNITIVE TRUST | + | EMOTIONAL TRUST | = | INTER-PERSONAL TRUST |
| Task-based | | Relationship-based | | Combined |

Great teams build interpersonal trust through rapidly accruing high levels of cognitive and high levels of emotion-based trust and layering on more of both over time. But what's the quickest way to build trust—do we focus on building emotion-based trust or building cognitive-based trust, or both at the same time? The populist approach, fueled by the surge of interest in transformational leadership, emotional intelligence, and psychological safety is to prioritize the building of emotion-based trust. Several writers including Lencioni have suggested this is the way to go:

"The first dysfunction is an absence of trust among team members. Essentially, this stems from their unwillingness to be vulnerable within the group."

—PATRICK LENCIONI[18]

His model for team building was for the team to immediately start building the capability to be more vulnerable. This was his advice to fast track the building of trust. As we shall see, this is not quickest route, though. In a team, especially in the more extreme teams, competence is paramount, so cognitive-based trust has a much higher currency than emotion-based trust. In some extreme teams, it's sometimes the *only* currency.

Our Trust Journey

Some of us are naturally more trusting than others. We were either born that way or we've had experiences growing up that have shaped us into trusting types or the untrusting types. Before we even meet someone, our trust levels are low, half full, near full, or somewhere in-between. Then, before we meet them, we gain knowledge about their competence, background, or reputation. Based on what information we acquire about them, we adjust our trust levels. Then, on our first meeting, depending on whether our initial hypotheses of their competence and integrity are confirmed or confounded, we alter them again. If I'm told my heart surgeon is renowned internationally for their work, my cognitive based trust levels rise. But if, on my first meeting with her, she reeks of whiskey, they will quickly diminish. We will also form emotion-based trust too based on how they speak to us and take an interest in us. If we are highly relationship centric, then this emotion-based trust will be more powerful. But for many of us, especially in the more extreme teams, where jobs are on the line and lives are at stake, emotion-based trust is likely, certainly in the early days, to be less powerful than the cognitions we form of their competence and their integrity.

When we start working in a new team then, it has been mainly our cognitive-based trust that has been building or falling. Our trust then rises in line with the reliability and the results we see compared to that which we were expecting.[19-21] Meanwhile our emotional levels of trust also start to move, depending on the degree to which we witness helpfulness, respect, and consideration. Over time, we continue to adjust both cognitive and emotional trust levels depending on what we experience. Ed and Luke, and then Ed and Cho, would have gone through this journey.

TEAM INSIGHT: *THE BENEFITS OF HIGH TRUSTING PEOPLE*

In recent years we have discovered that the best teams are composed of workers who start off with fuller rucksacks of trust.[i.e., 20-22] Higher trusting people bring distinct advantages over low trusting people. The benefits of employing high trusting individuals in a team are so numerous that's it's an absolute no-brainer to recruit as many of them as we can. For starters, they go about building trust quicker than lower trusting people,[21] tend to be more optimistic and extroverted (whilst pessimists and introverts can make excellent team members, both of these types have been found to be associated with superior team working),[20;21] and have a more pronounced internal locus of control, which is a posh way of saying they believe they can influence things more than they are influenced by them, so rather than seeing themselves as victims of change, they see themselves as participants or cocreators of it.[23] They are also more resilient and more adaptable. And they are more comfortable with speaking up and voicing their opinions.[24] High trusting individuals are also better at communicating and sharing their knowledge and are more active in pursuing the team's goals.[2; 20;21] Several researchers have also found that in *"short lived"* project-type teams, those that employ the high trusting individuals perform the best.[20;21;25] As I witnessed once in a very senior team, someone with a naturally empty rucksack of trust can be so cynical that they can actually consider the construction of a desired set of behaviors, produced by the team, for the team to work to, as controlling and inhibiting.[19]

For some of us over the course of our lives, we have grown to trust, while others have had it pummeled out of them. A heart gets broken by an unfaithful lover, and it's not just that person we can't trust, suddenly all men or women are untrustworthy, cheating bastards. This is a form of prejudice. The good news is that the way we trust is not fixed. As we get older, we get wiser, and our trust levels are less impacted by isolated moments and more influenced by the patterns we see.[20] As I say to my daughter Emily when her brother, Alexander, is annoying her, which he frequently does, *"He's not a naughty boy; he's just done a naughty thing."* I'm trying to convince her, and him, that a single instance doesn't define him as a person. No matter how idiotic he may have been, he's no idiot.

How Do We Build Swift Trust?

As we have seen, cognitive-based trust is often accrued *before* we even meet someone. Based on what we know about someone, we just assume competence and integrity from the outset.

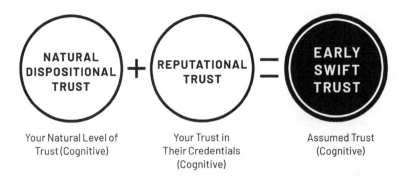

NATURAL DISPOSITIONAL TRUST + REPUTATIONAL TRUST = EARLY SWIFT TRUST

Your Natural Level of Trust (Cognitive)

Your Trust in Their Credentials (Cognitive)

Assumed Trust (Cognitive)

Andy was a flight commander for the RAF during the 2003 Iraq war. I interviewed him to better understand how he went about building a trusting team that could execute under the most extreme of conditions. The risks were high; during his posting, he lost two colleagues from friendly fire and over the course of the war, several aircraft were tragically shot down in battle. Andy reflected eighteen years later about the secrets of teaming in this extraordinary pressure cooker and the importance of "trust."

"You have to trust your team to do the job they're trained to do, and you have to trust others to do their jobs, too. You have to trust people to execute the plan we're all working to."

"I get that, Andy," I said, "but how do you build this trust? You hardly knew many of the people in whose hands you were putting your life and the life of your squadron." He said:

"You had to assume they were competent. They've all gone through training like we have in the UK. With some of them, we also trained together which also helped. Even if we didn't get to train with them, you know the selection and training we all go through to get into these positions, so you trust them implicitly."

Fran is a partner at a well-known global consulting firm that employs hundreds of thousands of people. Making partner was no easy feat. The race to the top was long, competitive, stressful, and very fierce. The average annual salary for partner in several global consulting firms is over a half a million pounds sterling with many more senior partners earning seven figures. So bright and ambitious consultants are keen to rise up the ladder and make partner. The partnership model means that any profits made by the firm are shared by the partners. As salaries are extraordinarily high, existing partners only want new associates in the firm who will add to their wealth, not drain it. So they make sure they are very careful in who they select into the partnership. Many consultants never even get onto the partner trail and many others fall by the wayside. Only the very best make it. Consequently, when a client meets a partner, they can expect quality. As Fran puts it:

"When I meet another Partner at the firm, I know what they went through to get there. I know straight away I am dealing with someone who is quality."

Andy and Fran generate a kind of trust called **"Swift Trust."** Coined by Debora Meyerson over twenty-five years ago, she noticed that in the more extreme teams, such as the military or emergency services where people are thrown together for a short period of time under the most intense pressure, they build trust remarkably fast because, essentially, they *have* to. [26] She also stated that in these teams, the way we build swift trust is more based on cognitive trust, what we believe others are able to contribute, than on emotion-based trust which is built on how we connect with values, personality, or belief systems. [26] We ask, "are they competent and can they do the job?" Meyerson, just like Andy, stressed the importance of assuming competence in the team from the outset as a means of accumulating swift trust. [26] And just like Andy, she stated that cognitive trust was initially more important than any other form of trust.

Swift trust is not just reserved for emergency services; however, it is increasingly being sought after in industry. We all have to do more in less time these days. Researchers have discovered that as a result of being so time crunched, teams simply cannot rely on the quality of their relationships to build the necessary level of trust required to team well. [19;20] In fact, they have found that the more pressure the team is under, especially the pressure of tighter deadlines, the more crucial is the role of trust in determining team success. [21; 27-31] Simply stated, the more pressure on the team, the more important trust becomes and the more important it is we rapidly accumulate trust in the form of swift or cognitive trust.

The nature of swift trust is that teams "assume it" first, then have it either validated or eroded based on what happens next. As it forms so quickly, it is recognized as very much a *conditional trust*. So swift trust is simply an early starting point to building deeper levels of interpersonal trust.

To convert swift trust to these more profound levels of inter-personal trust, teams have to be then able to layer on top of swift trust deeper levels of cognitive and emotion-based trust. To build the former, team members have to act reliably and consistently with the promises they make, and to build the latter, they have to be respectful, helpful, and caring toward others.[20] So we can conclude that for many teams, cognitive-based trust is more important in the early days, while emotion-based trust becomes more powerful over time. This makes intuitive sense. As Luke would testify with Ed, if we are treated particularly badly by someone, no matter how much we trust their competence, we will rapidly lose trust in them, sometimes irreparably so. And conversely, as Ed and Cho discovered, if the relationship endures through thick and thin, our trust levels can go through the roof, safe in the knowledge that we can endure our ups and downs.

*Building Same Page Trust is **the best** way to Turbo Boost Swift Trust.*

So, is the best way to build swift trust simply to employ highly trusting and competent people who treat each other well? Yes and no. If you can afford them, then happy days. However, this combination of qualities usually come at a price in the marketplace, and in any case, let's not forget that low trusting people can bring unquestionable value and shouldn't be discounted just because they are not naturally trusting. And let's also remember that high competence doesn't necessarily mean the team will gel. Several sports teams made up of superstars have had very poor seasons.

What about ensuring our selection practices are so demanding, that only the very best will get through, so we build the same cognitively based trust automatically assumed in the SAS or Navy Seals? Ensuring many existing team members are involved in the recruitment process is a great way to build trust early, but most teams simply don't have the resources available to them to put their "talent" through such a long, arduous, rigorous selection process.

What about, if you're the team leader, modelling the team leader "model" the way and trust everybody, and in doing so enable the rest of your team to follow suit to create a more trusting team? It will certainly help, but I've seen plenty of trusting team leaders in teams that are low in trust for reasons that have nothing to do with the team leader. And besides, this will take too long.

Why can't you just tell everyone, as I've heard so many times at team off-sites, to be more trusting? We forget, though, that humans don't *choose* the trust we give; it's more of an instinct.

Build Same Page Trust

You obviously need a more practical way to help build swift trust in today's more extreme work teams. You can't simply rely on reputation or the recruitment process to generate trust. Your answer lies in the sharing of *mental models*. Your team can do this by framing and sharing its thinking of how it wants your team to function and behave. Typically, conversations will include a shared understanding of the work that needs to be done, the strategic approach the team will take to achieve its goals, a shared understanding of each other's roles and the relevant experience you each bring to the problems that require solving. The sharing of mental models will also help you if your team works across the boundaries of your organization as "boundary objects" such as blueprints, plans, diagrams, or charts help teams literally share the same picture of what has to be done and by whom.[32] Your team is also wise to share its mental models of *what members expect to happen*, as we know this also boosts levels of team swift trust. This is especially important if you run Global Virtual Teams.[20; 21]

The act of sharing mental models helps the rapid building of cognitive-based trust.[33-35] Ed and Luke were not on "on the same page" because they possessed very different mental models on why they were walking, what the walk entailed, and how they were going to walk. Mental models concerning plans and roles are particularly important; when these are not shared, your team will suffer.[33-35] Agreeing on desired team behaviors has been found to not only boost levels of emotional-based trust, especially for the more relationship centric, but it also boosts levels of cognitive-based trust.[36;37]

The purpose of your team is another mental model, which when agreed upon, will also increase levels of cognitive-based trust.[38-41]

Building swift trust therefore hinges on your team sharing and consolidating a small but profoundly important number of mental models. When these mental models are not shared and thereby not reconciled, not only will trust be slower to build, but you will find that dysfunction becomes inevitable.[42]

Being on the same page is very much implied by Meyerson and other Swift Trust researchers, although never explicitly named, so I've taken the liberty of giving the trust it generates the title of "Same Page Trust." Meyerson and colleagues stated that swift trust erodes with *"deviations from or violations of group norms."*[26] For these erosions to take place, logically norms have to be present in the first instance. However, as Ed and Luke discovered, deviations from norms are much more likely to occur if norms are *assumed* rather than *explicitly* stated.

To build the swiftest of trust then, the best teams get these mental models agreed as soon as they possibly can. It turns out Ed and Luke had significant differences here. They had either assumed these differences didn't matter, or they had assumed they didn't exist. These assumptions proved to be disastrous because they triggered a whole host of trust drainers, notably hostility from Ed and resentment from Luke, which ultimately led to their downfall. When I spoke to Ed thirteen years after he started his walk, he had yet to make the connection between some of these symptoms and these root causes residing in these conflicting mental models. This is because nobody had told him about them. If he had a check list to work through with Luke, a code to work from, he would have been able to understand these connections at the time the issues were occurring and potentially taken steps to avoid them before it was too late.

So achieving Same Page Trust is very much like signing a bunch of teaming contracts. This might sound a bit unnecessary, but it really works. If we're working with a builder and we have a contract, something that we've both agreed on and signed up to—we're naturally going to be more trusting of them than if we didn't have something explicitly agreed.[43] The psychology is basic.

The problem is that we can think we're on the same page when in fact we're not. *"Do I trust you and do you have skills and the desire to do this walk?"* was all that Ed and Luke needed to convince each other that they were good to go. They would have scored high on cognitive-based trust, as they respected each other's competence and integrity, they would have scored high on emotional-based trust, as they were good friends, but they would have bombed out badly on Same Page Trust. This is because their initial swift trust was built on a number of assumptions about themselves that over their three months together, turned out to be false. Because they didn't understand how to reconcile these differences, their initial absence of Same Page Trust would have caused both their cognitive and emotional-based trust to diminish rapidly. If they had asked themselves from the outset, a different set of questions and looked at a different set of dials to properly stress test their cognitive trust, they would have realized it was actually built on crumbling foundations. If they had discussed their Same Page

Trust way before they took their first steps at the source of the Amazon,
alarm bells would have been ringing and they would have had some time to
reconcile the obvious differences that existed between them, or more likely,
not even started their walk together.

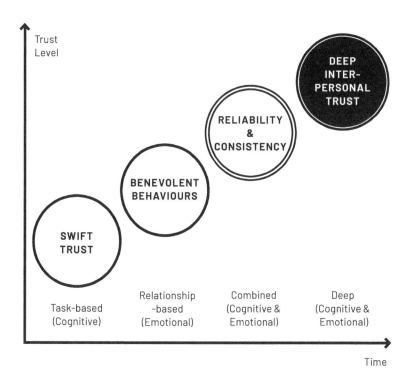

Ultimately, we convert Conditional Swift Trust to Deep Interpersonal Trust.

Go All in to Build Swift Trust

It makes sense then, as Meyerson advocated twenty-five years ago, that
teams go "all in" to accrue as much Swift Trust as you can muster. The
science tells us that your starting point is to rapidly make a bunch of task-
based agreements to ensure that you and your team share highly influential
"mental models." Agreeing why the team exists, what it is tasked with doing,

and how it will go about doing it builds rapid Same Page Trust which you can then convert to more powerful interpersonal trust over time.

Of course, the really switched-on teams make their agreements in ways that *also* generate relationship-based emotional-based trust. They go about making their agreements thoughtfully, respectfully, and assertively, but not aggressively. They start to build emotion-based trust from the moment they start to work together. But one thing they absolutely *don't* do is prioritise the building of emotional, relationship-based trust over cognitive, same-page trust. This is the mistake I've seen time and time again. Just like Ed and Luke, either the team under-estimates the power of getting on the same page, or they wait too long to do it, or they assume they agree on everything they need to.

So now our criterion for the code is extended. The introduction tells the story of Ed and Luke and of Ed and Cho and how the latter succeeded so famously while the former failed. Chapter One informs us that walking the Amazon is not too dissimilar to the reality facing many of today's teams. Chapter Two tells us our track record to date in building great teams is not great and postulated that a code would have helped teams like Ed and Luke to have succeeded, and this chapter describes the vital importance of swift trust to today's fast paced teams and how we generate it quickly. What we have actually done in this chapter is spell out the start of "the code."

TAKEAWAYS

1. Trust is a powerful driver of team success.

2. Trust is composed of cognitive (perceived levels of competence and basic integrity) and emotional trust (how well supported we feel by others).

3. Swift trust is conditional and rapidly formed, mainly through building cognitive trust.

4. We accrue cognitive-based swift trust before we meet someone, based on their credentials and their reputation.

5. We then accelerate the building of swift trust by "getting on the same page" and building same page trust with them.

6. The quickest way to build trust in a team is for the team to establish several shared mental models.

7. Swift trust is conditional and is converted to deeper levels of trust when our expectations of reliability, delivery, and benevolence are met over time.

Chapter 4

The Code

We desperately need that team building code. Most team leaders just like Ed and Luke are fine people who understand the basic elements of good team working. Without help we will only see them floundering in today's fast paced, relentlessly changing, digitalized world. They need that code to help them rapidly build the swift trust or to regain any trust that may have been lost. The problem is, there never has been a code that we can turn to. As we've seen we've had various "maturity models" that describe the life story of the team, and we've had various buckets of behaviors that we know work, but we've never had a code that reliably instructs us what to do and in what order, one that we can pass to any team leader to give them the best chance of succeeding. So I set about exploring the possibility that one actually exists and figuring one out.

The Story of Code Construction

Since 2016, a team of four psychologists here at TeamUp have been pouring over decades of academic studies and reading just about every book that exists in the field of team development in the quest to find that elusive team building code. We invested in work psychology search engines and employed an organizational psychology research company. In doing so we extracted data from literally hundreds of thousands of academic studies, published in respected peer related work psychology journals over the last 30 or forty years, with a primary focus on the most recent research.

We were scrupulous. We only wanted to learn from the very best science available. We didn't take much notice of esteemed journals like *Forbes* or the *Harvard Business Review*. Although highly respected publications, they are not actually considered "good science." Journals have an "impact factor" that gives us an indication of the importance they have in the scientific research community. The higher the impact-factor the more important, influential, and reliable the journal. The *Harvard Business Review* has an impact factor of only 1.27. To put this into perspective the highest rated journal, *Nature*, has a current impact factor of 41.456.

Unfortunately, academics have not always helped the cause. Have you read a published academic journal recently? If so, are you still breathing? If you understood the workable conclusions and it didn't drain the life out of you, I'd be pleasantly shocked. I've been reading academic papers for years and as a result, now have to attend anger management classes.

From this research, we identified several team behaviors that were found to predict positive performance outcomes and we identified a bunch more which predicted other behaviors that in turn predicted positive performance outcomes. In other words, we found the makings of some sort of code or sequence. We poured over the data, and I tore much hair out of my already balding head as we tried to construct a code that was based on science, but also satisfied the other criteria listed in Chapter Two. Remember, it had to be simple, measurable, comprehensive, enable swift trust to be built, and of course, able to put into a predictive sequence.

After much study and statistical testing to demonstrate its reliability and validity, we have identified a code that met every single one of the criteria we set. No other code is available, anywhere, that can claim to do this. We call it The TeamUp Playbook™, a purposefully simple, memorable four-part code for any team to apply with absolute confidence. It also passes the Amazon Walk Test because, as we'll see, it explains exactly what went wrong in Ed and Luke's team and what went right in Ed and Cho's team.

The Team Up Playbook

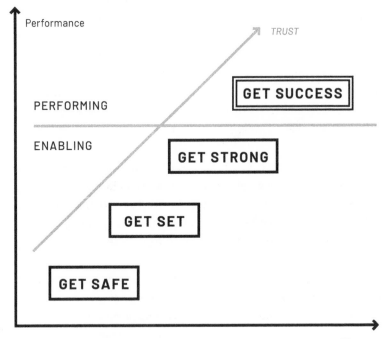

The Code in a Nutshell

First the team Gets Set by sharing and forming agreed mental models in order to rapidly build swift trust and to immediately propel the team forward. While it is making these agreements, it enters the Get Safe phase. Here it is more purposefully building trust, deepening relationships, and forming a climate where the team can freely exchange opinions and feelings and where it is able to learn. When the team accumulates sufficient psychological safety, it will then be in a better position to engage in value driving interactions defined by autonomy, commitment, and reliability in the third, Get Strong phase. It is these interactions that then produce the desirable outcomes we all want to see in the Get Success phase. Of course, the reality is that teams don't sit in any one phase of a linear journey at one point in time. Rather they occupy the Set, Safe, Strong, and Successful phases all at the same time, only at varying degrees of competence. However, when it comes to improving the way a team works, we absolutely advise leaders to follow the code in the order it is set out.

The code is structured in such a way that competence in each phase builds more competence in the next phase. In the team development journey, the team focuses its energy on developing its competence at each stage until it has reached a satisfactory level before then progressing to developing itself at the next phase.

The code doesn't stop there; there's a code within the overall code. Each of the three development phases are divided into three skill sets, each containing three behaviors. We therefore have three lots of three behaviors across three phases, totaling twenty-seven high performing team behaviors.

The code is therefore simple, comprehensive, measurable, actionable, sequenced, and builds swift trust, but is it scientific?

The Science Bit

All twenty-seven agreements and behaviors are taken from the hundreds of thousands of journals that we filtered and studied, so we know the content of the code is predictive of team effectiveness. The code clearly and unarguably has what we call "content validity." In other words, all the components all predict successful team outcomes.

But Does the Sequence Stack Up?

The sequence of the code also has content validity. Close examination of the scientific journals, as we shall see, suggests this sequence really does exist. However, we went one step further. We tested our code on twenty-three teams involving 178 team members. We found very significant concurrent validity. Regression analysis demonstrated that each phase significantly predicted the next phase across the code. Get Set significantly predicted Get Safe which significantly predicted Get Strong which significantly predicted Get Success. Furthermore, Get Safe significantly predicted Get Success and as the significance of the relationships between Get Set, Get Safe, and Get Strong with Get Success increased as we progress through the code, we have even scientific validation for the integrity of the code.

Our regression analysis also found something even more compelling. We found that competence in each *skill set* significantly predicts the competence in the next skill set. So competence in Mission significantly predicts competence in Plans which significantly predicts competence in Disciplines.

As we know, teams are highly complex emergent systems, so finding a code that works in the presence of multiple feedback loops is no mean feat.

Finally, at long last, we can now confidently say that leaders have a code they can confidently use to build their teams. One they can back. One that tells them what to do and in what order. Let's examine this order. You will see, it really is, after all the science that has been conducted, actually very much common sense.

Phase 1: Getting Set
MISSION, PLANS, & DISCIPLINES

The Three Skill Sets for Getting the Team Set. See page 77 for all nine behaviors.

The code starts with *Getting Set* so you can immediately start to build swift trust in your team. Doing so builds more rapidly crucial confidence and certainty in today's highly uncertain digitalized world. Getting Set is simply getting the team "on the same page." You want your team to know as soon as is feasibly possible that the whole team agrees on what it is doing, who's doing it, and how it will be done. You want those shared mental models out on the table, being kicked around, and ultimately consolidated. We know that things change fast these days, and so don't expect to stay set for very long. Getting set means being ready and able to reset.

To be on the same page the team has to make team agreements on nine different mental models, each of which we know results in team success.

You first want your team to agree on its mission by sharing the same understanding of its purpose, its vision, and its shared goals. Then you want your team to agree on its plans in the form of a high-level strategy, how it will influence its stakeholders, its core priorities, and as much clarity as you can achieve on who is broadly responsible for decisions and actions. Finally, you want your team to agree on its disciplines, namely how it wants to behave, how it wants to meet, and how it ensures it has sufficient skin in the game to be motivated toward achieving shared goals as well as individual goals.

Plans change, membership changes, roles change, and meetings become outdated, so we want you to continuously revisit these agreements to reset and to be sure your team maintains certainty, clarity, and confidence through continuous turbulence. If your team is a new project team, Getting Set is an especially natural place to start as it has been established that the way a team starts really can determine whether it ends up succeeding or failing.[1;2]

Why Get Set before Getting Safe?

We Get Set before we Get Safe in order to get the team moving and to build swift trust more rapidly. If this wasn't enough to convince you to start here, then consider a host of additional research we found to substantiate the logic of attending to the Get Set phase before the Get Safe phase. Firstly, when team members are aware of each other's goals (Get Set), we know it helps them to give each other more feedback (Get Safe),[3-5] and when they have visibility of each other's goals, it helps them learn more from each other[2;6] (Get Safe). We also know that teams who operate with both explicit shared goals and explicit shared rewards (both part of Getting Set) create more psychological safety than those who don't.[7] Did you also know that the more teams make up front agreements with each other (Get Set), the more psychological safety, trust, and cohesion they create (Get Safe)?[8] The logic for starting with Get Set before Get Safe also stacks up for the most demanding of all teams, the Global Virtual Team. It has been established that the stronger the identity of the global virtual team (identity is largely based on Getting Set agreements), the more psychologically safe and the more resilient the team.[9] In fact, any global virtual team that possesses both a strong identity and a strong shared purpose (Get Set) will also have a better tolerance for diversity (Get Safe) and will ultimately perform better[10] (Get Success). Our own validation studies also demonstrate that teams that Get Set are more likely to be Safer too.

Phase 2: Getting Safe
VULNERABILITY, EMPATHY, & LEARNING

The Three Skill Sets for Getting the Team Safe. See page 77 for all nine behaviors.

Most of us require some sort of safety blanket even if we don't care to admit it. Before we speak up, we want to be reasonably sure we will be well received, are entitled to say what we want to say, and that we won't incur a cost. When we feel "psychologically safe," most of us in possession of a beating heart then feel more able to interact in honest, direct, and authentic ways. There are of course some people who feel so permanently safe that they don't need much safety to express themselves. We call these people psychopaths.

Research by Amy Edmondson verifies that teams can build psychological safety by being vulnerable, being empathic, and via learning conversations.[11] Vulnerability skills include asking for help and saying how we really feel. Being grateful, being appreciative, and using humor are also forms of vulnerability as we take a personal risk when we do any of these. Empathy skills include sharing knowledge and offering help, respecting diversity of opinion, and listening for both content and emotion. The learning team is built by developing curiosity and asking great humble questions, giving descriptive feedback, and investing time reflecting on how the team is working together. Edmondson emphasizes how it is the learning created from psychological safety that forms the powerful bridge between psychological safety and performance.[11] For this reason, learning is the third and final skill set found in the Get Safe phase.

The work of some formidable team development authorities such as Tuckman, Hackman, Katzenbach, and Lencioni has now been extended. This code uniquely makes the building of psychological safety, *Get Safe*, a core and very central team development phase. Not one of this esteemed aforementioned group mentioned the term "psychological safety" in their approaches. This is not because they got it wrong; it's because it has only recently emerged as an important predictor of team success,[12] and these writers composed their models at least 20 years ago before a wealth of evidence has been found to support it. According to Project Aristotle, Google's research into what made their teams successful, psychological safety came out as one of the most powerful predictors they found.[13;14] Countless other studies also document its beneficial effects.[i.e., 15-19] Up until now, though, no code has existed that has placed psychological safety into a team building sequence and broken it down into three core skill sets.

If Getting Set is predominantly about building swift, cognitive-based trust, Getting Safe is much more about layering on generous portions of emotion-based trust. As we know, swift trust is very much conditional; it's based on what we expect to happen. If your team is not psychologically safe enough, associated falls in emotional based trust can completely destroy overall trust levels. As we'll see in the next chapter, this is exactly what happened between Luke and Ed.

Why Get Safe before Getting Strong?

Just like the evidence behind attending to Getting Set before attending to Getting Safe, the evidence behind Getting Safe before attending to Getting

Strong is utterly compelling. When team members feel safe they are more likely to take what Edmondson called, "interpersonal-risks."[11] It is only by taking such risks that teams are able to have the better, stronger, and tougher conversations. On the other hand, if your team is registering low levels of psychological safety, it will likely have less clarity of thought, more destructive conflict, less learning from mistakes, less innovation, less collaboration on shared goals, experiment less, and be less assertive.[11;20-27] The evidence of the Safe/Strong axis is indisputable; to be strong, you must have first banked a number of safe interactions. Our validation studies also support this finding, that teams that are safe are more likely to be strong.

Phase 3: Getting Strong
ACCOUNTABILITY, CONSTRUCTIVE TENSION, & EXPERIMENTATION

The Three Skill Sets for Getting the Team Strong. See page 77 for all nine behaviors.

The rubber hits the road in this, the third and final developmental phase. The previous two phases may be extremely helpful, but neither actually drive tangible commercial value. They simply prepare the ground for value to be driven in this phase. In the *Get Strong* phase, we want your team to engage in proper value creating interactions, inside and outside of your team boundary. These interactions will be defined by influence, leadership, and a deep-seated desire to strive forward to achieve individual and shared goals. You will want your team to be outcome focused—to know what they want to achieve and what actions have to be taken to drive the team forward to goal success. And you want the team to be taking these actions without you jumping on their back. In this phase, your team is better able to manage their emotions so they don't become too consumed by success or failure. They are very much in control of themselves. This phase is characterized by strength of character to influence the agenda, the courage to stretch out of comfort zones, and a persistence to keep experimenting.

Clients usually start their conversations with me by going straight to this phase, *"We need more ownership across the team,"* or *"I'd like to see the team taking action instead of continuously checking in with me,"* or *"we're playing it too safe—we need to have more challenging conversations with each other."*

In this third developmental phase, you want your team to be accountable by being able to work alone or in sub-teams without feeling they have to refer back up to you, to be prepared to make verbal commitments, and to give early warning signs if they are unable to make these commitments.

Getting Strong is also about creating constructive relationship tension by being prepared to hold others to account, handling tough feedback well, and proficiency in influencing those in and outside the team.

You will also want to build an experimenting team, one that takes action without having all the information in hand, can innovate, and that tries different ways to resolve inevitable conflict. This is probably the phase where any talent you have within the team will most likely show up. Some of your team may not actually require that much psychological safety to operate well in this zone. We are all different; however, research tells us that most of them will need to feel safe to thrive here. Your team will be characterized by decisiveness, influence, and a willingness to act on limited data.

Why Get Strong before Getting Success?

This is the only axis in the code that connects behaviors with actual performance measures, so what we want to be sure of here is that the nine behaviors in the Get Strong phase are each known to predict performance outcomes. You can be reassured that they do, either directly or indirectly. We all know that collaboration, autonomous working, giving early warning signs, commitment making, reacting well to feedback, holding others to account for poor performance, influencing, taking action without all the information, resolving conflict, and being creative are all known performance correlates. And we also know, from our own research, that,

consistent with the science, the strongest predictive relationship with Get
Success was with this final developmental Get Strong phase.

Getting Success

The fourth *Get Success* phase is unique as it is the only purely outcome
phase, whereas the three phases are all means of achieving these outcomes.
The primary outcomes you will see will be delivery and results. That is
predominantly what leaders get paid to produce. But are results the only
outcome you value? Don't you want a team that enjoys its time together
and has excellent mental health? One that helps other teams succeed
in the organization? That profoundly trusts itself? That has a wonderful
reputation? That converts its creativity into profitable innovation? That has
learned to learn so that it is future proof even without you at the helm? That
is wonderful at pivoting and resetting itself? Each of these outcomes also
define the Get Success phase.

GET SUCCESS	SCORE
DELIVERS	
1. Our meetings and interactions are highly productive, enjoyable and efficient.	
2. We consistently deliver on our commitments to those inside and outside of the team.	
3. We prove that we truly value the team agenda as well as our own personal agendas.	
TRUSTED	
1. We profoundly trust each other.	
2. We have proven to be a resilient and unified team even under the most extreme duress.	
3. We have a great reputation and our stakeholders really do believe in us.	
ADAPTABLE	
1. We are adept at converting our creative thinking into innovation and value.	
2. We are consistently effective at pivoting & resetting.	
3. We are fast learners.	

ALL NINE POSITIVE OUTCOMES OF SUCCESSFUL TEAMING

1 - strongly disagree, 2 - disagree, 3 - neutral, 4 - agree, 5 - strongly agree

Below 3.2: Requires Urgent Improvement, 3.2-3.8: Requires Some Improvement,
Above 3.8: Team Strength

Trust Builds through the Code

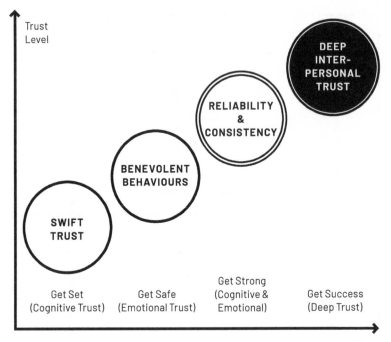

So there you have it. We have found our Holy Grail. You finally have a trusted team building code. One that ticks all the boxes. One that you can apply with confidence, no matter what your team does, where it works, or what level it sits in your organization. A code that is simple and memorable yet rich in scientific rigor. A code that is fit for the time in which you and your team exist. One that, as we shall see in the next chapter, perfectly explains what went so abysmally wrong with Ed and Luke and at the same time what went so exceptionally right with Ed and Cho.

TAKEAWAYS

1. We have a code that meets all the criteria required to help any leader to build a high performing team. It is simple and memorable, comprehensive, measurable, and actionable, sequential, scientific, and rapidly builds Swift Trust.

2. This is a "world's first"—no other team development code exists that achieves all of this.

3. The code comprises three development phases, Get Set, Get Safe, and Get Strong, with each phase building on the previous to successfully deliver the fourth and final phase, Get Success.

4. When you Get Set, you get your team on the same page by sharing mental models of the team's mission, plans and disciplines, and agreeing on them. It includes being ready to reset.

5. When you Get Safe, you build respectful, supportive relationships and accrue important psychological safety by being vulnerable, displaying empathy, and engaging in learning conversations.

6. When you Get Strong, you harness all of that certainty, confidence, trust, and psychological safety so that task and relationship centric conversations can coexist to produce accountability, constructive tension, and experimentation.

7. When your team is well set and ready to reset, feeling safe, and interacting strongly, you will see success flow as your team performs at its best, delivers well, and adapts.

8. Although you will set about improving the team in this order, you want to be encouraging the team to act in safe and strong ways from the outset.

9. When you follow the code, your team will also automatically be doing their bit to contribute to a "team of teams."

Chapter 5

The Code in the Amazon

Unfortunately, Ed and Luke were most likely destined to fail. Using the code, we can now see they were misaligned on so many fundamentals before they set off that it triggered multiple conflicts which neither of them had the maturity nor capability to reconcile. The code highlights the agreements they did not make in the Get Set phase, how these then caused Ed to act in ways that destroyed psychological safety in the Get Safe phase, and how this then translated to unresolvable conflict in the Get Strong phase which then predictably culminated in Luke leaving the walk.

When we look at Ed and Cho, however, we see the polar opposite. We see shared mental models, swift trust, and agreements throughout Get Set which helped generate feelings of safety in the Get Safe phase translating to high functionality and a remarkable Guinness World Record in the Get Strong and Get Success phases.

Getting Set

The best teams share a common purpose—or at least individual purposes that don't conflict—but Ed and Luke had different reasons for walking the Amazon that did conflict. Ed wanted to walk the Amazon partly to honor his late father by raising funds for a poignant charity, but mainly to help him transition into a career of adventure and survival. Having left the army and having drifted a little in the trekking industry, Ed wanted a new career, and he saw the walk as a potential entry ticket. Luke, on the other hand, just wanted an enjoyable experience. This meant he was always going to approach the walk very differently than Ed in terms of the goals he wanted to set, the responsibilities he wanted to take on, and the way he wanted to conduct the walk. While Ed wanted to steam ahead and get across as fast as he could, Luke wanted to take it easier, walk steadier, and stay longer in the towns in nicer hotels. They didn't share the same goals.

Because their goals were different, Ed set off on the walk as fit as a fiddle and kept himself trim by not eating too much at the towns they stopped in. Luke arrived a little less fit, a bit heavier, and wasn't so bothered about keeping the weight off, especially in the hotel stays. He clearly didn't regard being very fit as part of his role, whereas Ed did. Luke also didn't want the hardship of carrying his own rucksack, so he used the guides and any available horses or donkeys to relieve him of this burden.

Luke also felt it acceptable to hitch a ride on the horses from time to time to avoid holding up the walk and to preserve his energy. Ed felt this was against the spirit of the walk, so he insisted on walking every step of the Amazon.

From the outset, they were operating from very different mental models with differences in their understanding of the plan, their roles, their responsibilities, and their desired behaviors. They were most definitely not on the same page.

There was also no upfront agreement on how they would review how the pair of them were getting on together. Who could blame them? They were two friends walking the Amazon. Surely, they could work things out as they went, couldn't they? Clearly, they couldn't. The frustration that these differences created built up. Without an agreed mechanism to review not just their progress but how they were feeling about how they were "teaming," these conversations never actually happened.

Did they have skin in the game? Were they both equally motivated to make the walk work? I don't think so. Luke had a career as a paramedic lined up, so the walk wasn't anywhere near as important to his future career as it was for Ed. This asymmetry would have mattered. Ed was simply hungrier and more motivated to "suffer" than Luke would ever have been, which became evident as the walk progressed.

So when we review the Get Set phase of the code and apply it to Ed and Luke, we see implicit, not explicit disagreements everywhere. The code highlights they were just not on the same page and that they didn't know they were not on the same page. If they had applied the code, it would have directed them toward having the necessary conversations to try to manage these differences. It would have raised a number of red flags which if not resolved, would have predicted serious dysfunction, which is exactly what happened.

Ed and Cho, on the other hand, were very well set, sharing several mental models and operating very much from the same page. Cho's purpose for completing the whole walk and to extend his five days to nearly two years was very much aligned to that of Ed's. Like Ed, he wanted to better himself and make a fundamental change in his life, one for Cho that was characterized by exiting a depressing cycle of earning money from hard forestry work and then spending it all on hard drinking and a well-known class-A drug found in South America. So like Ed, Cho really was "up for the cup," with significant skin in the game and was prepared to do whatever it took to turn his life around. He didn't mind suffering and according to Ed, shared his commitment to do whatever it took:

> *"Cho used to say, 'if we die, we die' and it was a running joke between us, and we would repeat this over and over again. We really did mean it. Both Cho and I would never have given up. We were prepared to do whatever it took to make it to the end of the Amazon."*

With Luke gone, Ed found himself solely in charge. Those who co-lead or have to collaborate on shared goals with peers where there is no formal leader would testify that this makes life, especially decision-making, much simpler.

> "When Luke left, I could do the blogs as I wanted to do them— to be authentic and real—to be less jokey with not so much fooling around."

So with Cho, the purpose and goals were agreed, they had skin in the game, and they were aligned on how they were going to walk. Ed and Cho were on the same page when Ed and Luke so clearly weren't.

Getting Safe

The code tests for vulnerability, empathy, and learning and gives direct feedback according to the nine behaviors that make up these three skill sets. Luke left because none of these were in play and the atmosphere was so toxic, he just couldn't take it any longer. I've interviewed so many team members over the years who have complained about at least one of these three.

Ed uncomfortably but freely admits responsibility for the toxic atmosphere created with Luke and does so with a deep sense of sadness and regret. He's moved on since the walk, grown up, matured, and learned a lot about himself. But at the time, he had, in his own words, the emotional intelligence of a child in a man's body.

> "I was picking up on all the small errors he was making, criticizing his skills. I was probably more intelligent than Luke and I used that to my advantage to undermine him. Much of this was very subtle; I'd touch very lightly on what he was not so good at and used it to unsettle him. I was constantly cross checking his navigation and picking on every little mistake, draining his confidence. I was constantly reminding him he wasn't good enough. I think subconsciously, I just wanted him off the

expedition as he was slowing me down...It was part of me that
I'm really not proud of. I could see several years later, when I
took some therapy, what I was doing. I was just too immature to
recognize it at the time."

Such powerful words. Such vulnerability in action. But was there
vulnerability at the time of the walk? None at all. Neither Luke nor Ed
asked each other for help, nor shared how they were feeling. There were
long periods of silences, and no feedback was exchanged. Ed certainly
didn't show much appreciation and gratitude for what Luke brought,
both of which the code recommends as a form of vulnerability. Back then,
there wasn't a shred of vulnerability about Ed. He was a "proper man"
in a very outdated, old-fashioned sense of the word. Being a big, tough,
rugby-playing, and ex-military, what else would you expect? Instead of
admitting or facing his own fallibilities, weaknesses, and fears, he did the
opposite and made sure he drummed into Luke that he was strong, utterly
capable, and superior. More damaging to Luke though was his negativity
about Luke's weight, fitness, speed, navigation, Portuguese, and probably
much else, too.

"His skills trumped mine, especially his rope and kayaking
skills. But I just wanted to poke holes in him. I projected my own
limitations onto him. I paid little attention to his ability to lighten
the mood in the villages, to take out juggling balls and make the
children laugh."

Was there empathy in the team? Luke was clearly not having a good time,
but Ed wasn't too concerned. And I'm sure that Luke didn't feel he had to
empathize with Ed's frustration. He hadn't signed up to a hard and fast
walk, so why should he have to feel he had to apologize or help Ed deal with
his frustrations? As for Ed, he just didn't have the maturity to see anything
other than the jungle in front of him and the goal he wanted to achieve:

"I was wrapped up in myself, only thinking of what I wanted and
being a selfish bastard. I was being narcissistic."

Clearly Ed wasn't that concerned about helping Luke. Humor, so important in the more extreme teams and very much part of the code, was also in short supply:

> *"We were joking around, but there was always an edge to it; I was mainly sarcastic and cutting."*

Was this a learning team? Of course not. How could there have been any learning if there was no constructive feedback going on? Silence, anger, and picking holes are not learning conversations.

> *"When he made navigation errors, I fed off them. I think it was just boiling for a fight."*

Apart from one occasion, when they tried to clear the air, no attempts were made to discuss how they were working together or how they could better support each other. All in all, then, the code tells us that the psychological safety between Luke and Ed would have been paltry.

Cho and Ed, on the other hand, felt much safer together. Cho was so much more competent than Luke at walking and dealing with the terrain. As a result of the greater cognitive-based trust this would have generated, he received far less hostility from Ed than did Luke. This helped Ed be calmer, more composed, and more pleasant to be around as he believed the mission wasn't so much at risk. As they progressed, their emotional trust then started to layer on, although Ed admits he was so caught up in himself, even this took time.

> *"It was only when we were joined on the walk by a friend of mine, and I saw them chatting over the campfire one night, that I began to notice something about Cho, and it was then that I began to really appreciate and see something special in him."*

This would have helped Ed to then be more vulnerable with Cho.

"There was one time when I was particularly annoyed at Cho. We were not making great headway and going round in circles. I let Cho know I wasn't very happy, but not in a very nice way. Cho said nothing. He decided to teach me a lesson. He set off up the mountain at breakneck speed and to show him I wasn't going to be beaten, I kept close behind him. He kept his speed up and I kept going right behind him, refusing to let him get away from me. Eventually utterly exhausted, we collapsed on a branch of a tree. After a few seconds we just looked at each other and burst out laughing at the ridiculousness of the situation. I apologized to him. We completely killed any tension and resumed the walk."

Humor appeared elsewhere, too.

"I remember dropping a machete in a fast-flowing river after a mix up with one of our guides, Raol. It was the only machete we had amongst the four of us. We just stared at each other and then broke into smiles as we realized the craziness of the situation. It was a bonding moment."

And where there was little learning taking place between Ed and Luke, it was already occurring between Ed and Cho.

"We took turns to go upfront, as it was tougher work, hacking away and clearing the ground for the team to walk through. When Cho was leading, just like with Luke, I'd be challenging his decisions. Cho got pissed off, so we discussed a better plan. We agreed that whoever was upfront would not have their decisions challenged."

Ed, Cho, and the guides built a team defined by more vulnerability, more empathy, and much more learning than that built between Ed and Luke. The code predicts this would most likely translate to stronger team working, which is exactly what happened.

Getting Strong

The code points to accountability, constructive tension, and experimentation as being crucial for long term and sustainable success. We know that there's a feedback loop here; if the team is executing these three skill sets, then the trust levels shoot up thanks to boosts to both emotion-based trust and cognitive-based trust. A team that experiences itself delivering on its promises and meeting the expectations it sets itself is one of the most powerful ways to accumulate trust. Unfortunately, as Luke and Ed discovered, the reverse is also true. Ed felt Luke was not "executing" well and we know what happened next. Partly as a result of the low levels of safety between them, they experienced extremely destructive tension. Constructive tension requires that we say what we want, without being unduly personal. And if necessary, we confront the behaviors not the person behind the behaviors. Ed admits doing the polar opposite:

> *"I projected a lot of my frustration and anger I was feeling at the time onto Luke. Much of this Luke didn't deserve. I wasn't honest enough with him."*

As we know, this tension was so toxic it became the main reason that Luke left.

With Cho it was so different. They were on the same page, felt safe with each other, and Cho was also more willing to confront and challenge Ed than was Luke.

> *"We had employed a guide, and I had serious concerns about his navigation skills. After a bad day when we kept back tracking, I told Cho I didn't think he was any good and was going to fire the guide the next morning. Later that evening, Cho came up to me and told me to go easy on him. It was impossible to know which way to go, he said, so mistakes were unavoidable and not that costly in the grand scheme of things. He told me he was a really good guy and that although it's my decision, he advised me to not fire him.*

" I thought about how tough I'd been with Luke and so I listened to Cho. He ended up staying with us for several weeks and proved to be a brilliant person to have in the team."

Getting Success

The Ed and Luke team failed to achieve their mission when Luke left, but they were also making slow progress, losing trust, and not showing signs of adaption. These are the big three outcomes of the Get Success phase. The code would have predicted this to have happened given the shortfalls described across all three preceding phases.

Cho and Ed walked for over two years together and achieved their mission. I asked Ed about how his relationship with Cho also matured over this time, and whether they had improved their speed, their trust, and their adaptability.

"We really bonded. We learned to support each other... and no question about it, we got faster and faster. We just got better and better at getting through the flooded forest. We understood each other so well and developed systems to make the best use of our skills. We became very comfortable with each other, and this translated into more speed."

"What about experimentation?" I asked, "Did you become more innovative?"

"There was loads of innovation. We found a way to make washing lines out of natural resources so we could dry our clothes over our night fires. You can't imagine the difference putting on warm dry socks makes.

"Cho was also creative with his fishing. Piranhas are so vicious they eat through the line near the hook so you can't catch them,

so you have to have a bit of wire that connects the hook to the line to stop this happening, but we ran out of this wire. So one evening, when we were starving hungry, Cho came up with this idea to sew together safety pins from my sewing kit to make a makeshift wire. He came back that night with a load of piranha which we ate that night.

"On another occasion, our GPS had broken, and I worked out that by digging into the menu of our satellite phone I could get a bearing within two square km of where we were. It wasn't that accurate, but it meant we could at least track our overall progress which was really important."

I didn't have to ask Ed about trust. It was clear there was a deep and profound level of trust and a life-long friendship had been created. Cho has since come over to UK to stay with Ed and played in his rugby team.

Overall, then, the code passes the Amazon test with flying colors. It uncannily explains how dysfunction in one phase caused dysfunction in another. It explains why Ed and Cho succeeded and why Ed and Luke failed.

But would it have made any difference to the chances of Ed and Luke succeeding if they had used it from the outset? It would have helped but the different mental models that existed between Ed and Luke in the Get Set phase were probably irreconcilable. It would have required considerable emotional self-awareness, extraordinary self-control, and excellent collaboration skills to have managed these differences. At that time, as Ed bravely admits he just didn't have the maturity or the skill set to do this.

If we were to transport modern-day Ed back in time to the start of the walk in 2008, unquestionably he would have acquired the emotional intelligence to have given him and Luke a fighting chance of bridging their differences. He has worked hard on his humanity and leadership since the walk finished. I can see these in the way he conducts himself in First Man Out, his latest series on the Discovery Channel. The fact he was prepared to take my request for an interview and reveal all the worst parts of him quite freely was testament to his willingness to still look in the mirror and to strive to better himself. Ed is no longer a proper man in the old sense of the word; he's a proper man in the very contemporary meaning of the word. He's still tough, uncompromising, brave, and as hard as Amazonian teak, but now he combines these qualities with self-awareness, brutal honesty, and humility. He's less about Ed and more about the team. His willingness to share his story, warts and all, so that others might benefit from it exemplifies this. He may no longer be on the most challenging of journeys from one end of the Amazon to the other, but he's embarked on another one, in many ways just as brutal—one of reality facing his own demons and learning to deal with himself.

PART 3

Real Teaming in the Digital Age

Chapter 6

Digitalization and the Code

> "As we enter the 'second machine age,' digitalization continues
> to expand and accelerate, translating into some absolutely
> stupefying statistics."
>
> —ERIK BRYNJOLFSSON AND ANDREW MCAFEE[1]

A few years back, while on vacation, we visited the theme parks in Orlando, Florida. For three whole days we gorged ourselves on the most thrilling theme rides and the highest-octane roller coaster rides we could find. The first day was wonderful and I thoroughly enjoyed myself, but by the end of the third day I found myself utterly ruined. My wife Caro, sensibly decided early on that she'd already overdosed on adrenaline and reverted to happily watching the rest of us ride the more adventurous ones without her. Like a fool I continued to chase the adrenaline. The children, of course, were in bliss; they loved all the rides, especially the roller coasters and especially Sophie, my middle daughter, who loves climbing. Along with Caro, they took great pleasure in seeing my face turning greener and greener as the hours passed. To get my own back I told them that we would all be going to Western Super Mare for our next years' holiday. "It's even got a pier," I tried to reassure them.

I discovered we don't just experience physical sensations during roller coaster rides, we experience the emotional ones, too. From the anticipation of queuing up, to the tension of being strapped in, the excitement of the ascent, the fearful dawning that there is no going back, the anxiety of rising higher and higher, the sheer panic of the steep descents and seemingly impossible bends, to the joy of making it home safely. Some never start the journey; some want to do it all over again.

We've been riding a roller coaster of change since the 1990s, but in this new age of Digital Transformation (Dx), this ride has become ever more extreme, with hair-raising ascents, unfeasibly fast turns, and death-defying gravity drops. Some of us love it, some of us just about cope with it, and some of us, after taking so much, rather struggle with it all.

We all know by now what change means—like Ed and Cho, who rode their own roller coaster through the Amazon jungle, we have to be resilient, able to cope with ambiguity, and be very adaptable. And like Ed and Cho, we must remember that individuals don't adapt alone—we adapt with others in things called "teams."

So what can you expect to be the impact of Dx on your team and which parts of the code will determine whether you end up being a winner, or a victim of the Dx age?

Expect More Dx

We define Dx as the cultural and operational transformation of our organizations via the integration of digital technologies with processes and competencies. It is occurring at all levels of the organization, across all our functions and across whole industries and ecosystems. And it will come as no surprise that it is on the increase. In the Gartner Digital Enterprise 2020 Survey, 67 percent of business leaders agreed that if their company did not become significantly *more* digitalized, it would no longer be competitive. [2] So our organizations have been busy constructing and revising their digital transformation roadmaps. At the end of 2020, the research form IDC forecast that by 2023, 75 percent of organizations will have comprehensive

Dx implementation roadmaps, up from 27 percent today. We can expect,
according to the research, to experience "true transformation across all
facets of business and society."[3]

Expect Widespread Organizational Change

Buckle up for the ride, the future is one of uncertainty and unprecedented
technological change in Cloud technology, Artificial Intelligence,
Automation and Robotics, edge computing, big data, advanced analytics,
systems of intelligence, machine learning mobile, the Internet of Things,
and a raft of other emerging technological realities. The Internet of Things
or IoT, the next stage of the Internet, is still in its infancy, but you can expect
it to be the glue for the majority of future transformational evolutions.

IDC expects accelerated digital transformation investments to culminate
primarily in business model reinvention as we try to future proof our
organizations, but we can also expect huge transformations in how we:
interact with our customers; hold our data; use our data, do our work, and
where we do our work. In a recent survey of over 3,600 IT leaders, 46 percent
of them believed that their business would change their products or service
offerings or indeed their business model in a "fundamental way" during the
next three years.[4]

Expect Industries to Reshape

Thanks to digitalization, the lines between industries are also now
becoming blurred and companies, rather than sticking to their knitting,
are diversifying into new industries and producing brand new types
of products and services. We are already seeing changes in business
functions; business processes management, optimization, and automation;
business ecosystems between companies and other companies and

regulators; and the way businesses manage and revalue their assets such as customer intelligence. The impact of Dx goes way beyond the organization, though. It is impacting the behavior of consumers and reshaping entire industries. We have seen this in both the retail and manufacturing sectors. Retail especially is one of the most rapidly transforming verticals and is leading the way in technological advancement so that it appeals to today's 24/7 consumer. In the UK we've seen a catalogue of well-known high street shops, who have been too slow to adapt, go out of business. We can also expect "holistic transformations," incorporating various ecosystems especially in regard to sustainability.

Expect Big Data to be at the Forefront

The explosion of Big Data has been a game changer as it allows us to calculate, at lightning-speed, huge amounts of data over a very broad range of fields, enabling the creation of machines that are able to learn. It is expected to herald a "second machine age." Big Data collectors now include Google, Facebook, Apple, Amazon, and IBM. Learning machines, fed by big data, will begin to perform tasks that were previously unimaginable, such as diagnosing sicknesses, driving vehicles, forecasting epidemics, and restoring sight to the partially blind. The growth of Big Data has been exponential: it has been calculated that 90 percent of the world's data has been created in the last two years with 1.7MB of data created every second by every person during 2020. Every day, 2.5000000000000000000 bytes (I'd like to meet the person who did the counting) are produced by humans; this is estimated to reach 463 exabytes by 2025. Each day there are 95 million photos and videos shared on Instagram, 306.4 billion emails sent, and 500 million Tweets made. By the end of 2020, 44 zettabytes (multiply 44 by 44, and keep multiplying by 44 another 69 times) will have made up the entire digital universe.[5] The global big data market is forecasted to grow to 103 billion US dollars by 2027, more than double its expected market size in 2018. With a share of 45 percent, the software segment would then become the largest big data market segment.[6]

Expect More Advanced Machine Intelligence

In Japan, there are 1,662 industrial robots installed per 10,000 employees in car manufacturing.[7] Their continued and increasing integration into our workplaces is an inevitability. Compound annual growth rate of the global commercial robotics market between 2000 and 2025 is projected to be 13.2 percent, with the demand in 2021 to be $9 Billion in the US and $5.35 in China.[8]

Google appears to be leading the way in AI. They had only two deep learning projects back in 2012, but by 2017 these had rocketed to over one thousand. Ray Kurzweil, a director of engineering at Google and well-respected futurist, predicts 2029 as the date when AI will pass a valid Turing test—achieving human levels of intelligence—and that during the 2030s, tech will be invented that can go inside your brain and help your memory. He and others have set 2045 as the date for singularity,[9; 10] where there is no difference between humans and machines. Soon we will have widespread use of computer translations, self-driving cars, deep neural learning, and sex robots.

According to most experts, Machine Intelligence is already superior to human intelligence in low level tasks, such as stock picking at supermarkets. The experts agree that it won't be long before they also surpass human performance at high level tasks (HLMI) such as answering the questions we might ask a travel agent. What they don't agree on though is when this revolution will occur, with estimates varying from 2040 to 2081).[11] Fifty percent of experts are also 75 percent sure that it would only take another 30 years before we achieve superintelligence—where machine intelligence becomes *more* intelligent than humans in *all* tasks.

Summary of the Future of Digitalization

1. Expect a spate of continuous digital transformations

2.   Expect significant restructuring of organizations

3.   Expect industries to be reconfigured

4.   Expect Big Data to get Big

5.   Expect Machine Intelligence to erode blue collar jobs

6.   Expect more subject matter experts (SMEs)

So the future of work will be largely defined by tech and its continuous, rapid, and accelerating development. But what exactly will this mean for your team teams, team working and the way your team has work with other teams?

Broadly, the impact is two-fold:

1.   It puts pressure on mental health.

2.   It will change the landscape for teaming, with several team "types" becoming more prevalent.

More Job Uncertainty and More Pressure on Mental Health

It appears that white-collar workers will have to adapt and apply their intelligence differently while blue-collar workers face the prospect of being replaced by armies of robots. A huge survey conducted in 2014 involving 1,896 global AI experts concluded there would be a significant negative impact on blue-collar employment and less skilled white-collar workers. [12] Many believe that highly skilled workers will be OK, but 50 percent of the population, with lower IQ and less skills, will be forced into low-paying, less creative, problem-solving-type jobs or into no job at all. [13-15]

Others, though, are more bullish claiming that technology will create more jobs [16] and will free us from day-to-day drudgery, allowing work to be more positive and socially beneficial. We control our own destiny as a society, they say, and we will adapt by inventing new types of work and making use of skills that make us human.

Basically, no one is sure what the impact will be and when we will feel it. However, one thing we can all agree on is that the future as a result of AI will be very different. We can expect change and we can expect uncertainty.

Tomorrow, I facilitate a workshop for a leader who is working seventy-hour weeks, driving several Dx work streams, who fears for his job, and who has several of his team members who are very close to a breaking point. He's suffering and his team is suffering, and these two things are related. My client Bill is not alone. The research tells us that the distraction caused by Dx to leaders like Bill threatens the implementation of corporate strategy they are responsible for implementing, reduces the time people like Bill have to build self-awareness,[17] and increases the blurred lines between their work and non-work domains, just as Bill is experiencing.[18;19] Bill's distraction is also compromising his ability to be creative and to solve problems—also evident.[20]

With job uncertainty[21] and the very real threat of removing meaningful relationships from our places of work,[22] automation and AI also present a real threat to mental health. The AI gurus have tried to get around this by trying to humanize their robots. Measure, adapt, and teach (MATE) robots are able to watch the emotional state of the person they are talking to and change how they approach the interaction, and assembly robots are being given artificial eyes[23] as it helps workers more quickly engage with them and do so with smiles on their faces. I wonder if this also works with children, vacuum cleaners, and dishwashers.

But isn't all of this small potatoes when we consider the humanity of it all? Sherry Turkle writes in her book *Together Alone*:

> "The full richness of conversation is replaced with the functional bare-bones... Technology 'short-changes' you out of real conversation. Loss of real conversation has led us to develop artificial intelligences, robots who 'feel like real people.' Machines that seem to care about us. We expect more from technology, and less from each other."

Over one-third (37 percent) of us are technophobes, and researchers have found that technophobes are three times more likely to be fearful of becoming unemployed and three times more likely to fear not having enough money in the future than non-technophobes.[24] They are also 76 percent more likely to feel something awful is about to happen as a result of Dx. The link to mental health is plainly obvious. Technophobes have 95 percent greater odds of not being able to stop or control worrying when compared to others. Unfortunately, the fear of losing one's job and being replaced by a robot will, for some, be a source of clinical depression.

TEAM INSIGHT: *MENTAL HEALTH AND LAVATORIES*

Every team I work with these days is under pressure of tight deadlines. It wasn't like this at the Defence Logistics Organisation in 2004 when I was working there as management consultant. The DLO is responsible for purchasing all the materials and equipment used by the UK armed forces on and off the battlefield. If you ventured into their lavatories wanting more than a pee, there were chairs you could sit on while waiting for one of the three cubicles to become free. How thoughtful. Rather than return to your desk, be productive, and then return a little later, you could take the opportunity to rest your weary legs from the ever so long walk to the loos (fifty to one hundred yards) and sit in peace for a few minutes. But the generosity didn't stop there; next to these chairs there was a pile of magazines you could read while you were patiently (or impatiently) waiting for a free cubicle. Why sit down and twiddle your thumbs when you can sit down and have a bloody good read? Naturally, most people ended up taking their magazines in with them to finish whatever they were reading. This meant you'd often have to wait for a cubicle to be free for longer than you'd hope for. No matter; the pile of magazines meant there was plenty of reading material to keep you occupied. At the time, I wasn't sure what was weirder, a culture that was so relaxed that it enabled people to wait for their loo visits in comfort, or the people who were quite happy to relax and read their magazines only meters from others doing their business.

Looking back at this now, I'm far less dismissive of magazines in the loo than I was at the time. It gives a welcome break from the pace of work. Mental health continues to be a growing concern and unfortunately, fueled by Dx, we can expect it to get worse.[25]

A New Landscape for Teaming

Digitalization and all that constant, fast-paced, and emergent change will require us to change the way we team. We can expect to see the landscape of teaming to change, probably forever. Expect to see more emphasis on teaming and more: agile teams, cross-functional teams, hybrid or virtual teams, and more inter-connected teams.

Expect a Growing Emphasis on Team Working

We can expect both the centrality of team working to the organization and the principle of "leader subservience to the team" to become more the norm. We will see in Chapter Eight that this doesn't necessarily have to equate to servant leadership, as others have recommended.[26] Rather, it will require a transaction between leader and team so that both parties feel comfortable with the deal they explicitly make together.

Ego is often construed as a negative leadership attribute, yet a good, strong, and healthy ego is an essential bit of kit for most leaders.[27;28] The best leaders enjoy taking the reins and want to influence. The problem is that over the years, as described in chapter one, egos have just gotten out of hand. It starts way back, as soon as we become a leader, organizations, the media, and social media then unwittingly take us on a journey of ego expansion. We're almost brainwashed to see leaders as VIPs. Organizations don't help when they refer to leaders as "talent." Who is not going to feel at least a little bit important with that label? We become far too heroic, even if we think we're not. It's got to a point now where leaders who are humble and distinctly un-heroic are regarded and hailed as heroic simply because they aren't. As a result, faux humility is everywhere.

Back in 2006, I was consulting at the BBC and was struck at how hard it was to build a sense of team-ship in the news and the programs departments. Producers had to "line-manage" famous presenters who were earning ten times their salary. Egos just got in the way, and for a while, the BBC used to tolerate the most obnoxious behavior from their "talent" simply because they were "talent." When Jeremy Clarkson, one of the highest earners at the BBC, was fired from *Top Gear* in 2015, it was allegedly for thumping his producer in a row about not being able to get a late-night steak at the hotel his producer had chosen. The BBC made an honorable and values led decision to exit Clarkson, but back in 2006, he may well have kept his job.

Times are changing, though, and I forecast a slow but steady shift away from seeing our leaders as heroes to seeing teams as the real heroes. Individualism isn't going anywhere any time soon; I'm simply forecasting more steps being taken to guard against it. For us to embrace and thrive in the new age, we've little choice. We have to evolve in this way.

Expect More Agile Teams

On the February 11th, 2001, at The Lodge at Snowbird ski resort situated in the Wasatch mountains of Utah, seventeen world-renowned software development gurus met to ski, relax, and try to find common ground on how to best develop and deploy software. After three days together, the Agile Manifesto was born. I doff my cap to them for producing such groundbreaking work, especially from a bunch of men (the IT industry is still lagging in its diversity) holed up in a ski cabin in the middle of ski season. In that environment, the less driven of us would have produced mainly aching legs and a number of almighty hangovers. But not this lot. They changed the world of work forever. The next day, Valentine's Day, conveniently marked the precise time that software engineers at

organizations around the world started to fall in love with the 11 principles
of team working that made up the Agile Manifesto. Organizations have
been implementing agile ever since, especially in more recent years when
it has really taken off. Agile teams self-organize themselves, deconstruct
hierarchy, and repeatedly iterate in a do-learn—do fashion and the agile
methodology has now migrated beyond software development and
become the norm in many other areas of the business, especially in change
functions. It has been estimated that 83 percent of large corporates in
Western Europe are adopting agile working methods,[29] and 42 percent
of these are implementing agile in non-IT teams. Nearly 75 percent of
companies surveyed predict that agile working will be the norm in the
future. Agile has been used to create new programming for radio to develop
fighter jets, improve marketing, transform human resources, and especially
to speed up the relentless march of major transformations in companies.

> "The rate of change is so fast that the team delivering the tech
> or the business is 'the asset' and not the tech, product or service
> being produced."

—STEPHEN DENNING

Notice the centrality of "the team" to Denning, one of the contributors to the
Agile Manifesto and a now world-renowned expert in Agile ways of working.
I'm sure I'm not alone in finding it quite astonishing that he, along with his
esteemed colleagues, placed team working as absolutely front and center
of excellent software engineering. Did he consume too much Jägermeister
in that ski hut? Not so. He and his colleagues were onto something here.
Denning makes the point that the art of agile leadership is to mitigate
against leader error and dominance by leveraging the full potential of the
team. As he points out, agile is primarily about avoiding perfectionism,
moving quickly, and executing at speed. Gaining the full support of the
team and translating it into value generating outcomes is its ultimate
challenge. In agile, therefore, the balance of power between the team leader
and the team dramatically shifts toward the team. In doing so, agile is truly
leading the way we want the rest of our organizations to behave, to embrace
the notion that the leader is not as relevant as the team they lead.

Expect to Team in a Team of Teams

In his brilliant book, *Age of Agile*, Denning summarises what he believed to be one of the most important concepts underpinning the agile movement—that the agile organization is really a team of teams:

> "When the whole organization truly embraces Agile, the organization is less like a giant warship and more like a flotilla of tiny speedboats. Instead of a steady state machine, the organization is an organic living network of high-performance teams... In effect, the whole organization shares a common mind-set in which the organization is viewed as a network of high-performance teams."

—**STEPHEN DENNING**[30]

Researchers have since confirmed that the innovation coming out of innovation hubs or cross-functional innovation teams produces much more value when organizations are comprised of inter-connected teams.[31]

Building a team of teams was also something that General Stanley McChrystal recognized to be essential if he was to successfully turn the Joint Special Operations Task Force into an entity that could defeat a very elusive and resilient Al Qaeda. McChrystal fervently believed that traditional military methods, more aimed at maximizing efficiency, had to be replaced by teams purposed instead to maximize adaptability.

> "We dissolved the barriers—the walls of our silos and the floors of our hierarchies—that had once made us efficient. We looked at the behaviors of our smallest units and found ways to extend them to an organization of thousands... We became a 'team of teams'... Almost everything we did ran against the grain of military tradition and of general organizational practice. We abandoned many of the precepts that had helped establish our efficacy in the twentieth century, because the twenty-first century is a different game with different rules."

—**GENERAL STANLEY MCCHRYSTAL**[32]

Technological innovation is not just forcing us to collaborate more, it
is enabling us to collaborate more. Leaders and their teams are now
expected to engage with collaborative tech, not just stare at it. Digital
knowledge-sharing platforms such as Google Drive, Trello, and Slack
are now ubiquitous as they enable problem solving in multi-location and
geographically dispersed offices.[33] Futurists have even forecasted a time
when team members will be represented by avatars who grow in size or fade
away based on the quantity and quality of their participation.[18; 34] With or
without avatars, one thing is for sure: teams will increasingly have to work
with other teams, and team members will have to work more collaboratively
with members of their own team and of other teams. "Flat" organisation
charts will be brochures displaying simplistic interactions, when the reality
is one of more organised chaos.

The Brochure and the Reality of Team Structures

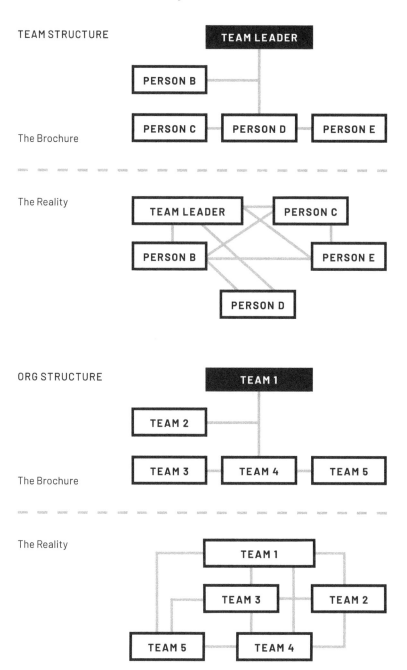

Expect More Cross-Functional Teams

Digital channels lower barriers to entry, which increases competition and ultimately leads to the commoditization of industries. Thanks to digitization, more companies are now having to compete via efficiencies and innovations in the supply chain and in how they differentiate their customer service. Product differentiation and brand are becoming less crucial. But who exactly will drive enhanced end-to-end customer experience, better supply chain efficiencies, and profitable innovations? Software Engineers? Change functions? Front line? Middle Managers? It will vary from organization to organization, but cross-functional teams (CFT) will almost certainly now be front and center in the new digital world. The importance of highly functional CFT's in our organizations is not to be underestimated, as when they work well with other teams, we know that these relationships tangibly influence customer satisfaction levels[35] as well as helping the organisation to learn.[36]

Expect More Virtual and Hybrid Teams

Those of us who have worked through COVID-19 can relate to what virtual team working actually entails. We explore how to build the virtual team in the next chapter. One thing is for sure, the trend towards virtual working is only to keep rising.

EFFECTS OF DIGITALIZATION ON TEAMS

1. Teaming becomes more important

2. Agile teams will increase

3. Growth of cross-functional teams

4. More teams of teams

5. Virtual and hybrid teams will increase

Building Adaptability

There is a common consequence arising from this changing teaming landscape. It's the insatiable demand for adaptability. It is your team's adaptability that will determine whether you are ultimately successful.

The code provides you with a tried and tested route to making your team adaptable. You start with getting it set by ensuring your team is clear on what's expected and on the same page in relation to its goals, roles, and disciplines, then leveraging this confidence to build high levels of psychological safety (so it becomes safe) before finally utilizing the learning arising from this safety to be more autonomous, and more able to experiment, to try things out and to rapidly learn from what happens (becoming strong). All of this is what the science tells us to do to build the adaptable team.

So let's add to our understanding by exploring what the research also tells us about how to adapt in a digitally transforming world

Embrace a More Empowering and Distributed Leadership Approach

One of the unquestionable consequences of the digital age is the requirement for teams to be able to move at tremendous pace. The ability of an organization to monetize Big Data provides a perfect example. Organizations have to fast track the commercialization of Big Data before it becomes obsolete. The clock starts ticking the moment they get their data. All the research suggests a more empowering leadership approach is the best way commercial races will be won. The act of Getting Set entails agreeing what this empowerment looks like. Getting Safe builds the environment and climate to enable this empowerment to be taken up, and Getting Strong is where we see the empowerment in action.

Empowerment is not news to the agile community. They are trained to apply a light-touch rather than controlling leadership approach as they know it works better.[37] Agile teams employ "scrum masters" who ensure the agile principles and values are upheld and who clear obstacles out of the way so the team are free to work things out for themselves in order to achieve the goals it sets itself in real time. Just like the military teams, they are not without certainty, though. They are on the same page when it comes to knowing their mission, goals, roles and responsibilities and the disciplines required from them.

Similarly, the best cross-functional teams also have leaders who don't confuse accountability with control, who distribute their leadership throughout the team, and who empower team members, individually and in sub teams to act more autonomously. What seems to be particularly powerful is the leader who combines a more empowering leadership approach with the ability to enthuse the team with strong sense of shared purpose of why it exists and what it is contributing.[38] It seems combining purpose with empowerment is a very potent combination for cross-functional teams.

Stephen Bungay in *The Art of Action*[39] proposed that on the battlefield, one of the most hostile, complex, and fast-moving of places to work, soldiers were more likely to succeed when they were empowered to be free to act in real time to events happening right in front of them, without reverting back up the chain of command. The term VUCA—that which is characterized by Volatility, Complexity, Uncertainty, and Ambiguity—actually originated from the military[40] in describing the situation the US Army faced in the first Gulf War. More latterly, General McChrystal in his fight against Al Qaeda following the second Gulf War embodied perfectly the same distributed leadership approach encouraged by Bungay. He called it "empowered execution," and it came to mean to his Command "as long as something supports our execution, and it is not immoral or illegal" it could be done without referral back up the chain. McChrystal freely admits in his book he wasn't even aware of many decisions being made beneath him. But he backed every one of them.

A distributed leadership approach is not just intuitive, it is also supported by bucket loads of science. Without question, empowering leadership helps fast moving organizations adapt better.[41-43]

TEAM INSIGHT: *THE EMPOWERMENT DEAL*

Empowerment is not a one-way street. It exists as part of an agreed transaction, ideally made in the Get Set phase. I advise the team leaders I work with to strike an explicit *"empowerment deal"* with their teams. I regularly run an exercise where I ask the team to reveal what they most want from their leader that they are not getting enough of. Then I ask the team leader to reveal what they most want from the team that they are not getting enough of. They barter and haggle a little bit and they end up with an agreement where ten times out of ten, trust and empowerment are central components. It's a deal because each party is contingent on the other to uphold their part of the deal. It's a proper transaction. Making this kind of deal would be less relevant to an agile or military team. They have institutionalized empowerment already and as it is taken for granted the empowerment transaction happens almost unconsciously.

FROM TEAM LEADER TO THE TEAM	TO TEAM LEADER FROM THE TEAM
+ Come with a solution not just a problem + Don't escalate unless you absolutely have to + Make decisions yourself + Manage my expectations + Ask for help and use me as a sounding board + Don't give me any surprises + Be prepared to make some mistakes – but make sure they're not catastrophic ones	+ Get out of the way! + Trust us + Manage the stakeholders to help us achieve our shared goals + Provide us with insights and knowledge you have to help us + Be there when needed + Don't beat us up if we occasionally get it wrong

+++ ← **TABLE SUMMARIZES A TYPICAL EMPOWERMENT DEAL BETWEEN THE TEAM LEADER AND THE TEAM** → +

Be Very Wary of Getting Bogged Down in Detailed Planning

Ed and Cho had a rough plan to get across the terrain, but no more. There were just too many imponderables to make any detailed planning a worthwhile endeavor. Bungay also described how in war, battle plans largely go out the window after first contact, and that following a detailed plan is not just a waste of time, it can be downright dangerous. To avoid falling into this trap, he recommends organizations adopt a more mission-centered leadership approach where commanders would describe to their teams, the mission, or purpose of the "manoevre," the outcomes they wished to achieve, the main effort or most important thing to bear in mind, and a broad-brush plan to achieve it. Commanders would then get out of the way and leave the "how we're going to deliver the plan" bit to the teams on the ground to work out themselves. Before returning to the front line, the teams would feedback their understanding in a "brief-back" to ensure no wires were crossed in translation. They were not left to sink, they knew they could check back in for guidance or reassurance whenever they needed it, but essentially, they were free to execute the mission as they saw fit. Bungay was clear though, that for this to work best, the *whole* organization had to adopt it, which is exactly what General McChrystal successfully dedicated his time to achieving.

In the same way, teams now have to accept that, largely as a result of the speed of tech development, a granular plan may not always be possible. Better for you to let go and give your team space and freedom to react much more to what's in front of them.

Be Crystal Clear on Expectations

In the cross-functional team, leaders don't fully "own" their team members, so team-first thinking becomes impossible—the only member of a CFT who can expect to be universally loyal to that team is the team leader. Clarifying expectations therefore becomes even more important, as they provide a much-needed means of harnessing attention. Research findings confirm that the most successful CFTs have leaders who invest in the necessary upfront time ensuring the team has clearly established goals, an agreed means of influencing their stakeholders so that they get the resources they need, and a set of team norms that include operating with crystal clear deadlines. In other words, the best cross-functional teams operate with the shared mental models advocated in the Get Set phase. Knowing what is expected clearly helps them build at least some certainty in a very uncertain world.[44-47]

Build Psychological Safety and Safeguard Mental Health

As described earlier in this chapter, thanks to rapid change, job uncertainty, and reduced social time, the mental health forecast, as a result of Dx, is sadly not looking so good. The code tells us that in order to build adaptable teams, leaders must first build psychologically safe teams. The same goes with safeguarding mental health—it's born out of safeguarding psychological safety.[48]

We must remind ourselves that leaders are not therapists, even though sometimes it might feel like you ought to be. Having good levels of psychological safety doesn't guarantee good mental health in your team. Depression and anxiety are clinical conditions that for some have nothing whatsoever to do with how their team is working. People are mentally ill for other reasons. However, you can minimize the risks of these conditions taking shape and thereby help those that are suffering cope as best they can. Building the vulnerable and empathic team is one way you can achieve this especially in this world of Dx.

TEAM INSIGHT: *POSITIVE CONTAGION*

When we are mentally ill, we experience negative emotions such as sadness or anxiety. We know that emotions are contagious.[49-54] We want to be building climates of positivity, appreciation, gratitude, and humor.[55] These won't be enough to prevent mental health issues, but they just might be lifelines for some.

Make Team Empathy a Priority

Empathy is regarded by many as one of the most important team working competencies.[56] It enables us to pick up the emotions of others, to reassure them that we understand how they feel and think, and ultimately and most importantly, to respond in helpful ways. Reading facial expressions, noticing tones of voices, observing the words used in conversation, the patterns of behavior—these are all part of this "A-List" competency. Unfortunately, mainly driven by Dx, our empathy levels are declining.[22]

There is no denying the impact that tech is having this decline.[57;58] Within five minutes of waking up, at least 32 percent of teenagers have reached for a smartphone or electronic device, with 36 percent waking up at least once in the night to check it.[59] Tweens (children aged eight to twelve) average slightly more than four and a half hours of screen media time each day. Teens (thirteen through eighteen) average nearly seven and a half hours on screens, excluding time spent in school or on homework.[60] It's not just the millennials though; Apple found, Gen X spends 169 minutes on their phone per day and Baby Boomers spend 136 minutes—totaling over a month per year![61] According to 2019 research by global tech care company Asurion, the average American user checks their phone every ten minutes and up to ninety-six times a day.[62] Digitalization means we are on screens a lot more than we used to be. While information is flowing faster between us and we are better able to connect with each other via all this new tech, the quality of our communication is falling. The outlook doesn't look bright. Experts believe we'll see less skill in face-to-face interaction in the workplace going forward.[63] The winning team leaders of the future will therefore be those who actively prioritise and ensure the presence of empathic team interactions.

Organize the Team to Learn

They say a monkey never makes the same mistake twice. I don't know about that (and I speak as someone with a slightly hairy back who happens to like bananas). But I do know that digitalization means adapting and adapting means learning, so the speed at which teams learn will naturally become a major source of competitive advantage in the Dx age.

Amy Edmondson writes so eloquently about this in her book *Teaming: How Organizations Learn, Innovate, and Compete in the Knowledge*

Economy.[64] She describes how companies have for a long time been organizing themselves to execute and now they have to organize to learn. To help learn, teams need to experiment and to help experiment teams need to adopt a learning mentality. We have a feedback loop here. It really will determine the AI winners and losers. Edmondson is one of many other researchers who believe it will be the organizations that make learning central to their cultures. She believes they will be most likely to succeed by reducing the time it takes to turn their ideas into action.[65] This is the very same mentality that McChrystal brought to bear on his task force. Central to his cultural transformation was becoming "organised to learn and adapt" rather than being "organised to be efficient and in control."

As we'll see in Chapter Nine, teams can learn in a number of different ways. One of these, learning through *sharing* knowledge, seems to be particularly important to the CFT, more important in fact than having that knowledge simply *available.*[66] In other words, your team will only really benefit from the knowledge that its members hold (let's not forget we tend to fill a cross-functional team with experts) if they *share* this knowledge with others. It seems in the Cross-Functional Team, sharing really is caring. With the psychological safety generated, and as exactly as the code predicts, studies confirms that the CFT is then more innovative.[67;68]

Execute on Empowerment

This is the manifestation of the empowerment deal described earlier. While Dx requires leaders to empower and distribute their leadership so the team can take swift action without referral back up the chain, it will only work if those empowered meet the team leader halfway and act on this empowerment. It is the "execution" part of what General McChrystal called "empowered execution." The Dx research entirely supports this. Google researchers found that their best teams not only had team leaders who distributed their leadership across the team, but they also had team members who used their initiative to take the leadership without waiting to be instructed.[69;70] The best Google Teams, when confronted with blockages, issues, or problems, took it upon themselves to resolve them rather than look upwards to their managers.

Get Comfortable with Collaborative Tension

Dx means that teams will have to solve more complex situations with themselves and with other teams. Humble adaptive thinking rather than more certain positional thinking is required. Very recent research tells us that teams will have to learn to interact differently than before if they are to do this well. It will require your team to be especially proficient at habit- or pattern-breaking in the collaborative and problem-solving spaces. This competence, very much part of the third phase Get Strong, will only be possible in your team if it engages in open dialogue and members share their ideas, thoughts, and feelings about how they are tackling emerging complex situations together.[71] As we know, and consistent with the code, these are all part of getting safe. Problem solving and collaboration in the Dx phase clearly supports the Get Safe to Get Strong axis of the code.

This form of constructive tension, known as the "meta-position" in Gestalt psychology, occurs only when the feedback, rather than being about what is being discussed, centers on *how* it is being discussed *while* it is being discussed.[72] Two of the greatest authorities on influencing and negotiation, professors William Ury and Roger Fisher from Harvard University called this "going to the balcony." They described how someone is able to disassociate themself from the "play" they are acting in with someone, by imagining they have moved to a balcony, to observe themselves.[73-75] They do this during the interaction to get an imaginary "third-person" view of what is actually happening. By breaking well-practiced patterns, your team, if it is facing a Dx transformation, can be better at problem solving.

Build Team Adaptability before You Train Individual Adaptability

We know that teams these days have to be resilient and adaptable, resilient to bounce back from adversity, and adaptable to be able to make the most from new and arising situations.[76] Resilience is closely related to adaptability,[77-79] and over recent years, this is probably why it has been been a very popular training course that organizations have provided for their staff.

Popular doesn't mean well-informed, though. We are kidding ourselves if we think individual training programs aimed at boosting resilience are the best route to building adaptable teams. That's like giving a weight training program to an Olympic sprinter and telling them that's the best way to run faster. It may help them run a bit faster, but it's missing the fundamentals of how they acquire speed. In the same way a sprinter works on their core stability, balance, and ability to relax their muscles when sprinting, the code advocates building adaptability from the ground up.

First, we go the Get Set Phase, and particularly the Re-setting part. You will recall that getting on the same page, which is what the first Get Set phase is all about, primarily centers on the team sharing a series of mental models, or frameworks, of what it is commissioned to do and how it is going to do it. Well researchers have very recently found that it is the ability of the team to change its mental models that also helps them to adapt and change.[76;80;81]

Now let's go to the Get Safe Phase and the part of code that predicts that the acquisition of psychological safety will enable learning and adaptability. Teams who monitor, give feedback, and support each other during periods of adversity and make changes to how they work together based on this learning have been found to be the most resilient and adaptable.[76; 82; 83] And consistent with the Get Safe part of the code, the most resilient and adaptable workers were not just able to self-motivate and maintain their own levels of confidence, they went out of the way to motivate and build confidence in others, too. Individual resilience and adaptability appear very much to be functions of effective team working.

To build adaptability in our teams and be consistent with the code, we need to Get Set and Get Safe first. From this more stable position, we can then think about training personal resilience skills across the team. The best of way of doing this is to train adaptability and resilience skills *with* the whole team present. Remember: people lose more weight in teams than on their own, suffer less pain from cancer treatments when they are part of a cancer treatment team, do more exercise when they are part of an exercise team, and are more likely to give up smoking when they do so in groups of like-minded people.[84-92] All of these exemplify how resilience and adaptability are very much team sports.

Create a Positive Emotional Contagion to Build the Adaptable Team

"There is no doubt my mood affected the crew. When I was positive, they sailed better and when I was tight or grumpy, the crew became tense and sailed slower."

—**DEE CAFFERI,** *VOLVO OCEAN RACE SKIPPER 2017*

Just as Dee states, when leaders project positivity and optimism, they produce better learning better adaptability and better performance. This is especially the case if they are respected and the team looks up to them.[93-100] Positive mood then spreads across the team because we've known for a while that teams act like petri dishes, spreading positive emotions from one member to another. More recently, there is now evidence that mind-set is also contagious.[101;102] One person's attitude about learning and adaptability may well influence others in the team.

Yet again, the code is supported here: optimism and positivity support the building of psychological safety, and psychological safety supports the building of adaptability.

Adaptability as a team sport is gathering momentum. Some researchers believe that without team-level resilience, teams simply won't adapt to the adverse unstable environments to which Dx is subjecting us.[76] Only in the most recent years have researchers found that whole team resilience is greater than the sum of individual resilience levels across the team.[51;76;82] Let's not forget that the most important element of team working is picking the right people to be in the team in the first place. Recruiting resilient team members who are naturally high in perseverance will help build *team* resilience. Helping your team frame their change experiences positively will help their less hardy teammates also bounce back from adversity.[76]

How Teams Thrive in Dx

PHASE	ACTIVITY
Getting Set	1. Empowering and distributing leadership 2. Engaging in high-level rather than detailed planning 3. Being crystal clear on expectation setting
Getting Safe	1. Prioritizing the building of psychological safety to combat mental health 2. Safeguarding threatened empathy levels 3. Becoming organized to learn 4. Creating positive emotional contagion
Getting Strong	1. Executing on the empowerment deal 2. Tolerating and thriving with collaborative tension 3. Building adaptability and resilience at the team level

TAKEAWAYS

1. The effects of repeated digital transformation and widespread organizational change is changing the teaming landscape.

2. Mental health is likely to be put under more pressure.

3. It will be more important for your team to work well as a team and to team with other teams in a team of teams.

4. Only the most adaptable teams will excel.

5. Employ adaptable people and build adaptability through the phases of the code and you will build your adaptable team.

Chapter 7

Virtual Teaming and the Code

How have you found working virtually recently? COVID-19 has meant we can now all answer this question. No doubt your answer will probably include both positives and negatives. The positives are likely to include the following: we don't have to commute; we have no early AM alarm clock calls; no long unpleasant, overheated, overcrowded trains or tubes where we are forced to stand up under the smelly arm pit of an unwashed stranger and no bumper-to-bumper traffic. Nor do we have late night arrivals back home, feeling so worn-out and emotionally spent that all we can give our loved ones is an exhausted grunt or two. Is it any wonder why 73 percent of workers report the positives of virtual working outweigh the negatives?[1]

There are negatives, though, and we can't ignore them. Most people complain they are more isolated, find it hard to maintain healthy levels of productivity, and experience more conflict/stress in their teams. Understanding these will help you apply the solutions required to fix them.

The Challenge of Isolation

It can be lonely working alone and feelings of isolation can be very real.[1] Even though we can laugh at the memes and jokes flying around on WhatsApp, many of us miss the fun, banter, and camaraderie we only experience being physically present with others. We miss the nonverbal cues that tell us how others are feeling and the feel-good we get from responding to them. Feelings of loneliness and isolation ensue which then means we are less able to contribute, innovate, and be as effective as we normally are.[2] Along with financial worries, feeling isolated has been reported as being one of the main reasons why mental health in the UK has worsened substantially during the pandemic. Ed experienced this very issue in the Amazon; feelings of remoteness, being desperately short of funding, and being forced to interact with his sponsors by email all conspired to make him feel both isolated and depressed. Compared to pre-pandemic levels, in the first half of 2020 alone, mental health overall has worsened an average 8.1 percent and even higher in young adults and women.[3]

The Challenge of Productivity

A CEO I work with pushed back against introducing a working from home policy. When I asked him why he said he was worried about "people taking the piss."

To some degree I could understand his sentiment. Friends make bunny ears when saying they are "working" from home. Not any longer, though. It's actually the reverse that my CEO ought to be worrying about—mental and physical stress caused by *over work*, especially for those who are naturally hard working and who struggle to know when to stop. At home, we don't have the same boundaries afforded by a commute such as a natural change of clothes or a physical move from the office to our homes.[4;5] And as there are more misunderstanding occurring in the virtual team, we are more likely to be spending time reworking, especially on the more complex tasks and on our detailed project management activities.[2;6-10] Rework causes more stress for all of us.

Many of us struggle without the structure and routines of the office environment, finding it harder to motivate ourselves in the face of countless home distractions. We feel guilty we are not achieving what we'd like to be achieving, but it's not for a lack of trying. Focusing on a screen hour after hour is so tiring. When I spoke to a client the other day, known for her boundless zip and energy, it was as if someone had dimmed her lights. It was late in a day of end-to-end VC calls, and it really showed. (It's very possible, of course, her low mood was simply because she was having to talk with me.)

The Challenges of Conflict and Trust

As we saw in Chapter Three, trust is crucial to a team, and the sooner we build it, the better. In the virtual team, this is especially important, so much so, that for some teams who haven't formed it quickly enough, it has completely derailed them.[11] Low trust forms one part of a potentially very vicious cycle that the virtual team in particular has to contend with. In this cycle, low trust creates more conflict which creates lower trust which creates more conflict and around and around we go. This vicious cycle is especially dangerous for the virtual team because not only does it typically experience more conflict than the non-virtual team,[e.g., 12-15] but acquiring the necessary trust to minimize this conflict is also harder to come by. Researchers have found that the level of trust in a team is inversely proportional to the frequency of face-to-face interactions across that team[6;9;16;17] and that the level of relationship conflict is similarly inversely proportional to the number of face-to-face interactions in a team.[18] So building trust in the virtual team, where the face to face is time minimal, is seriously compromised.

The virtual team is even more challenged to resolve this conflict as team members in a virtual team become bizarrely more stubborn. Researchers have found when we work virtually, we are less likely to change our minds to accommodate the views and perspectives of others than in face-to-face teams.[15]

To make negotiation and collaboration even more challenging, researchers have also found it is more difficult for team members to disagree with each other on a conference call or via email.[19;20] So in the virtual team, we will also get more unresolved conflict which then creates a higher intensity of negative emotions, which in turn causes team members to be less helpful and less thoughtful to each other, further driving down even more levels of trust.[21-25] Surrounded by all this conflict, team members then doubt the competence of the virtual team to perform well.[13]

If leading the virtual team is a tough gig, it's a relative walk in the park compared to leading the global virtual team (GVT). If I had a medal to hand out for acts of bravery in the field of leadership, then I'd give one to any leader of a GVT. All the challenges and conflict we see in virtual teams are magnified in the GVT, thanks to time zone and cultural differences.[14] In a recent survey[17] of 1,372 respondents in eighty countries working in GVTs, each representing a range of businesses of different sizes, the top five conflict areas were found to be (in order):

1. Colleagues not participating
2. Slower decision-making
3. More time being spent on speeding up decisions
4. Different role expectations of team members
5. Disappointing action follow-through

Trust is so important to the virtual team that the research concludes that as team leader, you will **only** be successful if you are able to effectively resolve the inevitable and emerging conflict.[26]

It all sounds doom and gloom, but a virtual team can win if it purposefully and quickly builds trust and the skills to leverage it when it occurs.[19;27;28]

We have seen how important swift trust and cognitive-based trust are in Chapter Three. It's apparent from all of this research that the stakes are higher in the virtual team, and that finding a way to effectively lead the virtual team is now crucial, especially as the trend toward virtual working will continue to increase, long after COVID-19 has been dealt with.

The Trend of Virtual Working

Even before the pandemic sent us all back home to work, 85 percent of us have at some time worked in a virtual team and almost 20 percent of us spent our working day interacting with other virtual teams. You will have noticed that the virtual team bandwagon has been well and truly gathering speed prior to COVID-19. A recent study by IWG surveyed 18,000 business professionals across ninety-six international companies and concluded that two-thirds of people around the world work away from the office at least once every week.[29] An analysis of the American Community Survey (2005–2018) by Global Workplace Analytics found that regular work-at-home has grown 173 percent since 2005, 11 percent faster than the rest of the workforce (which grew 15 percent) and nearly forty-seven times faster than the self-employed population (which grew by 4 percent).[30]

At the beginning of the chapter, I asked how you have found working virtually. If you answered "isolated," you're not alone: 41 percent of corporate virtual teams never actually meet in person, and 28 percent of them only meet once a year.[17]

If you answered the question with "challenged," that would also make sense. Over recent years, we've also seen the growth the Global Virtual Team (GVT), 48 percent of organizations with virtual teams now report that half of their teams had members living in other countries,[17] up from 41 percent in 2014 and 33 percent in 2012. Not only that, but many of us are also working in more than one virtual team as 63 percent of respondents surveyed reported that they work on one to three teams and 22 percent stating they work on at least four virtual teams.[17] The GVT is clearly a more complex entity to manage.

We've been working more virtually because it suits all parties to do so. It enables companies to get the best access to the best global talent, allows round the clock customer service, speeds up their response times to global market demands, reduces travel costs, and most importantly for some of us, allows team members to spend all day in our pajamas.[16] All of these (maybe not the pajamas bit) are obvious sources of competitive advantage. According to research led by Stanford professor Nicholas Bloom, remote working increases productivity, lowers attrition, and improves concentration levels. He found that workers were less likely to take sick leave or prolonged breaks from work. He also found that employers saved an average of $2,000 per employee each year just on real estate costs. [31] More recent research into the effects of COVID-19 induced virtual working supports the view that organizations get more from their employees, with 77 percent of people in the US saying they work the same or more hours, and 69 percent reporting their productivity levels are the same or higher. [32]

Pre-pandemic, the forecast was that by 2028, 73 percent of all departments will have remote workers. [33] In light of COVID-19, this figure is expected to be much higher. [34] Lockdowns have done wonders for discovering the benefits of virtual working. Lockdowns have been singularly responsible for sending levels of virtual working through the roof and with it, the share prices of Zoom, Microsoft, and Cisco. The expectation is that the "new normal" will be a more hybrid model of team-working, a blend of office and remote working.

For our leaders then, the very real challenge of leading the highly effective virtual team will only magnify. The complexity of building a virtual team is so high that some experts believe that leaders of virtual teams require special training. [35]

Getting the Virtual Team Set

"The immediate goal of the virtual team is to build levels of Swift Trust."

—BRAD CRISP & SIRKKA JARVENPAA [36]

Clearly, our leaders need a bit of help and to be reassured that this help is based on sound science. While most of the online and training advice flying around concentrates on building psychological safety and making sure everyone is feeling looked after, consistent with the code, the science actually directs us to the more mundane, less sexy, more transactional, Get Set phase. The science tells us that when we get this right, and we build that all important swift trust, the virtual team will not only work better, but it will also be more able to create the compassion that so many virtual team members are crying out for. Chapter Eight provides you with a mini manual on how to do all of this. The remainder of this chapter is dedicated to sharing what the science tells us about how to best lead the virtual team. You will see that, once again, this research seamlessly supports the sequence of the code.

Recruit High Trust/High Task-Oriented People

As we know, you start building your team by first ensuring it is set. You do this by sharing a bunch of important mental models in the "Get Set" phase. In doing so you build "same page trust" which in turn contributes to the building of swift trust. Before this trust journey takes place though, you have to be sure you put the right people into your team.

In the virtual team, the science tells us you are best recruiting task-orientated people because they build their trust much more quickly than high relationship-oriented people.[37] The most successful virtual teams also have more practical "doers," people who like to form plans and make things happen fast, rather than the "completer finisher" types who are more prone to perfectionism and who can slow things down.[37]

Prioritize the Building of a Team Identity

Team identity is how we identify with the team and how positive we feel about being part of it. It is based, amongst other things, on what the team stands for and where it is heading, two shared mental models that the code suggests we share in the Get Set phase.

Teams with strong identities work more effectively together.[39] Building a team identity will be important to you as it will protect your virtual team from inevitable conflict.[40]

The challenge is that building a virtual team identity is not easy,[14;41] particularly for the GVT, where multicultural diversity will most likely be the primary cause of conflict.[16] Language differences, ethnocentrism, clashes between individualistic and collectivistic values, and different interpretations of the same facts all play their part in the conflict we see in the GVT.[16] Researchers have found that only those GVTs who carve out the necessary time and emotional space and who invest in the communication technology to build and safeguard their identity are able to nullify the cost of these conflicts.[41] It doesn't help that not enough team leaders have been adequately prepared to lead a Global Virtual Team. While 96 percent of GVT leaders rate themselves as effective or highly effective in leading their teams, only 34 percent have actually had proper training to do so.[17]

So how do you build a team identity? Easy, you start by getting everyone on the same page.

Immediately Get the Team on the Same Page

The data tells us that getting on the same page helps builds team identity and this strong team identity will then help your team build the all-important team trust. What we know is that the best virtual teams share the following practices.[40]

1. First, they invest in the tech required to connect together to have proper conversations.

2. Then they gave the necessary time to actually agree on:

    + Their purpose;

    + Their shared goals;

    + Their preferred ways of working together.

As we'll see in Chapter 8, these are all mental models making up the Getting Set phase.

They then give each other sufficient time to reflect on the degree to which they are meeting these agreements (Get Safe) and they ensure they are delivering on these agreements by taking accountability (Get Strong).

In other words, the science confirms that you follow the sequence of the code to build your team identity.

Explicitly Define Decision Making Responsibilities

No team risks a lack of clarity more than the virtual team where the risk of miscommunications is so much greater. So the advice coming out of the research is simple, consistent and stark: to avoid what the Dyers called "violated expectations," make it crystal clear who is making what decisions in the team. Make it absolutely bleeding obvious who's making the calls.[37;42-44]

Google did their own research into what made virtual teams work well with their famous Project Aristotle.[45] They found that their highest performing teams were those that were most clear and certain of their roles and decision-making responsibilities.[45-47] Interestingly, the stars of their class invested the necessary time, especially early on, to create their clarity. Once again, the code points you in the right direction, get your roles and responsibilities mental model crystal clear from the outset, then continue to clarify them as you go along. This is exactly what Google's star teams did.

TEAM INSIGHT: *INTERLINKING AND OVERLAPPING GVTS*

It is extra important that each member of your GVT team understands each other's roles and responsibilities. Further studies have found that it is important to establish that all of the roles and responsibilities of a GVT are interlinked and to design them so that to some extent they are also overlapping.

In this way one team member can step in for another in an emergency. So, while everyone within the team needs to have clear roles and sets of responsibilities, in high-performing teams it is common to find that the team members have a secondary set of skills. Go ahead and do this because this interlinking, overlapping arrangement will make your GVT more resilient, more flexible, and more successful.[48]

Agree on Target Norms

Andy Cotton is one of the world's most renowned big wave surfers. At Nazaré in Portugal in 2011, he towed legendary big wave surfer Garrett McNamara into a wave that measured seventy-eight feet high. Several years later, Garrett returned the favor and towed Andy into one reputed to be eighty feet. By anyone's definition, these are jaw-dropping-sized monsters. When a wave that big hits you, it can, and has taken lives, so team working is essential. One person is on the cliff looking out and giving instructions to a jet skier who tows the surfer onto waves that are travelling way too fast to paddle into. There's also a safety ski on the shore, just in case the jet-ski capsizes, which it frequently does. Andy told me how in training, if he missed the pick-up zone or towed in too steeply on the jet ski, even if the way was only ten to fifteen feet, Garrett would let him know about it:

> "Treat every wave as an eighty-footer, Cotty. You gotta get focus 100 percent on getting the entry right on the minnows if you're going to get me onto the monsters."

The science advises us that to minimize conflict in any team, but especially the virtual team, just as with Andy and Garrett, it's a good idea for team members to agree, upfront, a shared vision, including shared norms, customs, or ground rules.[49]

When you set team norms and then display them, you will of course perform better. But something else will happen when your team meets normative expectations, they will build more profound levels of trust.

However, the research is also true. When you set norms, you put a stake in the ground which can also bite you in the back side if you don't meet it. Researchers verify that trust will either grow or shrink depending on whether a team feels that its normative expectations are met.[50] So set them, but make sure you meet them.

Make an "Empowerment Deal"

Just like agile teams and any team operating in a VUCA environment, the best virtual teams have leaders who employ a more empowering leadership style.[51] As expected though, empowerment in the vitual team is not a one-way street. In a recent study exploring the success factors behind successful global virtual software development teams the best teams were characterized by the team leader proactively sharing the decision making across the team **and at the same time** team members, experts in their field, being proactive, and sharing leadership among themselves.[52]

What was also interesting was that of all the teams in the study, the one that came out best happened to operate in an authoritative organizational culture.[53] In other words, a team that smashed product development time by a massive 30 percent actually managed to strike an empowerment deal while operating in a culture defined by autocracy and command and control. If this team leader could build an oasis of empowerment in a dessert of command and control, why can't others do the same? This study alone gives all virtual team leaders hope.

We also know that virtual teams who operate *without* distributed leadership will ultimately fail because of a failure to learn and adapt,[53;54] especially those involved in the more complex, fast-moving environments.[35; 54] As Amy Edmondson states, the best teams these days are as much organized to learn as they are organized to execute.

So the science unequivocally supports the empowerment deal described in the last chapter between the leader and their virtual team.

And it's not just you as team leader who can share your leadership more. If you were to encourage the more senior members of a team to hold back their natural instincts to speak and instead give space to the more passive or shy members to contribute, you will find the team becomes more reslient over time too.[55]

So why don't virtual team leaders distribute their leadership more? It's because leaders simply underestimate their reports' ability to deal with the empowerment they are thinking of giving them.[56] As a result, leaders tend to hog the decision-making authority, essentially denying their team the autonomy to do a better job together.[56]

Here we can see just how important it is to get the whole virtual team on the same page. Consistent with what the code prioritizes, we see clarifying the mission, the plan, and the disciplines all helping the virtual team to perform better. We also see how important it is to establish all of these to build a team identity strong enough to help mitigate the inevitable conflict we get in the virtual team. All this takes time and I endorse the claim of the Dyers that doing all of this may mean the virtual team leader has to invest 50 percent more time than the co-located team if they wish to be equally as effective.

TEAM INSIGHT: *HOW TO DISTRIBUTE LEADERSHIP*

So here is some advice for you to ensure you distribute **and** your team takes up what you distribute, so you form this distribution deal with your virtual (and non-virtual) teams. You will notice how task-oriented these are:

1. Make it clear that *your* job is not to tell them how to do *their* job.

2. Make it clear that you require them to clarify between themselves decision-making roles and responsibilities and that you will only step in if they're struggling to get consensus.

3.   Ask them to communicate to you clear measures
     of success.

4.   Ask them to feedback their progress to the whole team.
     The baton is on them to demonstrate their progress to the
     team, not just to you.

5.   Be absolutely uncompromising on reliability. Agree
     with them to ask for support or to flag up issues before
     deadlines not afterwards.

6.   At the conclusion of VC calls, instead of you summarizing
     actions, ask team members to do this.

7.   Ask them how you can best support them to deliver so you
     don't set them up to fail.

HOW TO GET THE VIRTUAL TEAM SET

1.   Recruit high trusting and task-oriented people.

2.   Focus on building a team identity.

3.   Build same page trust by agreeing on purpose, goals
     and ways of working.

4.   Make decision-making roles and
     responsibilities explicit.

5.   Strike an empowerment deal early with the team.

Getting the Virtual Team Safe

The code informs us that having acquired the security and trust from getting on the same page in the Get Set phase, your team will then be more able to build psychological safety. As we'll see in Chapter 9, the virtual team now has to place a high priority on demonstrating empathic and learning interactions if it is to Get Safe.

Create Highly Supportive, Empathic, and Positive Environments

In the Get Safe phase you move from being very task focused to focusing on relationships. Doing this will serve you very well [57]. No more so than when it comes to distributing your leadership as part of your empowerment deal. Research involving forty global teams shows the empowerment deal is much more likely to reap you benefits if you are *also* supportive and good at communicating.[58] When you check in on how the team are feeling and you offer them your empathy and support, you are boosting trust. The most successful GVT leaders have been found to build environments consistent with the Get Safe phase of the code, namely: communication, support, timely responses, and constructive feedback.[59;60]

It is well-accepted in the scientific community that leadership is probably the most determining factor of psychological safety in a team;[61] however, virtual teams, or any teams for that matter, cannot rely solely on leaders to build safety. Researchers[62] examining virtual teams have identified additional ways for the whole team to contribute to a more positive, less conflictual, and more supportive environment. They have found that the three skill sets of the Get Safe phase, vulnerability, empathy, and learning, all support better team working.

1. Apologizing if you've upset others (vulnerability);

2. Going out of your way to clarify where you are coming from in order to avoid misinterpretations and confusion (empathy);

3. Not waiting to receive feedback but actively reaching out to receive it (vulnerability);

4. Sharing the positivity about the good things you see in others (a form of vulnerability, that has been found to be particularly helpful in virtual project teams).

Sharing knowledge is also especially important in the VT. Team members who proactively share their knowledge really do increase the chances of virtual team success.[63-66]

And it's not just knowledge that the virtual team is advised to share, but feelings, too. Very recent research testifies that virtual team members can be trained to better manage and share their emotions which then reduces conflict in the team.[67] This gives us all hope as it shows we can all improve our emotional intelligence.

And let's throw in the sharing of positivity, too. We know positivity works in digitally transforming teams—as we have found that those that share their positive emotions about working in their virtual teams contribute to the building of a more resilient team.[68]

All of this sharing of knowledge, emotions, and positivity ensures the mood is empathic, positive, and appreciative and as result the virtual team develops an even stronger team identity than created by getting everyone on the same page in the Getting Set phase.[69] Consistent with the code, it really does help to get the virtual team safe once it has successfully got itself "set."

Encourage Team-Level Feedback

"Reflexivity" is a posh way of describing the ability of the team to feedback on *how* it is working and not just *what* it is doing or achieving. It specifically refers to feedback provided by the "whole team" on the whole team. It's also another term that people like me use to make ourselves sound more intelligent than we really are. Reflexivity enables team-based learning to take place. Team based learning is very much part of building the psychologically safe team. The research on it is stark and compelling. Teams that feedback and have high reflexivity significantly outperform those that don't,[53; 70-76] and when the virtual team reflects on how it is upholding those normative agreements made in the Get Set phase, the research confirms that conflict levels fall and levels of trust correspondingly rise.[19;20;27]

Reflexivity also does wonders for creating the "connected" team. This is not to be confused with teams that run the Mafia, although in many ways very much like them, the "connected" team possesses both a strong identity and a sense of community. "Feeling connected" has proven to be an important predictor of creativity in virtual teams.[77] Just ask the Mafia: the "horse's head," the "concrete shoes," and the planning of the Valentine's Day Massacre—they're all creative examples of the highly-connected team. And if I ever did a gig with any team in the Mafia, you can bet your bottom dollar I'd be very much praising them for this.

Proactive reflexivity is also especially important for the GVT. When members of a newly formed GVT openly discuss their cultural differences and how they may play out in the team journey, it helps them perform better.[37;50]

So the advice from the science is clear: if you run a virtual team, turn your attention to getting the team safe but only after you're satisfied it's reasonably well set, and only then go to town on building empathic relationships before then focusing on developing the learning team.

HOW TO GET THE VIRTUAL TEAM SAFE

1. Encourage diversity of views by asking someone by name or by throwing it open... "Who would like to express a different or opposite point of view?" or "What are the pros and cons of this?"

2. Model vulnerability by saying how you feel and where your personal challenges lie.

3. Say what you like and what you appreciate about big

and seemingly insignificant things. Crack a joke. Sometimes it's important to be positive even if you don't feel positive. Your mood is contagious.

4. Listen and restate what you have heard to confirm understanding.

5. Ask how others are feeling—run a few VCs where you allow the team to vent just how they feel.

6. Get the team to show others around their house or office. Help them get to know each other a little.

7. Ask your more senior and outspoken team members to give space to the quieter ones.

8. Take time to check in during your 1:1 meetings on how people are really feeling and what you can do to support them. Don't rush through this.

9. Share successes—no matter how small.

10. Apologize if you've upset others.

11. Go out of your way to clarify where you are coming from in order to avoid misinterpretations and confusion.

12. Don't wait to receive feedback but actively reach out to receive it.

Getting the Virtual Team Strong

So far, you've ensured your virtual team is set and on the same page, you've started to build swift trust, and you are beginning to form a strong identity, which is growing stronger and stronger as you start to amass psychological safety. Having put these foundations in place, the code tells you that you are now in a better position to ramp up the quality and quantity of value creating interactions that characterize the Get Strong phase. Here's what the science says about how to do this for the virtual team. Chapter Ten will elaborate on how to get strong for all types of teams.

Explicit Accountability is King

"When you meet your workmates by the water cooler or photocopier every day, you know instinctively who you can and cannot trust. In a geographically distributed team, trust is measured almost exclusively in terms of reliability."

—ERIN MEYER[78]

We know that we build the most cognitive-based trust when we see reliability in action. Our trust plant grows when watered by kept promises and upheld commitments. In witnessing supportive and benevolent behaviors, we can also feed our plant super powerful plant food to generate powerful and influential emotional based trust. Without reliability, any of the trust accumulated from getting on the same page and this emotion-based trust will be pretty much ruined. Plants need watering. Ultimately, trust requires action not just words.

So the best virtual teams ensure they follow through on the empowerment deal made in the Get Set phase. Team members simply pick up and run with what they have been empowered to do. They are proficient at working autonomously without checking back in with their leaders.[79] They clearly and explicitly commit to their actions. They say what they are going to do, they do it, and then they communicate they have done it. The team leader follows suit. To not just commit to what you are going to do and by when, but to continuously summarize team commitments and team achievements as they are achieved. Making the implicit explicit is very much the order of the day for the virtual team.

Researchers have found that this explicit clarity helps build certainty and trust in the virtual team, and the more the team trust's itself, the more the team benefits from the extra trust generates from this certainty.[80;81] Google also understand that demonstrating reliability is crucial in the virtual team setting, their most successful virtual teams have been those also making the implicit explicit, the ones who have actively shared their actions and their progress.[46;47]

So to help this trust progression occur, the advice from science is to bang out what your virtual team is going to do, who's going to do it, and what your virtual team has achieved. We see the Get Set-Get Strong pathway of the code very evident here.

TEAM INSIGHT: *HOW TO REDUCE EMAIL TRAFFIC*

The sheer volume of emails has been known to be a very real root cause of conflict in the virtual team, especially the GVT.[16] This conflict is not from a lack of trust, nor from misperceptions, nor from a lack of clarity, but from too many emails stealing vital time. The antidote? The team has to set itself the task of reducing its email traffic. Using other forms of communications such as Slack, less CC'ing, and consciously headlining whether the email is "FYI" or "To Action" can all help.

Be Cautious with Constructive Tension

Providing negative feedback can be so challenging that some of us avoid it like the plague. In the virtual team, it becomes even more of challenge though and you have to tread very carefully. Online, it is easy to make inaccurate interpretations of what we see and hear, based on our mood level and what we imagine about what is being said. Perception is reality, but our reality can become distorted. This is especially true when we read emails. I am sure I'm not alone in having to reread an email several times to work out its tone. Even then, I can judge it negatively when there was no need to. Depending on my mood, an email can easily set off my "inner chimp" and I, probably just like you, can become more sensitive and needlessly touchy.[82] The problem with exchanging negative feedback over email is that it's a terrible medium from which proper dialogue can flow. In email, we only really engage in exchanging our positions. This is not dialogue. And it's time-consuming to construct what we think is a point well-made only to go back and forth clarifying, adding, posturing, attacking, and defending on the basis of what we get back. Giving negative feedback or resolving conflict over email is a bloody nightmare. Best to avoid it. Pick up the phone or book a VC.

For the virtual team, accumulating the necessary trust to have constructive Zoom call conversations is the practical answer. But this is not easy. The science confirms that if we exchange performance-related feedback in the virtual team, then there *has* to be sufficient trust present to enable our feedback to be received well.[65; 83] It also tells us that exchanging performance feedback will only result in learning, the main reason why we give it in the first place, if the team members exchanging the feedback actually trust each other.[56; 65] Interestingly, as teams get more virtual, the more important trust becomes in feedback conversations.[83]

So we have to be sure we have the trust to engage in the tougher performance conversations, to be able to hold others to account and to challenge those with whom we share our goals. And we know from the code that we accumulate this trust from the previous stages, cognitive-based in getting set, emotion-based in getting safe, and more profound inter-personal trust when see reliability combined with benevolence, particularly in the getting strong phase. Patience and Diligence is required in the virtual team as all this takes a little longer and the trust is so much easier to lose.

The message is clear on the role of Getting Strong for virtual teams. Sure, you have to keep experimenting, but the research tells us your most important priority is to ostensibly demonstrate accountability and reliability. You have to do this while navigating the building of constructive tension very carefully. It's important that tough conversations take place, but the trust very much has to be there.

HOW TO GET GET THE VIRTUAL TEAM STRONG

1. Emphasize the importance of reliability

2. Endorse reliability by asking the team to declare their commitment to a course of action: on a 0 - 10 scale

3. Encourage reliability by making sure you explicitly state the actions agreed and summarize those that have been achieved

4. Advise the team to give tougher peer-to-peer feedback only when you feel they have acquired sufficient trust to do so

5. If you are going to give negative performance feedback, make it descriptive with lots of examples and emphasize the importance of this to the team

6. Maintain your composure and positivity under duress—you set the emotional tone

7. Avoid sending negative feedback emails. Give your more challenging feedback by VC or at a minimum by phone and encourage the team to do the same

8. Enforce good email etiquette to reduce email volume

TAKEAWAYS

1. Virtual teaming will continue to increase beyond Covid.

2. Use the code to build your virtual team—the science supports it.

3. The main challenges for the VT are productivity, conflict/ trust, and feelings of isolation.

4. It is especially important for the VT to share and agree on its mental models in order to progress through the Get Set phase.

5. Make whatever is implicit explicit—state clearly what's been agreed and especially what's been achieved.

6. Building psychological safety helps reduce conflict and misunderstandings in the VT.

7. Avoid, if possible, tough conversations online and in front of others unless trust in the team is extremely high.

8. Leading the virtual team requires more time and thought than leading a co-located team.

PART 4

How to Use the Code

Chapter 8

How to Get Set

The concept of setting the team sounds counterintuitive. Many of today's teams are in such a constant state of flux, so how can we expect them to Get Set and stay Set? We clearly can't, yet if Getting Set also means being "ready to reset," then Getting Set makes eminent sense.

Getting everybody in your team on the same page from the get-go and keeping them there is what Getting Set is all about. We want your team to feel as certain about where it is going and how it's going to get there as is feasibly practical. We want clarity of what your team can expect from each other. We want them to rapidly build swift trust by *actively* building same page trust. We want your team to be ready to excel at building psychological safety. All of the above define the Get Set part of the code.

A great example of a company that understands the importance of this first part of the code is Netflix. In his storytelling book, *Extreme Teams*, Robert Shaw describes how companies like Netflix, Pixar, Whole Foods, and Patagonia have each developed team working cultures, and in doing so have grown into hugely successful organizations. Netflix stands out. Their transparency and consistency are extraordinary.

In 2009 they published their "Culture Deck,"[1] which outlined their corporate culture, a kind of manifesto for what they stood for, what they expected from anyone working there, and what employees can expect from Netflix in return. The Culture Deck still exists today, and the Netflix transaction remains crystal clear.

Workers at Netflix are expected to be hardworking, unforgiving, and ruthless when it comes to standards and results. Netflix makes it quite clear it is happy to pay whatever it takes to exit people who fail to hit the highest of standards...

> *"Adequate performance gets a generous severance package."*

They employ their famous "keeper test" in which managers are expected to justify keeping people in role by answering this question to a bunch of other managers at performance review time:

> *"Which of my people, if they told me they were leaving for a similar job at a peer company, would I fight hard to keep at Netflix?"*

Netflix has a reputation for being very tough, but they are unashamed of the standards they seek and are crystal clear on the people they want to hire and keep. In fact, they shout about it in their Culture Deck[1]:

Our High-Performance Culture is not right for everyone.

Many people love our culture and stay a long time.

They thrive on excellence and candor and change.

They would be disappointed if given a severance package; their relationship at Netflix is marked by mutual warmth and respect.

Some people, however, value job security and stability over performance, and don't like our culture.

They feel fearful at Netflix.

They are sometimes bitter if let go and feel that we are a political place to work.

We're getting better at attracting only the former, and helping the latter realize we are not right for them.

There are consequences of thriving on excellence, of course. Ernie Tam had been a top performing Netflix engineer for six years, when one day he was summoned into his manager's office on a Monday morning in 2015 and told "You're no longer a star performer." An HR representative then entered, discussed Mr. Tam's severance package, and took possession of his laptop. "I just left the office and never came back," Mr. Tam said. "For a period of six years, I was a star performer, then all of a sudden I was not." Mr. Tam was taken back, because previous bosses, consistent with the Netflix rhetoric, had given him time to improve and develop:

> "We develop people by giving them the opportunity to develop themselves, by surrounding them with stunning colleagues, and giving them big challenges to work on. Mediocre colleagues or unchallenging work is what kills progress of a person's skills."

Yet notice the clear additional message that at Netflix, don't expect to be spoon fed. Mr. Tam's development was very much in his own hands and clearly this time he hadn't developed fast enough. Mr. Tam is one of many at Netflix who have been fired *before* they have been able to develop themselves. Perhaps a more realistic assumption held at Netflix is "you don't have time to develop; you've got to be excellent at everything you do." This unconscious belief might explain why employees put very long, brutal hours in, so they can maintain excellence at all times in order not to get fired. It might also explain why managers are fearful of losing their own jobs if they are not seen to exit enough of their team.[2]

Netflix argues their culture is not as cutthroat as some make out. In 2018, they pointed out they were ranked second on Comparably's "Happiest Employees" list (an index comprised of anonymous employee feedback). [3] They also quote a total turnover amounts to 11 percent a year, which is below the 13 percent annual turnover for technology companies (according to a 2018 study by LinkedIn[4]). Others point out that the happiness result and the relatively low turnover have more to do with the fact that Netflix pays very high salaries, in some cases doubling the pay of new recruits and awarding six-figure raises at salary reviews. They also promise a great reference to those that leave to help them secure other roles.[2] It seems, for all the pressure of the job, people don't want to leave Netflix. To me, that seems like a very transparent deal.

The Getting Set Approach

The process of Getting Set is similar to the aims of the Netflix Culture Deck, as it is about creating some form of certainty and "same page thinking." Yet it is different too, as unlike the "Netflix Way" which is a non-negotiable manifesto thrust upon the entire organization, Getting Set is series of agreements constructed by a team for that team.

The Get Set manifesto states why the team exists, what it is tasked with achieving, and how it is going to achieve it. The Get Set Phase revolves around the team making nine agreements and in doing so, ultimately sharing nine mental models that ensure it's on its way and rapidly building that all-important swift trust.

GET SET	SCORE
MISSION	
1. Our purpose is clear to us and to our stakeholders. 2. Our goal are SMART and are either clearly owned by individuals, by sub-teams or the whole team. 3. We share a vision of what we are trying to achieve.	
PLANS	
4. We agree on a high-level plan to achieve our shared goals including the way we'll communicate to our stakeholders. 5. Team member roles and responsibilities are clear and understood, especially for the goals we share. 6. We agree on our priorities and we are ready to swiftly re-prioritize if we need to.	

DISCIPLINES	
7. Our meeting structures (frequency, timing, invitees, preparation, and agenda-setting) enable both individual and shared goal success.	
8. We agree on our target behaviors and how we will maintain them, including how we would like to be led by our leader.	
9. We have sufficient "skin in the game" to ensure we are motivated to collaborate with others with whom we share goals.	

THE NINE AGREEMENTS MEASURING GETTING SET.
1 - strongly disagree, 2 - disagree, 3- neutral, 4 - agree, 5 - strongly agree
Below 3.2: Requires Urgent Improvement, 3.2-3.8: Requires Some Improvement,
Above 3.8: Team Strength

These nine agreements are all interconnected. Having a purpose will help you form your goals and without your goals in place, it will be hard to clarify the ownership of responsibilities required to land these goals. Our in-house research confirms that teams that are clear on their mission are more likely to be clear on their plans which in turn means they are more likely to be clear on their disciplines. This is illustrated by a real example involving one of my clients, relayed to me by several members who witnessed it.

Julie has the last agenda item, but it's squeezed on time. She's already annoyed before she starts speaking. She holds a forecast constructed from a series of meetings with other team members, and presents a financial challenge of being £250 million overspent. Peter says the figures are too simplistic and claims that much of the overspending sits with the business who are loading their costs onto the team. Jamie chimes in—the original plan was too optimistic, and the size of the challenge is far more onerous than originally thought. We have to push back—the transformation program will be compromised if we don't continue to invest. The mission has to come first. Julie gets more agitated. "You just don't get it, guys." she remonstrates angrily, "We have no choice, we have to hit this number! You lot are not taking accountability—go back into your businesses and find the bloody savings!" She fumes. Rob is getting angrier by the second. He's done what he can to shed cost, now he's being shouted at and accused of not caring, and by someone he doesn't even report to. He says nothing to avoid a confrontation. Sue, the team leader agrees but says little to emphasize the importance of meeting the financial challenge. She's been there before— she knows she has to rock the boat to affect the change, and not sticking to a naïve budget is fine. She also knows that if they don't keep the CFO and CEO happy—her job and the whole program is on the line. Eventually they all agree to look at their costs again. It's another frustrating meeting and not one person leaves happy.

We can see how the **purpose** of the team was not universally understood— was it to turn the organization around, or was it to turn the organization around to an agreed budget? The two are quite different. Some believed they weren't going to be captives to a budget when, by the nature of the task, they didn't know how things would turn out, while others believed there was no question of deviating from what was agreed.

As the purpose of the team wasn't agreed, the goals were also less clear. Did they have to hit this number? There were different views on this, largely stemming from the difference in understanding the team purpose. What's more, the team hadn't agreed whether the financial **goal** they were told to hit, was a shared goal or a goal that only Julie owned. Of course, they would have claimed it was a shared goal, however their behavior belied this. The financial shortfall appeared to sit with Julie, not with the team. She was the one calling the shots. She was the one leading the discussion, most of the room were quiet, and every one of her previous forecasting meetings were scheduled by her office, not by other members of the team. There was no evidence of "this is our goal, let's work it out together."

This goal ambiguity then created different expectations of their **roles and responsibilities**. Julie gave the impression that the financial delta sat with her to fix, even though she didn't believe this to be true, while the team did little to reassure her that they were leading the charge on this too. Julie became anxious and angry about their apparent lack of ownership so naturally being a good leader, she took even more ownership, which only made things worse. Sue, the team leader, meanwhile was nowhere to be seen. She'd already contracted with the team that they were to make as many of the decisions and to work things out as much as they could without her. Great in theory, but there's a difference between empowering and laissez-faire leadership. Eventually she recognized she had to step in and at least emphasize they had to work this out. But she failed to realize they were stuck and needed more of a steer. So instead of being decisive and adamant about their collective responsibility, certainly in a way that reassured Julie, she simply pushed it back to them to sort it out. As team leader, she had also failed to establish any meaningful **skin in the game** for teaming to take place. There were zero consequences being applied to her team members for not leaning in together and collectively solving the problem.

The way the **meeting** was structured further fanned Julie's flames as she was thinking, "How could Sue put a £250 million gap in the financials as the last agenda item in a meeting that regularly runs over time? What does this say about how important the financial shortfall is to Sue and the team?" Yet Julie hadn't realized that she was fully capable of influencing the agenda. In transactional analysis parlance, she was oscillating between persecutor and victim.

The **norms** this team had already set were not being upheld. This was because they were simply not front of mind. And this was because they had failed to reflect on them at the end of their previous meetings, as they had originally committed to do. So although they had contracted to be direct and not to withhold opinions or feelings, Julie, who was feeling distinctly isolated, chose to avoid disclosing this in favor of only communicating her anger. Nor did she challenge Sue and ask her to take a more definitive stance. Rob felt very angry at being shouted at but chose to keep quiet. This would have generated the unhelpful assumption that their agreed team norms weren't worth the paper they were written on.

This story, relayed to me by several team members, illustrates how getting on the same page is a multifaceted endeavor. Without agreement in one part, the team's struggled to form agreements in others. As a result, emotions can run very high which in turn then impact the trust and psychological safety across the team. The emotional charge in the room meant that the team were less equipped to resolve its conflict. The team were floundering in the Get Safe phase, which contributed to sub-standard psychological safety which in turn compromised the ability of the team to collaborate and manage arising tensions. In this story, we see the opposite of Getting Set to Get Safe to Get Strong. We see the root cause of the team fracture orginating in the Get Set phase, just as the code predicts.

It also summarizes the spine or, more accurately, the back-brace of the Get Set phase—as these building blocks are inter-connected—which when absent, can prove to be so costly. Much of my early work with a team is to help them construct this back-brace. If you've tried to make a plan without first understanding the precise outcomes you wish to achieve, you'll appreciate that the challenge isn't just what goes into the back-brace, but the order in which to build it. Fortunately, both common sense and science helps us out here.

How to Agree on the Mission

One of the most influential researchers and writers on teams, the late Richard Hackman[5] made the acquisition of a shared purpose one of his top six conditions for successful teaming. Subsequent research has validated the importance he placed on defining team purpose.[i.e., 6-9] More recently, the success of Sinek's book *Start with Why*[10] exemplifies not only his excellent writing, but the growing appetite we have to understand why we exist and what we stand for.

The case studies in the Dyer's[11] book also emphasize the importance they place on defining a shared mission, including defining the shared purpose and the shared goals *between* teams. They recognized that when a shared purpose is established in a team, the goals and accompanying plans can then be agreed from which the appropriate meeting structures and behavioral norms could then be identified. In doing so, they perfectly described the core elements of the Get Set phase in motion, starting with agreeing on the team's purpose.

It's actually not that difficult to agree on the purpose of a team in the form of a statement. Hackman recommended that this statement emphasize the contribution the team makes. He emphasized it had to be easy to understand and challenging to achieve in order to convert it into more of a motivational mission. The way to generate a purpose statement is to work through a three-part statement:

1. What does your team uniquely do or deliver?
2. Who do you do it for?
3. Why do you do it?

TEAM INSIGHT: *CREATING A PURPOSE*

I have found it takes about an hour of debate to construct something that reasonably ticks all the boxes. Finesse this with a few iterations after the meeting and you'll get a purpose statement fit for purpose. Watch out for the curse of team wordsmithing, though. This can take hours and hours.

Here's an example of a great Purpose Statement from a team responsible for change:

We enable profound improvement in how the organization delivers change in order to accelerate the safe delivery of what matters for our customers, our colleagues, and the Group, by challenging convention, providing better method, and transferring capability.

To make the most of purpose statements like this, I advise teams to regularly refer to it in their decision making, to check any new team goals align with it when they are made, and to pull out the statement and discuss it to help recharge energy, excitement, and passion, especially in the tougher times.

Identify Shared Goals

The Mission part of Getting Set includes one of the most important skills of a team. To be able to set goals and agree which of these are shared goals and which are not. If goals in your team represent a pizza, are your team bringing individual pizza slices to you that add up to one big pizza at the end of the year, or are they working more closely together to bring "joint" pizza slices and segments?

Many years ago, I worked as the sports psychologist to Southampton Football Club, a Premiership football team that was at the time managed by the legendary ex-England international Glen Hoddle and his likeable assistant John Gorman. Glen and John combined very well together. Hoddle was the strategic thinker and Gorman organized practice and built a great team spirit. The season I worked with them I saw first-hand how well they collaborated, helping Southampton achieve their highest ever end of season league position. When they separated to manage different clubs, neither found anywhere near the same success.

At Southampton we focused on shared goals in the sub-units of attack, midfield, and defense. We wanted the players to understand they had a joint responsibility for each of these sub-units. Some of these shared goals sat between these subunits. Making 90 percent of passes required a) a good accurate pass and b) good movement by the receiver to get in a position to receive the pass. Pass completion is a proper shared goal—it requires both an unerring pass and the movement of the receiver to get into a space to receive it. To bring these goals to life, I would sit with each subunit, such as the attack comprising James Beattie, Marion Pahars, and Kevin Davies, and we'd talk about what they required from each other to help them achieve their shared goals. I'd do the same with the midfield trio and the defensive units. Then I'd work with Glen to help him pay attention to the shared goals of the whole team such as retaining possession and set piece marking. We managed to engender a collective sense of responsibility amongst the team, where egos, in a very real sense, became diluted in favor of the overall team agenda as team members realized they were dependent on each other for individual and team success. When you consider the typical millionaire young Premiership football player, this was not easy. If shared goals can be understood amongst so-called "prima donna" football players, they can be understood anywhere.

We also embraced the concept of setting performance goals. Studies show that teams perform better and develop more resilience over time when they set SMART performance goals.[12-15] The achievement of a performance goal means we can control and influence it. For the players at Southampton this meant not winning, or scoring a set number of goals, or anything else that they couldn't really influence or control. It meant striving to make 90 percent of passes, putting 75 percent of crosses into the "danger zone" or tracking back and defending when they lost the ball.

In their highly pragmatic book *The Discipline of Teams*, Jon Katzenbach and Douglas Smith[16] focused on the "hard stuff" more than the "soft stuff" and brought to our attention the difference between a "leader led goal" and a "true team goal." Where leader led goals are more like individual pizza slices, true team goals are proper shared goal that requires a very different type of leadership and teaming to guarantee success. More recently, emanating from agile working, we have we have OKRs (or Outcomes and Key Results), which are goals described in outcome format. Whatever type of goals a team has in front of it, the most important question a team can ask itself is this:

Which of these goals require us to really collaborate together, and which are mainly individual endeavors requiring a bit of support?

TEAM INSIGHT: *CLARIFYING SHARED GOALS*

When I ask where the shared goals exist across a team, I will
often get either an array of different answers or just confused
faces. Automatically, this tells me the necessary clarity
of where teaming is most important in that team is almost
certainly missing. The clarity of inter-team goals is often
equally vague, which is of real concern given most teams
now operate in teams of teams. Understanding where team
members are dependent on others in and outside of team for
their mutual success really is *the* bed rock of team working.
The discipline of virtual teams, cross-functional teams, and
even inter-organizational alliance teams requires this kind of
up-front clarity. The Dyers emphasize the growing importance
of alliance teams. They also strongly advocate clarifying the
shared goals, which tasks sit with which goals, and which roles
and responsibilities sit with which tasks, all classic Getting
Set conversations.

As we'll see in the next chapter, understanding goal
dependency supports the art of humble dialogue that Edgar
and Peter Schein so fervently advocate. As we will see in
chapters nine and ten, it is humble dialogue that really opens
the door to creativity, coordinated action and value adding
collaboration. Once again, we see Getting Set helping us to Get
Safe which then helps us to Get Strong. We see the validity of
the code coming through.

So after you form your purpose, you can then start to identify
your shared goals. You don't need to work out every single
shared goal that exists—just five or six of the most important.
My experience is that if you can work well on these, and in the
right way, then you will most likely collaborate well on their
other shared goals too.

INDIVIDUAL PIZZA SLICE GOALS	SHARED PIZZA SEGMENT GOALS
+ You each bring a slice of pizza to the table - all the individual slices of pizza add up to 1 big team pizza delivery.	+ You contribute to a pizza segment which requires you to "really" collaborate and "do work" with others in your delivery team.
+ Although you have to collaborate with others to deliver your pizza slice, essentially you and your department do most of the work.	+ If one of the delivery team fails, the whole delivery team fails.
+ The buck stops with you and you only. The team leader holds you alone accountable for success or failure.	+ The delivery team members, not the team leader, hold each other accountable for the delivery of their shared goal.

How to Agree on the Plans

You've agreed your purpose and your goals, so now let's work from some kind of plan to achieve them. It sounds simple enough, and sometimes it really is, but for many teams, this is where a blockage in the Get Set phase will occur. Of course, formulating strategies, plans and priorities are not one-off activities; they require continuous updating. It's been obvious to me that different team members require different amounts of certainty to feel comfortable. I've seen several senior teams in a pensions business stall on their plans because the executive team to which they report wasn't clear on the overall company strategy. I've seen situations where plans coming down from "on high" have been so short lived, and subject to so much change, that teams have purposefully ignored them, knowing they'll only change again.

The fact that there is so much uncertainty and one team's strategy affects another's adds significant complexity to the planning challenge.

Let's also not forget that the ability of a team to agree on its plans is also related to how that team is able to work together. Unlike all the other elements of the Get Set Phase, which are more like simple agreements, the planning element requires good dialogue skills and process to be done well. Essentially, the ability of the team to be proficient in the Get Safe and Get Strong phases come to bear on this particular part of the Get Set phase. So in some respects, it makes sense to first develop the dialogue skill and the psychological safety *in order to* plan. However, without a trained facilitator in the room to point out patterns and to coach the team to improve its process, most teams can't wait to build safety or more advanced communication skills. Under pressure of time, they have to be able to work from some kind of high-level plan from which priorities will emerge and change over time. That is why the code and the science behind it advises the team Gets Set before it Gets Safe. Achieving some kind of certainty that the team is either on the right track or is getting on the right track is really what this part of Getting Set is all about.

Organizational Ambidexterity

Organizational Ambidexterity is the ability of an organization to exploit a current business model while simultaneously exploring future opportunities. Organizational ambidexterity does not necessarily need ambidextrous employees,[17] in fact organizations do better when they separate their functions that are involved in exploitation and explorative activities.[18] For many teams, though, this separation is just not possible. Many leadership styles have to do both. Similarly, smaller businesses just don't have the resources to separate these roles; they are forced to explore and exploit at the same time and with the same people in the room. These teams don't have the luxury of working on their aircraft in the hangar, they have to change their engines while flying at 35,000 feet.

Teams operating in the explorative domain have to be able to make decisions in complex, chaotic, and disorderly environments[19] while those who are tasked with exploiting what they already have make their decisions in more simple and complicated situations. This requires immense decision-making versatility as many have to exploit as well as explore. In complex situations where there are unknown unknowns, teams can't rely on collecting data, analyzing it, and then making plans, they have to probe around not knowing what they'll find before they then find it and respond accordingly. This is what Ed and Cho had to do quite regularly: walk until they met a threat, then decide there and then how they were going to deal with it. In chaotic situations, cause and effect are so unclear it makes no sense for the team to probe around. It's best they just take an action, any action, and iterate on the back of whatever emerges. Here, the team is attempting to move into a complex situation, where it can become aware of emerging patterns from which it can then act. In situations of more extreme disorder, the team has no idea what decision-making domain it is in and no way of finding out. The only option may be to break down the decision into constituent parts, allocate them to one of the four other domains, and then see what happens.

Ambidextrous Decision Making

DISORDER			
1	**2**	**3**	**4**
SIMPLE	**COMPLICATED**	**COMPLEX**	**CHAOTIC**
BEST PRACTICE	GOOD PRACTICE	EMERGENT	NOVEL
Sense	Sense	Probe	Act
Categorize	Analyze	Sense	Sense
Respond	Respond	Respond	Respond

Teams have to be able to flex their decision-making approach.

Teams today, in light of Dx especially, have to be able to convert their goals into plans in many of these different decision-making environments and all at the same time. That's some challenge.

Whatever decision-making situations faced by the team, the research tells us that some certainty is important, even if the plan is not to have a plan or to set about forming a plan. Getting Set simply means the whole team is on the same page, is doing what it can get a plan, and is ready to re-plan if required to do so. I have seen plenty of teams do this well, and I've seen plenty of teams struggle. As long as the team have bright people, are prepared to dedicate the right amount of time to the task and have some steer from others they rely on in the organization of where the business is heading, this is a challenging but eminently feasible team task.

TEAM INSIGHT: *GETTING READY TO RESET*

A crucial component of Getting Set is the ability of your team to re-plan and to be ready to pivot. In the Get Set phase, your requirement is not actually to pivot, but simply to be ready to pivot. I have found that a helpful way to build confidence and certainty that the team is ready to do this is for the team to ask itself:

1. What scenarios might emerge that will require us to rapidly change direction?

2. What do we have to do so that we are ready to initiate a change in direction if one of these scenarios presents itself?

3. How do we want to react when we get our curve balls?

Getting on the same planning pages also entails collaborative stakeholder conversations with those outside of the team who influence the team's ability to achieve its goals. Peter Hawkins recommends bringing "outside in" thinking here, where it is the stakeholders of the team that we must especially engage with, to help us construct our purpose, goals, and plans so they are constructed with their agendas in mind more than our own. Stakeholder conversations simply have to be prioritized, planned, and executed on an ongoing basis.

As we discovered in the last chapter on virtual working, the mentality of "just do it" also has to be applied to clarifying team roles and responsibilities and especially being clear on who's responsible for what decisions. This is one of the most important tasks in the Get Set Phase which first requires the understanding and agreement of which goals are shared and co-owned.

Roles, Responsibilities, and Empowered Execution

As General McChrystal emphasizes, it's not just individual goals that
require empowered execution, most goals in this increasingly complex
world are shared and these also require the boss to get out of the way to let
those responsible for collaborating on the same pizza slices or segments
of pizza to run the show without undue interference. In a shared goal, the
"true team" involved, as Katzenbach and Smith referred to it, influences
each other, challenges each other, supports each other, and brings the goal
home collectively. Only when they need help or they can't agree do they
seek direction from above.

As my client Julie discovered in the previous story, the dysfunction
experienced had at its core an abdication of responsibilities right across the
team. The shared nature of that financial goal necessitated a very different
set of responsibilities than those imagined by the team. Julie had passed the
responsibility for making sure the topic had adequate airtime to the Sue,
the team leader, who herself had failed to recognize that when the team
was stuck on a shared goal; it was her role to try to help unblock matters.
Meanwhile, the rest of the team were in reactive mode, failing to show any
initiative for the shared problem, instead treating it as if it was solely Julie's
pizza slice. Each of these dysfunctions interacted with the other to raise the
emotional charge in the room, which, as we all know, rarely helps matters.

TEAM INSIGHT: *USE HUMBLE CURIOSITY FOR CLARITY*

Those responsible for shared goals simply have to have open
conversations, upfront and throughout the process, to clarify
roles and responsibilities. They can start the conversation at
one of their earliest meetings together. Then when it appears
there are blockages or ambiguities, it's a great page to
which to return.

*"Can I confirm what I think I'm responsible for here and what
I think you're responsible for?"* is a direct and challenging

question. Asked with genuine curiosity and humility, though, it will often reveal the root cause of conflict you are seeing in your team.

Clarifying roles and responsibilities is really not a difficult task, provided it is done in a non-telling kind of why. After all, if the same people have different understandings of what they're required to do, it doesn't mean they are lazy, stupid, or difficult. It usually means they've either been told something different, quite often by the same person, or they've applied unconscious filters (usually from past experiences) to the same message. "Can you get involved?" for some means "Can you run the show?" whilst for others it can mean "Shout if think I'm needed." The good news is that differences can nearly always be resolved, if not by those disagreeing then with the help of others involved, with the last resort having them spelled out by their boss.

How to Agree on the Disciplines

Now your team is clear on its mission and its plans. To be sure of completing the Get Set Phase though, and ready excel at building psychological safety in the Get Safe phase, you will want your team to agree on three important disciplines. These have been proven to support the execution of business plans: how your team meets, how it rewards itself, and how it wants to behave.

Meetings

You want the minimal governance time required to deliver the goals of the team including, especially if the team is highly interdependent, the time it takes for the team to feel well connected. Agreeing what meetings are necessary and how these will be constructed and attended will flow naturally on the back of the goals, roles, and plans you've already established. The process of the meeting—the way the team converses, makes decisions, and behaves—veers into the Get Safe and Get Strong phases. In these phases, you will especially want the norms the team signs up to being demonstrated. You will want to see all the Get Safe competencies in evidence and a climate high in psychological safety. That way, effective decision making, innovation, and collaboration will more likely flow. In the Get Set phase, we want your team to be very focused on the structure of its meetings and to be sure it is happy with the following aspects:

1. **Agenda Discipline:** is it fit for purpose and are right people in the room and ready to contribute?

2. **Empowerment Execution:** are the owners of the goals doing the presenting on their part of the agenda and those sharing the goals doing the challenging, probing, and responding?

3. **Shared Goals:** are team members presenting to each other rather than just the leader?

4. **Getting Safe:** has the team dedicated sufficient time to feeding back on how it is working together and what it is learning about itself?

5. **Sub-Teams:** are meetings taking place where necessary in addition to the whole team meetings, and are they fit for purpose?

6. **Team Leader:** have you and the team agreed your role at your whole team meetings and sub-team meetings?

7. Are the more **strategic** and long- and short-term planning requirements of the team accommodated?

8. **Resetting:** do your meeting structures allow your team to pick up, in good time, when some resetting or pivoting is required?

Skin in the Teaming Game

Apparently, an alarming percentage of parachutes were failing to open in World War II and the allies were losing too many unnecessary lives as a result. The parachute packing department was ordered to improve their reliability by the powers to be. The staff responsible for packing the parachutes said that they couldn't do this, that they were already doing everything they could, and improvements were impossible. So the commander told them that rather than hand them out to the soldiers, he would be initiating parachute testing and the staff would be randomly selected to make these test jumps. The reliability rate soon exceeded the demanded level.

The principle is not new of course. In his book *Skin in the Game,*[20] Nassim Taleb (of *Black Swan* fame) informs of us the earliest documented example, Hammurabi's law, was posted on a basalt stele circa 3,800 years ago:

> *"If a builder builds a house and the house collapses and causes death of the owner of the house, the builder shall be put to death."*

I'm very close to sending this quote to our builder.

Taleb demonstrates that only with skin in the game, can we ever achieve symmetry in our transactions. His challenge to Financial Advisors who offer us paid advice is this:

> *"Don't tell me what you think, tell me what's in your portfolio."*

Brilliant and simple. In the Get Set phase, providing skin in the team game is simply ensuring those who play a part in a shared goal, either stand to win or lose by their involvement. Organizations are excellent at pledging there is skin in the game when it comes to individual achievements, but it tends to stop there. They play relative lip service to guaranteeing there is enough cost/reward to the way their team collaborates on their shared goals, either within the team, and especially with other teams.

Money is the obvious currency of cost or reward. For many people, it is all they want. Most sales managers know the way to a salesperson's heart is via the bonus they stand to get from selling more. But it doesn't end there. It can include development opportunities, extra responsibilities, appreciation, or simply gratitude. Getting on the same page when it comes to ensuring there is skin in the team game is not that easy. Most team leaders hand reward and recognition to the HR department and accept the status quo. They don't fight for their corner. This is a big mistake. In doing so, they are not maximizing the chances of shared goal success. When challenged, just about every team I've ever worked with accepts that, actually, there's a lot they can do to influence the way their teams are recognized and rewarded.

As we saw in Chapter One, individualism is on the rise and not all individuals strive for the benefit of the greater good, but in many ways, who cares? If we ensure there is skin in the team game then the individualistic will win, the team will win and other teams in the ecosystems will also win. Skin in the team game maximizes the chances that everybody involved wins together.

Simple Ways to Ensure Skin in the Teaming Game

1. Make sure any *shared* goal involvement is *explicitly and sufficiently represented* in the performance review process.
2. Ensure in your one-to-ones that the amount of time you spend discussing progress on shared goals is reflective of the actual significance of these goals.
3. Ask questions about how the sub-team is working and what they are doing to help that sub-team work well.
4. Praise and hold to account the whole sub-team together, rather than pick off members individually.

Norms

We saw in the previous chapter, that regardless of whether teams are virtual or co-located, establishing clear norms helps those teams perform better. Part of Ed and Luke's downfall laid in not doing this. Ed wanted to walk farther and faster and was critical and harsh, Luke wanted to take it easy and desired a more positive climate. They didn't agree on how they were going to be together, instead, like so many teams, it was assumed. On the other hand, Netflix is crystal clear and takes great lengths to ensure the deal it makes with its employees is explicit and totally unambiguous. If they could tie a banner to the moon, visible from earth, articulating their norms, I've no doubt they would have done it by now.

The best teams bring the same level of clarity to bear, but at the team level. I advise teams to make these agreements with other teams inside and outside their organization with whom they collaborate.

As described in Chapter Six, I also find it a very worthwhile endeavor to agree leadership deals between the team leader and the whole team. Typically the team's requests include air cover, communications, and empowerment, while the leader will encourage decisiveness, courage, and problems that are also accompanied with solutions. When the deal is made, a mental model is shared, same page trust increases, swift trust follows, and as the team has participated in creating a shared output, the team also feels more emotionally connected. That's what I call a good deal for all.

TEAM INSIGHT: *FORMING TEAM NORMS*

I run an exercise where I ask the team to individually write down all the behaviors they most detest and vehemently don't want to see in their team (for example, *"unreliability"*). They then pool these behaviors, put them into groups or themes, give each group a "heading" of a reverse behavior (for example, "do what we say we'll do"), and then prioritize their eight to ten most important headings. These then form the basis of normative statements they most want from the team.

Getting Set in Action

Bill and Ben own a very successful, fast-growing, and award-winning property agency. Bill runs the team that wins the leasing deals, and Ben, the team of surveyors that prices the refitting and refurbishments their clients want. Both teams operate quite differently, bound by a different set of assumptions of how to work in their part of the business. Bill's team is innovative, fast, abrasive, bold, and daring. They have to be win deals, outthink the competition, and survive in a very cutthroat environment. They are incredibly successful, led by Bill, who has a reputation in the industry for being one of the most innovative, charismatic, visionary, and toughest businessmen around. Self-belief is one of his stand-out strengths, and it has enabled him to keep going when others have doubted him. Ben's team of surveyors are more introverted, quieter, diligent, and sensitive who value accuracy above all in order to avoid lawsuits made against the firm. Ben is well respected within the industry for his breadth and depth of knowledge, and for his strong moral stance to do the right thing, even it means saying "No" to demanding clients.

Recently, Ben's team has been losing several long serving surveyors, who have departed, complaining of being overworked, underpaid, and given a very tough time by Bill and his team. Bill resembles Ed in the Amazon—he sets the highest of standards nor doesn't suffer fools gladly. He and several senior members of his team have been berating Ben's team for not being quick enough to complete the work that his team requires to win their deals. Ben's team complain all they seem to get from Bill is criticism, impatience, anger, sarcasm, and non-negotiable dictates. There is not a lot of appreciation, dialogue, civility, help, or empathy for the situation they face. It feels to them as if they are just objects to enable the stars of the business to go do their magic. Bill has little time for their frustration, seeing it as a sign they don't set their standards high enough nor take sufficient ownership for the work that has to be done. He feels he has to spoon-feed them too much. He's fed up with them and their whining and is quick to anger when he speaks with them. Ben feels stuck in the middle. As a partner, he knows how important it is that the dealmakers are supported, and he knows that the brilliance of Bill is one of the reasons the business and his bank balance are doing so well. But he also knows his team are working all hours and are feeling distinctly unappreciated. He also can't afford to lose any more staff. Tensions between him and Bill are at an all-time high and he feels so stuck and depressed, he's not sleeping. It's not as if they can work this out between them as there are no formal meetings between the two teams. Ben's team would rather not have them anyway. At the last meeting, when one or two spoke up, they were rounded on and humiliated by a very angry Bill.

The story illustrates how shortcuts in the Get Set phase contributed to compromised psychological safety. There wasn't a common set of behavioral guidelines that bound their two very different sub-cultures together. This was proving costly as they shared goals and just as we found with Ed and Luke, underneath these goals were unclear roles and responsibilities. Bill's view of ownership of work was different than that held by the surveying team. There were also no meetings between them to ensure they were working well together. Those that they did have were characterized by Bill telling Ben and his team what he and his team wanted them to do. Following the code enabled Bill and Ben to bring their exciting vision for the business to the fore, clarify the goals they shared, agree on the responsibilities that sat with their teams, co-create a set of values and behaviours they could all sign up to and gain consensus on what type of meetings would enable overall team success. The Performance Review process was also redesigned to ensure all the team had skin in the game for honoring the norms agreed. Consistent with the code, trust and levels of psychological safety began to improve. With the basics done, we only then really started working on the dialogue and the way they were interacting together.

TAKEAWAYS

1. Getting Set is where we start our team development journey. It involves the team making nine sets of agreements with each other and remaking them whenever necessary. Several of these agreements are interconnected, particularly purpose, goals, roles, meetings, norms, and skin in the team game.

2. Form a purpose statement and regularly refer to it to help guide your decision making.

3. Make sure your team is crystal clear on the goals that are shared and who's sharing them.

4. Make the implicit explicit. This includes clarifying the high-level plan, roles, and responsibilities and your team norms.

5. Agree team leadership/team membership deal.

6. Ensure there is skin in the game, but remember it is difficult to do this if there is no obvious game and no obvious skin.

7. Getting on the same page builds confidence, certainty, and "same page trust." Equipped with these, your team will be more able to progress through the next two phases of its development, Getting Safe and Getting Strong.

Chapter 9

How to Get Safe

Greg Hill is a world-record-holding extreme skier who has achieved some extraordinary feats of courage, endurance, and skill. The owner of multiple world records, he told me a story about travelling to Pakistan to shoot a film of him skiing down a treacherous peak that had never been skied before. It entailed him ascending with a team of European skiers and a film crew up to a high point of 5,500 meters, before choosing a line and making his descent. As anybody who skis off-piste will know, his biggest risks were falling or setting off an avalanche. Both can be deadly in the extreme skiing game. Greg, like others pro skiers, trusts his technique not to worry so much about falling, especially in this descent as it wasn't that rocky. The risk of avalanche was significant though. The area was prone to having them and a lot of snow had recently fallen. Avalanches don't tend to respect how good a skier you are, they just kill you. His home playground was British Columbia, so he was not familiar at all with this terrain. This nearly cost him his life.

Greg and the team ascended, the climb long and tiring. Greg was aware that the team was getting weary in the thinning air and were keen to get some decent footage in return for their efforts. Eventually he reached the very top, picked his line, and dropped in. A few seconds later an avalanche was triggered. Avalanches can reach speeds of eighty miles per hour after just five seconds. Greg was just a statistic waiting to happen. Incredibly, he had the calmness, under threat of imminent death, to calibrate the safest place to ski to where he felt the avalanche would be less potent. He never made it, though; within seconds he was swept off his skis and down the mountain. Incredibly, he was still able to think rationally, and despite being tossed around like a rag doll, going head over heels under the snow, he tried to keep his head as near to the surface as possible. His body contorted, twisted, and turned with the movement of the snow. Then he felt the excruciating pain of his leg snapping. As he felt the surge slowing, still very much with his wits about him, and knowing that suffocation is a primary cause of death in avalanches, he put his hands in front of his face to ensure he created an air hole from which to breathe, also swimming and struggling to remain near the surface of the snow. When he did stop moving, he was completely frozen into in a tomb of concrete like snow. Luckily for him, he was on the surface and his head was out of the snow. He couldn't breathe as snow had got into and frozen in his mouth. Calmly, he waited for his body temperature to warm it up so that it would melt enough for him to be able to spit it out. He was then able to breathe and await rescue. Thanks to his calmness under pressure, and against all the odds, he survived, with nothing more than a broken leg. Greg knows he was lucky to be alive.

Speaking about it afterwards, Greg realized he'd made two big mistakes. The first was losing his perspective and succumbing to Kodak Courage.

> "I am not sure why my sensors didn't go off, but they should have. I was at the top, waiting for the sun to come out so I could rip it. When it did appear, the camera crew told me to drop in, so I decided to go. It was my first ever descent in Pakistan and I just wanted to ski the slope. The issue was there were not a lot of escape options once I had committed to the line. What I didn't do was ski cut the snow, ski a bit, then ski cut and stop until I was lower down the line. I wanted to give the cameras something from the top, so I just skied it."

The second mistake he made was not creating a climate in the team where the European skiers could feel safe enough to challenge his decision to ski that line without testing it first. The Euros were too much in awe of him. He was the great Greg Hill. Nobody questioned him. He told me what he most needed at that time was the voice of sanity. Back home, Greg's friends were not intimidated by him or his world records. Rather than fear the consequences of speaking out, they feared the consequences of not speaking out. But Greg didn't clock this. His humility got the better of him. He didn't see himself as a star, revered and able to intimidate. Greg admitted to me that he wished he would have impressed upon the team, the importance of speaking up and challenging him if they felt it compromised his or anybody else's safety. He would have set about building much more psychological safety.

The Getting Safe Approach

The code advises that to get the best out of your team, it's important to build high levels of psychological safety and to do this, it helps if we're on the same page, so your team is more able to be vulnerable with each other, be empathic, and learn together. The code then says your team is then able to leverage this safety to propel them into interactions that then really drive value. As we know, all of this is supported by scientific research. Of course, you don't wait for your team to be set before engaging in the skills that create psychological safety, you want to see these from the get-go. However, the code tells us that before you invest time specifically improving and developing these skills, you first ensure the team shares the mental models in the Get Set phase. Remember, the science supports this order of development.

Part of the reason you Get Set before you Get Safe is to calm your team down. The swift trust built from being on the same page helps to reduce levels of fear, agitation, and concern. As we saw with Ed and Luke, these compromise psychological safety. It doesn't end with Getting Set, though. Far from it, the ability of your team to manage its emotions in the way it interacts with each other, as we shall see throughout this chapter, will hugely influence its ability to build psychological safety.

GET SAFE	SCORE*
VULNERABILITY	
1. We are open about what we don't know and good at asking for help. 2. We use humor, appreciation and gratitude to create a positive and optimistic atmosphere. 3. We feel confident to say how we really feel, without fear of reprisal.	
EMPATHY	
4. We listen well, picking up on both content and emotions. 5. We respect diversity, encouraging contributions from each other. 6. We are generous at sharing our knowledge and in offering help.	

DISCIPLINES	
7. Our meeting structures (frequency, timing, invitees, preparation, and agenda-setting) enable both individual and shared goal success.	
8. We agree on our target behaviors and how we will maintain them, including how we would like to be led by our leader.	
9. We have sufficient "skin in the game" to ensure we are motivated to collaborate with others with whom we share goals.	

THE NINE BEHAVIORS MEASURING GETTING SAFE.
1 - strongly disagree, 2 - disagree, 3 - neutral, 4 - agree, 5 - strongly agree
Below 3.2: Requires Urgent Improvement, 3.2-3.8: Requires Some Improvement,
Above 3.8: Team Strength

How to Build Vulnerability

We know that to fuel learning, teams have to be comfortable being vulnerable by taking the time to reflect on how they are working together as a unit.[4] As we discovered in Chapter Six, learning and adaptability are very much team sports.

Amy Edmondson's research[5] demonstrates how being a little bit vulnerable with each other is one of the most powerful ways a team can build psychological safety, and for Brené Brown, a resident expert on the subject, it's an essential ingredient, not just for psychological safety, but also for creativity.

"Vulnerability is the birthplace of love, belonging, joy, courage, empathy, and creativity."

—BRENÉ BROWN[6]

All very well, but how do you go about doing it? Being vulnerable sounds horrendous doesn't it, like something terrible is about to happen? It doesn't have to be; in fact, it can be liberating.

Admit Imperfections and Ask for Help

In the previous chapter, we could see that property man Bill showed little vulnerability. He had unbridled self-confidence. Just like a heavy weight boxer, he'd never been interested in admitting his weaknesses. Vulnerability was the last thing he'd wanted to leak in his cutthroat world of winning property deals. What he hadn't clocked, though, was that he's more than a deal maker; he leads his organization. He hadn't taken his "deal making hat" off when he entered the office and had learned to replace it with his "leadership hat." He continued to swagger, talk big, and be impenetrable. Just like Ed when he started his walk in the jungle, he showed zero weaknesses and no chinks in his rather impressive armor.

The players at Southampton football club playing under Glen Hoddle would have agreed that a little bit of self-deprecation goes a long way. Glen used to intimidate them at practice, sometimes preferring to rely on himself to take the crosses at the practice sessions. What impact do you think that had on his players? Admitting imperfections is not that difficult. We just have to find a way to own up to things we're not so sure about or haven't done well and be open and explicit about things we're not that good at.

TEAM INSIGHT: *THE TOUGH CAN BE VULNERABLE*

Alex Ferguson, the most decorated soccer manager of all time, revealed how he used vulnerability to help break bad news to star players at Manchester United that he was dropping them.

> "I tell them 'Look, I might be making a mistake here'—I always say
> that—'but I think this is the best team for today.' I try to give them
> a bit of confidence, telling them that it is only tactical and that
> bigger games are coming up."
>
> —Sir Alex Ferguson[7]
>
> Notice how one of the toughest and most ruthless bosses
> soccer as ever seen, in his own words, "always" made himself
> just a little bit vulnerable when giving bad news to players.

Under duress when we are emotionally charged, we are also less likely to
hold our hands up, admit we don't know something, or convey we might
need a bit of help. One of my clients, Karen, a global Human Resources
Director, lived in fear of not being good enough, especially in the eyes of her
boss. Over time, she has learned to request more time, more information
or a little bit of help understanding what's being asked of her from those
who lead her. Appearing not to be in perfect control is a skill set that really
can be acquired. The breakthrough moment for Karen occurred when she
had the humility to realize she was actually dependent on others to achieve
her goals. Ed and Peter Schein term this moment "here and now humility,"
a kind of humility that transcends any traits of humility we may naturally
possess. They describe it as a *feeling* which occurs when we know we are
dependent on someone else in a situation. Some of us would rather risk
failure than admit we're dependent on others. When we share the reality
that we are dependent on others to achieve a goal, they more readily share
the necessary information required to achieve that goal.

Say How You Feel

Chapters One and Six describe a mental health crisis which very much
looks like it will get worse not better. Being able to disclose how we actually
feel is an important way to stay healthy and to seek the help we need
when we need it.

I feel vulnerable writing this book. It will soon be in the public domain, and I've no idea how it will be received. It could get panned and as a result, I might get panned. Sometimes I worry my writing is not good enough and sometimes I worry that by spending so much time improving it, I'm compromising the unity of my family and the success of my consultancy business.

As I've just demonstrated, being vulnerable is actually quite simple. It just requires candor and the sharing of important, truthful information about ourselves, which, in doing so, incurs a risk of being negatively judged. When we are vulnerable, we are more likely to build intimacy in our relationships and to draw people toward us rather than away from us.

In the budget discussion in the previous chapter, Julie became angry and accusatory because of what she considered a laissez-faire attitude toward a massive budgetary shortfall. The team who didn't understand the nature of this shared goal, the codependencies at work, and what ownership actually looked like only made her more angry. In that relatively low trust environment, Julie was the polar opposite of being emotionally calm, she was so charged, she simply couldn't access and display any natural empathy. She was agitated partly because she felt very exposed and partly because she expected more from her colleagues. In her mind, they didn't share the same sense of urgency and the same sense of ownership as she did for the issue. She was thinking "this isn't my sole pizza slice—we share this issue, so I shouldn't be the *only* one leading the charge here," "you lot should be much more on top of your numbers, it's complete joke you're so far out," and "this issue is so important, what the hell is it doing last on the bloody agenda!" These "should" messages, understandable as they were, made her exceptionally angry, and feeling like a victim, she turned on her persecutors with hostility and venom. Yes, everything she was saying was spot on, however, she would have had unquestionably more impact if she had instead exposed to the team her own vulnerabilities. To do this required her to reveal what was really happening inside of her and expose the reality of how she was *actually feeling*. This obviously included anger, but also, as she disclosed afterwards, feelings of isolation and fear. Sharing calmly this more intimate so-called "softer" information paradoxically may well have been much harder hitting. However, in the heat of the moment, she wasn't even aware of these innermost feelings, she was only aware of her more obvious anger, so in her agitated state, providing the team with this form of vulnerability proved to be way beyond her. She had also assumed, most likely unconsciously, that getting angry was the best route to achieve the outcome she wanted, which was to influence the team to engage in a discussion to solve the problem at hand. She was not alone here. Most angry people carry this assumption around with them. It turns out though that her assumption was incorrect. In fact, her anger achieved the very opposite outcome, it caused many of the team to close ranks around her, especially the ones whose budgets were the furthest out.

TEAM INSIGHT: *APOLOGIZING*

I've found apologizing to be a real stretch for some leaders, especially the more alpha types. One of my clients, Tim, managed a large team that invested in huge infrastructure projects. His portfolio accounted for more than £10 Billion. He told me that he felt it was a weakness to apologize. He'd been schooled in the investment banking world, where exhibiting this kind of vulnerability just wasn't done. His conviction was so ingrained, no doubt because he'd done very well in his career without apologizing, that when I politely confronted him with solid evidence[8-10] that timely apologizing actually helps teams work better, it did little to change his mind. To be fair, he did see the funny side when I apologized for wasting his time.

Be Positive, Appreciative, and Humorous

Not so long ago I was driving on a motorway and feeling a bit down in the dumps. In front of me was a huge semi-trailer truck with the sign "How's my driving? Call 08...."

So I called and the conversation went like this:

"Hello, what's the registration no and road you are driving on?"

"C455WRX. I'm on the M4."

"Why are you calling, sir?"

"I want you to know that your driver is driving quite superbly, possibly the best I've ever seen."

"Sorry, I don't understand."

"His lane control is spot on and not once has he strayed outside of the white lanes. He's magnificent."

"Oh."(sounding confused)

"And his indication is wonderful, so early and so precise."

"Ah, I see."(trying not to laugh)

"And get this, he is consistently staying inside the speed limit. It's quite extraordinary."

"That's great to hear."(now laughing)

"You can be so very proud of him."

"We are, sir. Thanks, then. Bye."(struggling to get the words out)

"No, thank you. Bye."

Time wasting? Maybe. But the call put a smile on my face and on that of the receiver, so maybe not. Who knows whether that driver received the over-exuberant but truthful feedback. (I hope so.) When we don't take ourselves or even the situations around us too seriously, it helps us cope with whatever life throws at us. Just ask any soldier how important gallows humor is to them as a means to staying sane and feeling as safe as they can when in the line of fire. In a way my phone call was my way of coping with a period of low mood. I certainly felt better for making the call, and judging by her reaction to my surprisingly enthusiastic feedback, I imagine the feeling was mutual. I've no doubt, in a strange way, we created, just for a few minutes, a nice safe bond between us. I see these bonds being formed in teams, too. The humor relaxes the team, and it can break the tension, especially if it is aimed out ourselves rather than others. It can be an incredibly powerful way to make people feel safe around us. With humor, we risk rejection or offending someone, especially in this very woke environment. Many of the most charismatic leaders I've seen over the years have combined self-deprecating humor with huge self-confidence, creating outstanding levels of psychological safety in their teams.

Positivity is the specialized subject of Professor Barbara Frederickson one of the world's most respected writers on the subject. Fredrickson has found something rather amazing about happiness. If we want to be happy, it's not such a good idea to cultivate a 100 percent "positive mental attitude," but rather strike a ratio of sharing three positives to one negative emotion. Frederickson's research[11] gives us permission to share with others any feelings we may have of sadness, despair, frustration, or anger, as long as these feelings don't dominate. In other words, it's good for us, from time to time, to admit we are not happy. There's also a ratio for positivity that seems to work for work teams too, it's called the Losada ratio.[12] The researchers observed the meetings and interactions of sixty teams and counted the frequency of positive statements and negative ones. Statements of humor and appreciations were recorded as positives while those belying criticism and concern were recorded negatively. They found that the higher performing teams, the ones with the best P&Ls, customer reviews and 360 leadership feedback reports, returned a ratio of positive behavior to negative of 3.2:1 while the more mediocre teams recorded 1.8:1. The very worst achieved a paltry 1:20 ratio. Although the study has been the source of some controversy in terms of its methodology, it provides further endorsement for appreciation and broadly supports the Frederickson's ratio.

Yet for many of the more critical leaders I've worked with, and I include myself here, being sufficiently positive, appreciative, and grateful can been a real challenge. For some of us, especially when under pressure, we are unable to be vulnerable in this way.

TEAM INSIGHT: *WE WANT TOUGH LOVE, NOT RELENTLESS TOUGHNESS*

I met Barbara, a young and inexperienced CFO at one of my first ever client engagements. She led a highly dysfunctional team, and her 360 leadership reports remains one of the most damning I've ever had the misfortune of feeding back. I remember quivering in fear before going into see her to share with her its contents. She responded to the feedback that was highly critical with:

"I expect basic standards, so why should I applaud them?"

Underneath her hardheadedness was the fear of driving complacency and of being taken advantage. Barbara had been trained to spot errors on spreadsheets and management reports. Perfectionism was drilled into her. Like so many other CFO's I've worked with over the years, her vulnerability behind her highly critical, unforgiving, mistake-pointing-out mind-set was a deeply flawed set of assumptions about how to best influence better team performance. Barbara was ultimately removed from her post. Her relentless negativity, pessimism, and criticism arising from maladaptive perfectionism ultimately cost her job.

A Word of Warning about Vulnerability

So vulnerability is helpful and there are several ways for teams to be vulnerable, but we also don't want too much of it either. Everything in moderation, as my wise old Gran used to tell me. If we are constantly appreciating, cracking jokes, asking for help, admitting our mistakes, apologizing, or over-sharing how we are feeling, it can come across as self-indulgent and cause others to question our competency levels. My experience is that most of us though, are more prone to under cook vulnerability rather than over cook it. Just ask Ed, Greg, Bill, or Barbara.

How to Build Empathy

"You will find sympathy in the dictionary somewhere between shit and syphilis."

—**ANONYMOUS**

Being empathic is very different from being sympathetic. Empathy is being able to see the world through the eyes of others and then responding in a helpful way. Whereas sympathy is very passive, empathy is much more dynamic, so people who have it pick up on the emotions and thinking behind actions, words, and silences, compute it, and then do something productive with it, all at the same time. It's a skill that is at the heart of emotional intelligence, but it's a skill that is not always easy to access, as it requires self-awareness and as we saw with Julie and the team, reasonable degrees of calmness.

Where was the empathy between Bill and Ben? The mood in their office, just like it was in the jungle with Ed and Luke, was overly cutting and too edgy. Positive feedback, courtesy, appreciation, and gratitude were all in short supply, yet that was what the surveyors, working their butts off, really wanted above all else. Humor was apparent, but it was sharp, sarcastic, and aimed *at* others rather enjoyed *with* them, so it came across as demeaning. There was no demonstrable willingness to help arising from Bill and his team. They thought that by throwing rocks, they were being helpful. OK, Ben's team were not assertive enough by asking for help. Their passivity only made Bill more irate, and understandably so. But was their reticence any wonder? Like Luke, they felt intimidated. Asking for help was only going to get them shouted at for being pathetic and weak. Feedback was one way and largely negative. And it revolved around the work being done, not on *how* the teams were working together. A classic (aggressive) defensive vicious cycle had emerged, where Bill, who hates passivity and defensiveness, reacted to what he saw with anger and frustration, which only caused more passivity and defensiveness. It was Ed and Luke all over again.

Empathy was in short supply when Julie was remonstrating with the management team over the budget shortfall. The team were under the most intense pressure to deliver the most substantial amount of change. They would have been more receptive to Julie's frustration if Julie had shown more recognition that they also had the most challenging of tasks, that to meet a budget set out months ago was in many ways an impossible ask. As we saw in Chapter Six, digital transformations are, by their nature, highly complex and highly emergent. Julie gave the impression she was operating with a "no excuse mentality," which the team felt was somewhat naïve. Don't forget, they were at the coal face and were more subject matter experts in digital tech than Julie, so they understood the risks of compromising long term success by making short term cuts to hit a preconceived budget. To one or two of them in particular, Julie came across as annoyingly arrogant.

At the same time, the team were also unable to diffuse the heat in the room by empathizing with Julie, by really noticing her anger, wondering what was actually going on inside of her, and then tuning into it. They were as un-empathic to Julie as she was to them. Having been beaten up, shouted at, and feeling unfairly treated, they were fired up with their own bunch of should's: "you shouldn't be shouting at us, you shouldn't be so aggressive, you shouldn't be lecturing us." Just like Julie, their reactions were understandable but fundamentally unhelpful. It just shows how, regardless of what level we are in the organization, it's so hard not to revert to our basic human instinct and react emotionally to the threats we see in front of us. Responding with emotional intelligence to threat, specifically with empathy, is a challenging ask. As we go up the organization, the egos get bigger and so the primitive threat reaction becomes even more pronounced. It's no excuse, though. As sports psychologist Steve Peters would say, we have to be able to manage our inner "chimps."[13]

If the team had the emotional intelligence to distance themselves from their own emotional reactions, then instead of getting caught up in the row that ensued, they would have imagined that behind Julie's anger was real fear and they would have explored what they imagined with what Ed and Peter Schein call "humble inquiry." Then they might have "reframed" the discussion away from the attack defend pattern toward a more constructive dialogue. Any one of the following would have helped:

> *"Tell us what's really going for you Julie, how are you really feeling?"*

> *"What do you imagine about us that is causing you to be so angry?"*

> *"I can see you are upset. How do you feel we are letting you down?"*

> *"What's it really like for you to be in this position in front of your stakeholders?"*

Training the team to "listen for emotions" is time well invested. We tend to listen for content, often not very well, so listening for emotions for many of us can be a real stretch. We can learn much from the field of therapy here. The greatest therapists and coaches like Carl Rogers[14] are trained to offer unconditional love and support to their clients. Principle amongst their techniques is simply feeding back what they are hearing. Summarizing doesn't just help confirm we've listened correctly; it also builds a bridge with the speaker so that they feel heard. They feel valued. They feel safer.

So the empathic team asks questions to understand, listens to what's being said, and then feeds back what they hear—both content and, where appropriate, emotions too.

> *"You're clearly pissed off, Julie, and you've got a right to be."*

That would probably have helped.

It was only when we discussed this interaction at a later team offsite that the team became aware of the pattern of attack and defend, and in doing so became more empathic toward each other and more able to work together to create a totally different dynamic. Julie started asking for help, rather than demanding action; the team started to offer help, rather than being in reactive mode; Sue, the team leader, started to attend budget meetings to help the team navigate priorities they couldn't navigate without her. Julie calmed down, the heat in the room dropped, and several months later, after we had applied the code, we measured levels of psychological safety and found they had grown significantly.

Meanwhile, Bill and Ben worked on their relationship, and Bill came to understand how his leadership role required a different modus than his deal-making role. With practice, he raised psychological safety, the surveying team learned to say "no" and struck a deal negotiating clearer prioritization which enabled them to make and keep more commitments. As a result, relations improved, staff stopped leaving and Ben got his sleep back. And importantly, Ben kept on believing in himself and winning in the marketplace.

So to build psychological safety, a team has to bring buckets of empathy to its interactions. We want lots of statements, conversations, and responses that tell our teammates that we understand and empathize with them, their situations, what's behind their thinking, the pressures they face, and the conflicts they have to manage. This doesn't mean we have to agree with what they say or do. The demonstration of the skills inherent in the third Get Strong phase will ensure this doesn't happen. It simply means we are able to relate to their world and *their* experience of it.

TEAM INSIGHT: *LISTEN OUT LOUD*

In reality, all nine Get Safe behaviors help to build empathic relationships, however, the cornerstone of empathy is listening. When we feel properly listened to, we feel safer with that person. The art of empathic listening includes actively restating what is being said and picking up and responding to the emotions being conveyed. Great listeners build intimacy through the process of listening. General McChrystal of Team of Teams fame understood this perfectly and went one one step further: he thanked everyone by name who briefed him, never criticized the quality of the briefings he received, and took the calculated risk of not just summarizing what he had heard but also his thinking about what he had heard. He made a habit of what he called "*thinking out loud*" at his daily briefings attended by his entire command. In adopting this practice, he cleverly simultaneously engaged in empathic listening while modeling vulnerability in front of what was surely a pretty hard-nosed command.

Respect Diversity and Knowledge Sharing

The importance of both of these in the Dx and virtual teaming world was evident in Chapters Six and Seven. Like all of Getting Safe, the role of the leader in setting the tone here is crucial. Encouraging contributions from all, avoiding cliques, and clearly demonstrating equity and fairness are must do's for the leader wishing to build psychological safety.

How to Build the Learning Team

Vulnerability and empathy both support better learning [15-20], which is why attending to learning is something you do after attending to vulnerability and empathy in the Get Safe part of the code. In Chapters Six and Seven, we discovered just how important learning is to success in digitalized worlds. It enables us to adapt to what emerges, which is so important when we can't plan or predict. Amy Edmondson in her book on teaming[21] suggests we have to now organize ourselves to learn when, to date, we've been taught to organize to execute. This paradigm shift makes eminent sense. For too long, we've learned only as a by-product of execution. In this digitalized mayhem, just as General McChrystal demonstrated, it's time we organized our structures and processes so we are better able to learn.

Little and Often Team-Based Learning Conversations

Team-Level Learning

Fig 1.1 Learning at the Individual Level

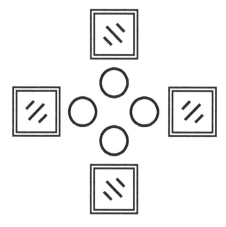

Fig 1.2 Learning at the Individual Level with the Team

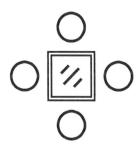

Fig 1.3 Learning at the Team Level

There is no more obvious place to organize ourselves to learn than at meetings. Meetings are like the family meals. When they go well, it's a sign the family are in a good place. When they either don't exist or are largely unrewarding, it's a sure fire "tell" that all is not well. But let's now add another filter, when they are not generating learning, we're also not running them well enough. The sad truth is that most meetings are not structured or led in a way that maximizes team learning. To do this justice requires the team, to regularly discuss its experiences, including its wins and its mistakes along its journey together, and then, from these conversations, extract useful knowhow it can then apply going forward. It's a way of helping the team adapt better to whatever is next thrown at them. It also de-stigmatizes errors which then encourages the team to experiment more. Doing this regularly is the key, not once or twice a year, but little and often, through the year.

Any learning conversation is a good conversation, but team-based learning is often the poor relation compared to individual based learning. Agile teams are the exception; they learn very well indeed because they have signed up to learn. Item number twelve in the original agile manifesto states:

No 12. At regular intervals, the team reflects on how to become more effective, then tunes and adjusts its behavior accordingly.

So as a result, they run what they call "retroflections" where, as a whole team, they shine the light on how they've been working together and what they can keep doing or do differently. They do this under pressure of time. Like cleaning their teeth in the morning, they form a habit, and they keep doing it, no excuses. Simple disciplines done little and often. The Dyers felt that team-based learning was so important they made it one of their core teaming competencies, uniquely referring to it as a "meta-competency." They also advocated the use of team-based surveys or diagnostics to shed light on where to focus the learning conversations. A quantum leap has to be made to make team diagnostics the norm rather than the exception. Our obsession with leadership 360 instruments prevents leaders from looking at the functioning of the teams they lead. Instead, they are predominantly only looking at one part of this system—themselves. And we wonder why teams don't work so well?

> **TEAM INSIGHT: *TEAM-BASED LEARNING IS A DISCIPLINE***
>
> We could learn much about team leadership and team-based learning from world class yacht skipper Dee Caffari.
>
> Dee holds the world record as the first woman to circumnavigate the globe, solo and nonstop, against the prevailing winds and currents. She is the only woman to have sailed nonstop around the world a total of three times and to have now completed six laps of planet Earth. In 2017/2018, Dee skippered the first mixed-gender youth team to take part in the Volvo Ocean Race (now known as the Ocean Race). Considered to be one of the most grueling yacht races, crews tackle some of the most formidable oceans on our planet, including the notorious Southern Ocean where the waves regularly hit 30 to forty feet, with some even reaching eighty feet. As one of the most accomplished sailors and skippers on the planet, Dee had this to say about team-based learning:
>
> *"We'd been on the boat for weeks. We had all got used to daily meetings which were mainly tactical. Then at the end of each leg, when we got onto shore, shattered and desperate for some sleep, the last thing anyone wanted to do was to get in a closed room and spend several hours debriefing what we, as a team, had learned from that leg. But I insisted on it, and we all agreed at the end of the race, it was one of the most valuable things we did together."*

Humble Inquiry

To really learn requires us to ask insightful questions at opportune times and in ways that helps illicit learning information. Unfortunately, plenty of teams I've worked with over the years have had members who have preferred to *tell* others what they already know rather than *inquire* about what others know. Yet we know that the best teams ask a higher ratio of questions than average or poorly performing teams.[12] Once again, our ability to be open minded is related to how emotionally charged we are. When threatened, we become more attached to the positions we hold and become more interested in defending our thinking sometimes by attacking the thinking of others. In doing so, we become less curious about what others are thinking. Some of us believe that if we were to be curious it would actually weaken our position, influence, and impact. Of course, it's the very opposite that is the case.

Ed Schein recognized nearly sixty years ago how emotions such as anxiety compromised our ability to learn. To prevent what he called "learning anxiety" during culture change programs, it was originally Ed who suggested we build "psychological safety" so the people that we wish to change can unfreeze old assumptions and reframe them into new, more helpful beliefs.

Ed and Peter Schein have since written extensively about the benefits of humbly asking questions instead of telling people what we think. They warn us that when we tell, we communicate:

1. We know more than others.
2. Our knowledge is the correct knowledge.
3. We have the right to structure someone else's experience for them.

However, when we genuinely and humbly ask, we empower the other person to provide useful knowledge and information, and in doing so, we make ourselves temporarily vulnerable. Not only do we receive more information we also build more psychological safety. Clearly, the two are linked.

Support Learning and Growth Using Descriptive Feedback Skills

There are few better experiences for me than seeing team members go beyond self-interest to actively support the personal growth and development of their teammates. Traditionally, the learning and development agenda has been placed firmly in the hands of team leaders and L&D departments who have tended to provide these resources for individuals rather than whole teams. I don't understand this. What better way to learn and develop than to do so with your teammates? What better way to boost levels of psychological safety?

For productive learning, feedback has to be exchanged on goals that are important to both parties. Just dumping feedback without first establishing it relates to a shared goal is unlikely to land so well. As Ed Schein points out, it's not so helpful if your tennis coach gives you unsolicited and negative feedback on your forehand if it is the backhand that you are practicing together.[22] The establishing of shared goals in the Get Set provides this crucial component of building psychological safety in the Get Safe phase. And as we'll explore in the next chapter, the best way to do this is to describe what is noticed and how we are feeling rather than evaluate what is happening and saying what we think "about" it.

The Getting Safe phase is therefore characterized by an attitude of being prepared to abandon certainty, an outcome that was so important to acquire in the previous phase of Getting Set. In Getting Safe though, there is now a quest for a psychologically safe climate and for the seeking of clarity, which can only really be achieved with humble inquiry. Through the art of listening more deeply to how others are responding with genuine curiosity and by taking an interest in what they have to say and who they are, profoundly deeper levels of intimacy can be created from which learning can then be more thoroughly achieved. It is this intimacy that enables the team to better shine in the next phase, Getting Strong.

De-Stigmatize Errors

Great performers, artists, and teams make plenty of mistakes and learn to embrace them, thrive on them, and even celebrate them. Not repeating the same mistake is important so great teams are also intolerant of sloppiness. But they don't treat all mistakes as the same. To be able to take the experiments required for adaption, they view certain mistakes as wonderful learning opportunities. Just ask James Dyson who worked through 5,126 failed prototypes between 1979 and 1984 before coming up with the dual cyclone vacuum design that turned him into a multi-millionaire.

> *"Failure is interesting—it's part of making progress. You never learn from success, but you do learn from failure. We have to embrace failure and almost get a kick out of it. Not in a perverse way, but in a problem-solving way. Life is a mountain of solvable problems and I enjoy that."*
>
> **—JAMES DYSON**[23]

Here's how you de-stigmatize errors at meetings:

1. Openly discuss failures and extract the learning.
2. Acknowledge the effort behind near misses.
3. Discuss the qualities demonstrated by an endeavor, even if it has failed.
4. Celebrate but don't over-celebrate the wins.
5. Celebrate but don't over-celebrate the losses.

TAKEAWAYS

1. Immediately endorse the nine behaviors that help to get the team safe and encourage the team to demonstrate them at whatever level of maturity your team are at.

2. Invest team time in improving these, but only after the team has reached a competent enough level in the previous Get Set phase.

3. First develop the vulnerable team by encouraging the team to:

   + Ask for help.

   + Reveal how they really feel.

   + Be positive and appreciative.

4. Then develop the empathic team by encouraging:

   + Listening for both content and emotions.

   + Sharing what you know and respecting diversity.

5. Then develop the learning team by:

   + Ensuring the team is being vulnerable and empathic.

   + Learning as a whole team and not just individually.

   + Humbly inquiring and being curious.

   + Building descriptive feedback skills and encouraging their use of peer-to-peer coaching and feedback.

   + De-stigmatize errors by openly discussing the learning gained.

6. As team leader, model all the vulnerability, empathy, and learning you ask for.

Chapter 10

How to Get Strong

This is a true story. Recently, a large corporation hired several cannibals to increase their diversity.

> *"You are all part of our team now," said Mary from Human Resources during the welcoming briefing. "You get all the usual benefits, and you can go to the cafeteria for something to eat, but please don't eat any employees."*

The cannibals promised they would not. Four weeks later, their boss remarked,

> *"You're all working very hard, and I'm satisfied with your work. We have noticed a marked increase in the whole company's performance. However, one of our secretaries has disappeared. Do any of you know what happened to her?"*

The cannibals all shook their heads, "No."
After the boss left, the leader of the cannibals said to the others,

> *"Which one of you idiots ate the secretary?"*

A hand rose hesitantly.

"You fool! For four weeks, we've been eating managers, and no one noticed anything. But now, you had to go and eat someone who actually does something."

If Getting Set is about sharing mental models to get on the same page, then Getting Strong is all about *doing* what's on that page. And if Getting Safe is all about building a climate where the team *feels* able to take some risks, have tougher conversations, experiment, and innovate, then getting strong is *doing* risk taking, *doing* tougher conversations, *doing* experimentation, and *doing* innovation. It's when the all the rubber gained in Getting Set and in Getting Safe actually makes contact with the tarmac and the team delivers its tangible value. The only way that a team can do all of this is if its members collectively stretch. Stretching defines this phase.

Getting Strong is about Stretching

```
┌────────────────────────────────────────────────────┐
│                                                    │
│  ┌──────────────────────────────────────────────┐  │
│  │                    SET                       │  │
│  └──────────────────────────────────────────────┘  │
│                                                    │
│      We all agree we're going to  have to stretch ourselves      │
│                                                    │
└────────────────────────────────────────────────────┘
```

```
┌────────────────────────────────────────────────────┐
│                                                    │
│  ┌──────────────────────────────────────────────┐  │
│  │                   SAFE                       │  │
│  └──────────────────────────────────────────────┘  │
│                                                    │
│       We're warming up our muscles and starting to extend       │
│                                                    │
└────────────────────────────────────────────────────┘
```

```
┌────────────────────────────────────────────────────┐
│                                                    │
│  ┌──────────────────────────────────────────────┐  │
│  │                  STRONG                      │  │
│  └──────────────────────────────────────────────┘  │
│                                                    │
│        We're all stretching out of our comfort zones together        │
│                                                    │
└────────────────────────────────────────────────────┘
```

The founder of Gestalt psychology Fritz Pearls recommended "contact" in all interactions, where we meet the other person with full awareness and see them for who they are rather than who we imagine them to be. In the Getting Strong phase, making contact becomes a bit edgier as our interactions are more influential. Maintaining adult-to-adult relationships and not reverting to parent-to-child relationships becomes a little more challenging. If we were jumbo jet pilots, we'd want enough contact to avoid having to abort, pull up, and circle back around but not too much that we create anxiety, or worse, crash and burn. We want good, solid, safe landings.

The Getting Strong Approach

"One afternoon at Aberdeen I had a conversation with my assistant manager while we were having a cup of tea. He said, 'I don't know why you brought me here.' I said, 'What are you talking about?' and he replied, 'I don't do anything. I work with the youth team, but I'm here to assist you with the training and with picking the team. That's the assistant manager's job.' And another coach said, 'I think he's right, boss,' and pointed out that I could benefit from not always having to lead the training. At first, I said, 'No, no, no,' but I thought it over for a few days and then said, 'I'll give it a try. No promises.' Deep down, I knew he was right. So I delegated the training to him, and it was the best thing I ever did.

"It didn't take away my control. My presence and ability to supervise were always there, and what you can pick up by watching is incredibly valuable. Once I stepped out of the bubble, I became more aware of a range of details, and my performance level jumped. Seeing a change in a player's habits or a sudden dip in his enthusiasm allowed me to go further with him: Is it family problems? Is he struggling financially? Is he tired? What kind of mood is he in? Sometimes I could even tell that a player was injured when he thought he was fine.

"I don't think many people fully understand the value of observing. I came to see observation as a critical part of my management skills. The ability to see things is key—or, more specifically, the ability to see things you don't expect to see.

"The minute staff members are employed, you have to trust that they are doing their jobs. If you micromanage and tell people what to do, there is no point in hiring them."

—**SIR ALEX FERGUSON**[1]

I know it's a bit dated and comes from a white male manager speaking about a male sports team, but Sir Alex Ferguson perfectly illustrates here what

the Getting Strong phase is all about. We see his coaching team having the
courage and the skills to challenge him about how much he was trusting
them; we see Ferguson initially not want to relinquish control because he's
obviously fearful they'll not do as good as job as him; we see him then get
over his anxiety, take a risk, and make an experiment to empower. Then
we see the coaches take the accountability they were given and pay back
the faith Ferguson placed on them by competently running the sessions.
Finally, we see Ferguson, after freeing up his time, being better able to
provide more value to the team. The story also illustrates the benefits of
this approach. The team went on to break Glasgow's football dominance
in Scotland, winning three league titles, the European Cup Winners Cup,
a Scottish League Cup, and four Scottish Cups. We also see in his quote the
three pillars of Getting Strong: accountability, constructive tension, and
experimentation, all combining to create these successful outcomes. The
common denominator in all three is "stretching" and being prepared, as Sir
Alex did, to move out of comfort zones.

GET STRONG	SCORE
ACCOUNTABILITY	
1. Individuals and sub-teams working on shared goals take action without unnecessarily referring upward. 2. We are effective at influencing those with whom we have to collaborate, both inside and outside of the team. 3. We habitually commit to do X by Y and we give early warning signs if we can't deliver on them.	
CONSTRUCTIVE TENSION	
4. When necessary, we can have challenging conversations with those whom we share goals. 5. We respond calmly and constructively to bad news, tough feedback, challenge or critique. 6. We are effective at minimizing and resolving inevitable interpersonal tension and conflict.	

EXPERIMENTATION	
7. We are prepared to step forward, take action and adapt, even when we don't have the clarity we would like.	
8. We bring creative and lateral thinking to our problem solving.	
9. We experiment and take calculated risks to try to deliver more value.	

THE NINE BEHAVIORS MEASURING GETTING STRONG.
1 - strongly disagree, 2 - disagree, 3 - neutral, 4 - agree, 5 - strongly agree
Below 3.2: Requires Urgent Improvement, 3.2-3.8: Requires Some Improvement,
Above 3.8: Team Strength

How to Build Accountability

Accountability is a broad-brush term that can mean any number of things. We want accountability for results, taking action, leadership, standards, getting the job done, taking a risk, not letting others fail... the list goes on.

This section of the code defines accountability more along the lines of taking purposeful action without unnecessary referral back up the chain. It's the "execution" part of General McChrystal's "empowered execution." We've seen how important this is in our digital age—controlling from the center just doesn't work so well. Chapters Six and Seven both testify that in this virtual and VUCA world, leaders are advised to distribute their leadership and empower their teams. More than ever, we want leadership *throughout* the team, not just *of* the team.

Attend to the Basics First: Get Set and Get Safe

A common mistake I've seen with team leaders is expecting their teams to be accountable without first building the foundations through the Getting Set and Getting Safe phases. That's like painting your house without an undercoat. The message won't stick. In the Get Set phase the team agrees what it has to be accountable for, why it's important, who else is involved, how we're going to be accountable, and what we get for being accountable. Getting Safe then builds on the cognitive trust and certainty accrued in the Get Set phase with emotional trust and extra confidence to execute on accountability.

All those shared mental models shared and agreements in the Get Set phase and all those relationships secured in the Get Safe phase will enable your team to extend itself and to take the interpersonal risks that define true accountability.

The Accountability Journey

SET
We all know what we are accountable for and what accountability we share

SAFE
We are building up the required safety to courageously take up the empowerment offered

---

STRONG

We are executing empowerment by taking initiative, making decisions and humbly asserting

---

Empower Individuals AND Sub-Teams

Clarys ran a very senior team of corporate finance bankers who she felt weren't working that well together. Her brief to me was to help them collaborate more with less reliance on her as the team leader, so they could generate more ideas and be more challenging with each other instead of relying on her to do both. Yet when I observed one of her team meetings, I noticed that all eyes were permanently fixed on her as she ran the show. Addressing individuals one by one, she shared with them her considerable knowledge, expertise, and insight while they each addressed her, and only her, with responses to her questions. The meeting was more of a series of public one-to-ones with the team presenting to her alone their individual slices of pizzas.

Clarys believed she empowered her team. She did, but only at an individual level. The concept of encouraging them to work in sub-teams to work on shared goals without her involvement was completely alien to her. Yet several team goals required four of five team members to collaborate together. She had not explicitly formed her sub-teams, encouraged them to meet together, present to each other, or challenge each other. Even though she couldn't see it, all the interactions revolved around her.

Good Empowerment Execution

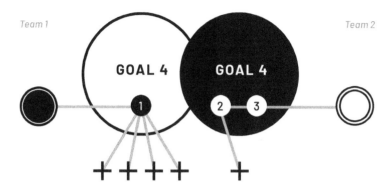

Bad Empowerment Execution

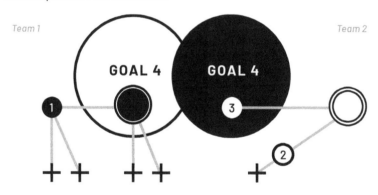

Goal 4 is shared between Teams 1 and 2
Any one 'in the goal circle' is showing 'proper ownership' of the goal

ACTUAL TEAM LEADER	GOAL OWNER TEAM MEMBER	CONTRIBUTOR (REPORTS TO TEAM MEMBER)
Team 1 ⬤	●	+
Team 2 ◎	○	+

Jacqui leads the distribution team of the insurance arm of a major UK institution and applies the same thinking. Unlike Clarys, she understands that empowerment is not just an individual transaction but occurs at the sub-team level, too. Refining the propositions, gaining new corporate pension schemes, or improving levels of customer service are all shared goals, better achieved in sub-teams than by mainly individuals. So she helps the sub-teams to be formed and makes them more accountable for the joint pizza slices and segments that they hand to her through the year. She doesn't confuse laissez-faire leadership with empowerment, though. She sees empowerment as a series of conversations, so she offers support, advice, and clears the path so that her sub-teams are enabled and supported. Ferguson did the same at Aberdeen, ensuring the right training equipment was available and by being highly visible and available to offer his advice when his coaches required it. Similarly, Jacqui focuses on influencing her boss, her stakeholders, and her peer group to ensure her team have the right propositions to sell and that other parts of the organization are directing their customers toward her teams so that they can assist them with their pension requirements. She also meets with her sub-teams and gives them her time. She does this in addition to attending to the whole team and holding regular one-to-one meetings. In doing so, she is *demonstrating* she values the concept of accountability at the sub-unit level. Unsurprisingly, Jacqui is seen as one of the brightest, talented leaders in the organization.

TEAM INSIGHT: *DON'T FEED THE ACCOUNTABILITY NEST*

A doting bird will go and fetch worms and give them to her screaming hungry chicks. Then, they'll scream again, and off the bird will fly to bring back additional worms. Ultimately, the chicks grow up, learn to fly, and hunt for their own worms. If the mother bird keeps feeding the nest, though, the birds don't acquire the courage or capability to fend for themselves. They are forever reliant on their mother for their survival, ultimately perishing when their mother is no longer around.

Too many managers feed their own nests in the same way. Jamie was one. Bright, helpful, diligent, and wanting to help his IT team, he couldn't stop himself from answering any question asked of him and fixing any problem they created. No matter what the topic, he was so bright, so experienced, and so fast that under constant pressure of time, he'd sort it. As a result, he'd created a dependency culture in the team as well as a succession plan problem. The gap between him and his reports in terms of capability was obvious. By getting the team Set and on the same page, especially by sharing goals in their sub-teams and meeting him halfway with their empowerment deal, the gap started to narrow, and Jamie saw a growing team rather than a dependent team.

Develop Humble Influencing Skills

Effective influencing requires one of the most sophisticated of so-called "soft skill" sets: listening. questioning, feedback, conflict resolution, empathy, rapport, emotional intelligence...the list goes on. Part of the challenge teams have is in actually knowing what great influencing, especially without positional power, actually looks like. This is where training helps. Many leaders require this training as they simply don't have the role models around them. Too many of our senior leaders are either a little too passive or, more often, too aggressive. Leaders these days have very few role models to follow in the art of principled, balanced, and assertively gentle influencing.

Take Steve Jobs, Elon Musk, and Jeff Bezos as examples. In the age of heroic leadership, these are our modern-day heroes. They have demanded excellence at all costs, yet are, or were, famously aggressive when it came to influencing the agenda. Steve Jobs could be notoriously demeaning, especially if he didn't rate someone. Nothing is wrong with the highest of standards, and even unrealistic standards can be timely, too—how many amazing breakthroughs have we seen as a result of dreaming the impossible?

Jobs was a perfectionist, especially when it came to design. It was all he really cared about. He applied no filters in his social etiquette. When he travelled to Japan, one of the more respectful and honorable modern-day societies, he famously wore jeans, sneakers, left the gifts his guests gave him behind, and never reciprocated with his own. He would also "sneer" at engineers and was known to tell them their work was "crap" in front of their colleagues. Any sniff of mediocrity, and he could rapidly turn into a nasty, demeaning bully. He once barked at an interviewee, who he immediately took a disliking to:

"How old were you when you lost your virginity"

"What did you say?" The candidate looked baffled.

"Are you a virgin?" Jobs asked.[2]

A brilliant man and role model in the art of product design he may have been, but a collaborator who influenced others to collaborate? An influencer who helped others influence? Forget it.

Like Jobs, Jeff Bezos also has ridiculously high standards but could also be famously aggressive and insulting. Three of his favorite sayings were:

"I'm sorry, did I take my stupid pills today?"

"Are you lazy or just incompetent?"

"Why are you ruining my life?" [3]

What about Elon Musk? Where does he stand on what he expects in terms of commitment to the cause?

"I asked Musk directly just how much he was willing to put on the line. His response? 'Everything that other people hold dear. I would die on Mars. If my wife and I have a bunch of kids, she would probably stay with them on Earth.'"[4]

He's not exactly diluting the standards here, is he? He'd happily die on Mars and abandon his family. Committed? Unquestionably. Unhinged? Probably. It came as no surprise when he very recently admitted having Asperger's syndrome, a condition characterized by feeling and experiencing empathy differently. He has my fullest respect for revealing this. However, just like Jobs and Bezos, he's another leader in a long list who can also bully their way to getting what they want. I would throw Donald Trump in here, too (I'd like to literally throw him in), with bucket loads of positional power and an unquestionable track record of being aggressive, belittling, and cruel to anybody who crosses him.

As Edgar and Peter Schein point out in their beautifully-crafted *Humble* series, the force of our messages increasingly seems to be taking precedence over the salient facts that define our realities and we find ourselves more and more resorting to forceful "telling" than engaging in the art of more "humble leadership."

So where do we go for inspiration? We need role models and leaders around us to show us the way, especially the more senior leaders. We need to see tough, respectful, and yet simultaneously humble and compassionate conversationalists in action, the sort of "radical candor" that Amy Scott writes about in her book and the sort of "humble leadership" that Edgar and Peter Schein describe in their books. Teams desperately need to see their leaders modelling a more compassionate form of influencing.

HUMBLE INFLUENCING AND COLLABORATION

1. Inquire and understand what's important to others and not just what's important to you.

2. Share feedback that you're understanding, so they know you know.

3. Share with them what's important to you and why it's important to you.

4. Explore options with them as best you can, so you both get what you want and need from the collaboration.

5. Present ideas and solutions but be open-minded to different ways of achieving what's important to you.

Encourage "X by Y" Reliability

We know that Swift trust is conditional, and that it is only realized when the team continues to be supportive and respectful, thus increasing emotion-based trust, while simultaneously proving it is reliable over time, delivering on its commitments to build cognitive task-based trust.

Great teams get commitment-making spot-on. They don't just commit to doing "X," they commit to doing "X by Y." There is a massive difference between "OK, I'll do it," and "OK, I'll do it by midday tomorrow." Not only does explicitly timed commitment making increase the chances of that commitment being actioned, it encourages the giving of early warning signs if deadlines can't be made, many of which we know can't be due to unforeseen circumstances. Taking care of the inconvenience of the impact of letting someone down is a validating team behavior. It models thoughtfulness, builds, and helps the team coordinate better.

How to Develop Constructive Tension

Your team will only be able to perform at its best if you and the team learns to tolerate temporary tension between you and the team and between the team members. Veterans of the Mac team learned that they could stand up to Jobs, but only if they knew what they were talking about. It was only with profound domain expertise that he would tolerate pushback, even admire it. I've worked with the most intimidating of leaders over the years. Formidable, hard-nosed, ruthless, unforgiving brutes, and they were just the same as Jobs. They'd respect you if you stood up to them and tried to influence them, but boy did you have to know your stuff and have the data to back it up. They sniffed self-interest in the form of defensiveness, uncertainty, bluff, or bravado a mile off, like red flags to a bull.

TEAM INSIGHT: *NORMS MUST BE SACROSANCT*

The importance of sticking to an agreed set of team norms can't be underestimated. Sam Walker's book *The Captain Class*[5] illustrates how he uncovered a common characteristic in the greatest sporting teams in history—that of the inspirational but uncompromising captain. These captains held normative standards as sacrosanct, regardless of whether the team was winning 8–0 or playing a seemingly innocuous practice game. As many Chicago Bulls and Manchester United ex-players will testify, both Michael Jordan and Roy Keane were examples of such captains. Keane was so normatively principled, he walked out of the 1992 Football World Cup because he was so disgusted by the standards of kit and training methods provided by the Irish coaching team. The Irish manager at the time, Mick McCarthy was operating from a very different *"page"* than the one Keane was used to being on at Manchester United. Claiming he couldn't influence McCarthy, he simply walked out. Whether you agree with his reaction or not, you can't help being struck by his commitment to the norms he held dear.

A bit of tension helps most teams perform better. The Dyers referred to it as "constructive controversy." I like the word "tension" as it relates more directly to how people are feeling about the controversy. When it is constructive, this tension guards against too much psychological safety which can cause "Group Think,"[6;7] a state characterized by complacency and insufficient internal critique. Valued by Jack Welch of GE fame, constructive tension, or "edge," as he called it, provides the team with this challenge, and fuels its creativity. I've no idea if Jack liked ABBA, but they produced some of their finest work in the years following both divorces in the two-couple band. I imagine Jack would have liked the title of one of the masterpieces they penned during this difficult time for them, "The Winner Takes It All," even though the song was really about losing.

Your team will create constructive tension by pushing itself onwards, challenging standards, and holding each other accountable, but, all the time, maintaining emotional composure. It can do all of this inside or outside its team boundary.

I have found the ability to have challenging conversations and to hold others to account to be one of the toughest skillsets a team can acquire. It requires a fundamental belief that's it is OK to have a challenging conversation with someone who you don't formally lead, the necessary psychological safety to have that conversation, and the technique to execute it well. That is some combination and explains why just about every team I've ever worked with has wanted to be better at it.

The courage to confront someone or something can be incredibly validating but get it wrong and suddenly we've a scene on our hands, which potentially could be long lasting or even permanent. It's why most teams play it safe and avoid the difficult conversations. But it also explains why most teams are also mediocre performers at best. The old adage applies: poor teams have leaders who fail to hold the team to account, average teams have leaders who do hold the team to account, but the best teams hold *themselves* to account.

Be Descriptive: Facts Are Your Friends

It became clear to me that Emma was at the center of things. Charismatic, popular, powerful, and somewhat intimidating if you got on the wrong side of her, her name kept coming up and not in a good way. Others in the team told me that she was "saying one thing and then doing another." Even Harry the team leader said, "She's the only one who isn't respecting my leadership." Not only was Emma a big personality, she was also a mood influencer and at the center of the goals of the team. So I decided to run an exercise that enabled the team to give feedback to all other members of the team, believing that this would enable them to speak directly to Emma, rather than about her, which was what they were doing. Apart from brave Martin, a more junior team member, Emma received very little feedback from the rest of the team during the exercise. All those criticizing her in private revealed nothing in the exercise. So I purposefully invited Harry, the team leader, to comment—surely, he would confront the elephant in the room.

Harry did speak but he chose to do so for other people—*"people* find you less available," *"others* have told me they find you hard to pin down." I prompted Harry, "Do *you* find Emma unavailable and hard to pin down?" He replied, "No, we're working fine." If the team leader couldn't confront Emma, what chance did the rest have? The implicit norm was set—"best not upset the apple cart, especially if it involves strong powerful characters."

The best teams describe what they see and notice and say how they feel. They offer less opinion and judgement and when they do, they do so tentatively, being careful not to state their opinions as facts. In doing so, they raise awareness, facilitate learning, and makes change and adaption easier. Pointing out, descriptively, that someone in the team has spoken out five times and each time it has been to either criticize, express concern, or disagree with someone (as I did recently with someone in a very senior Transformation team) is far more powerful than giving them your opinion that they are a "negative presence." The wonderfully reassuring difference between an observation and an opinion is that others cannot argue with an observation, whereas they can and probably will do with an opinion, and especially so if they are emotionally charged.

Our ability to be able to observe and describe is similarly compromised when we are the ones who are emotionally charged. In this more "aroused" state, we are more likely to think or even tell a person they are being a pain in the backside rather than calmly and objectively describe what we are noticing that makes us believe they are being a pain in the backside. Instead of telling them they have been missing deadlines, not saving documents in the right place, or turning up late to meetings without telling us in advance, we are more likely to greet them with a hostile face and leak the fact we are displeased with them in ways we're not even aware of. Maintaining composure is therefore an important skill for team members to develop in in the Get Strong phase.

Similarly, when I ask teams to tell me the difference between aggression and assertiveness, they will invariably tell me that with aggressive feedback, the person is attacked, whereas in assertive feedback, the feedback is aimed at the behavior, rather than the person. In other words, the feedback is not personal. When Julie shouted at the team during that budget discussion, "You're not showing any accountability," she would have had more success with stating, "I'm the one who's booking the meetings, not you."

When Bill said to the surveyors, "The standard of your work is crap," he would have had more impact if he said, "We're having to spend hours reworking your slide decks for client presentations."

Instead of avoiding giving feedback to the formidable Clarys for being too controlling, one of the members could have said, "I don't feel comfortable speaking up at our meetings."

Instead of Harry saying nothing to the notoriously slippery, charismatic Emma, he could have said:

*"You say you'll get back to me on something, but you regularly
don't do this. For example, the updated migration plan. I still
haven't received it. "*

In each of these, it is the facts that are exchanged, not opinions about the
facts. Feelings are facts, too, of course. If I say I'm upset, and I'm being
honest, then that's a fact that can't be disputed, even though the reason
for my feeling upset may not be accurate. You're annoyed I'm late for this
meeting as you think it's rude. However, I was late because I was helping
an old lady get back to her feet after a nasty fall. You weren't wrong in
feeling angry, but it turns out you were wrong to think I was rude. The
difference is crucial. Saying how we feel is not to be confused with saying
how we feel "about" something—which is just another opinion, albeit one
masquerading as a feeling. "I'm feeling demeaned" is very different to "I feel
you are being demeaning."

Instead of Julie shouting "you lot are letting yourselves down," she would
have created constructive tension with "I'm feeling exposed right now."

Knowing the difference between a fact, an opinion, and a feeling is the basis
of assertiveness in teams and runs right through all three development
phases in the code, coming to the fore most obviously in the Constructive
Tension skill set of the Getting Strong phase.

There are a host of other assertive skills to master here too, such as making
"I" statements rather than "you" statements, making requests rather than
demands, stating your interests while ostensibly trying to satisfy those of
others, are all to be encouraged.

The Journey of Constructive Tension

SET
I understand and accept I'm dependent on others to co-deliver my shared goals

SAFE
I see mistakes as learning opportunities

STRONG
I am influencing and asserting myself to ensure shared goal success

Respond Calmly

> "I will only work with a jet skier who is calm. I only chose them if they don't get too hot when the waves are big. In massive waves, it actually requires more skill to drive a jet ski slower than it does to drive it faster. They can't do this if they are 'hot' and if they are unable to be calm, as it compromises my ability to be calm, which I have to be, to get on and stay on an eighty-foot wave."
>
> —**ANDY COTTON,** *INTERNATIONAL BIG WAVE SURFER*

Influence, collaboration, and assertiveness starts with calmness, whereas aggression, passivity, and defensiveness are all driven by anxiety and fear, usually of failure. Julie realized that her ego got in the way, and she became too aggressive in the budget meeting. Similarly, we saw a lack of composure from Ben's surveying team, in the form of anxiety and a lack of assertiveness. To influence others and to be influenced by others, particularly when the collaboration involves the tougher conversations, we have to bring emotional self-control to the room, regardless of how intimidating that room might be.

Rob is the head coach of a well-known first-class professional rugby team in the UK. He's used to tension. When he first played professional rugby at the best rugby team in the UK at that time, he was immediately punched in the face to see how he'd react. Team training was regularly a series of punch ups, to help them build the physicality to compete with anyone they came up against. With their particular brand of rugby, they won everything that was possible to win. Who would argue that the tension they created, through their team punch ups, was anything but extremely constructive? Not for Rob in the long run, though. Now he's having to learn how to keep his cool more as a head coach in corporate environment of professional club rugby.

Rob is like so many other corporate team leaders I work with, still unconsciously assuming he's on the rugby field, receiving and giving metaphorical thumps on the nose and most likely, still being the school captain. In school, captains are selected because they are the best in the team or the most self-confident, or both. Under pressure, on and off the field, Rob can still revert back to influencing the agenda by shouting, admonishing, or aggressively holding to account. There's much more to him than this. But on occasion, just like countless other corporate managers out there, he can't help but revert back to type.

As Rob has discovered, corporate teams are very different than sports teams. In professional sports, the team is paid to win. In corporations, teams exist not to win alone, but in collaboration with other teams, so that the whole organization wins. Sports teams play better when their backs are against the wall, and are unified against a common "enemy," most often it's the press or disrespectful trash talking opposition. It's in the team's interest to "enemify." It brings out the best in them. Many corporate teams make the mistake of following suit, though. Like Rob, they subtly or unsubtly enemify other teams in their organizations. For Rob it's the club's "tie-wearing corporate boys" who, on occasion, wind him up. For other managers though, it's typically central services like HR, finance, or IT who are most frequently portrayed as incompetent, unsupportive, and useless cost centers. Leaders just like Rob set the trend with their subtle or unsubtle asides, jokes, taunts, and jibes. They may well be "projecting," failing to confront poor performance inside their team, or with their peer group, or with their boss, and instead projecting their dissatisfaction with themselves onto others, especially the easier targets. In competitive cultures, it's bred into them that it helps to put yourself up by putting others down.

In this digital age, we simply can't afford to enemify like this anymore. Not only does it pull people away rather than closer to each other, it also fires up our levels of cortisol and makes us more agitated. The emotional charge created closes our minds, makes us less humble and less likely to inquire and more likely to point a finger and tell. It perpetuates conscious and unconscious bias.

So the best teams keep calm, manage their "inner chimps," and learn to respond rather than react to threat. It's why emotional intelligence in your team is so important. How do you get teams to do this?

As we know, mood is contagious.[8-17] So when it comes to setting the emotional tone, the onus is on you to model calmness under duress, to have the equanimity to listen, inquire, and be open-minded rather than to react spontaneously by telling, defending, or attacking back. You model the dialogic skills required to get the team Safe. It also falls on the core members of your team, those who set the emotional tone. Every team has them. When they discover this for themselves, I've consistently found them to want to be able to adjust their tone for the benefit the team.

Employ Conflict Resolution

Effective conflict resolution is like influencing; it requires a multitude of interpersonal skills. The ability of your team to engage in these skills will depend on the commonality of the nine mental models in the Get Set phase and levels of psychological safety created in the Get Safe phase. The importance of a common mission and clearly established shared goals cannot be overstated. These will bind your team relationships together and gives those in conflict the motivation to sort things out for the sake of the greater good. Mick Jagger and Keith Richards have a track record of bust-ups; however, they have consistently managed to park their differences to ensure the Rolling Stones remains very much alive and kicking.

How to Build Experimentation

One of the most important qualities of today's teams is the ability to experiment—to try things out, to see what happens, and then, to be able to adapt accordingly.

The Experimenting Journey

SET
I agree to experiment to achieve my goals

SAFE
I see mistakes as learning opportunities

STRONG

I experiment and take risks in order to achieve my goals

If you want to build a team that *can* experiment, then develop your team in the order of the code to help you build a team *to* experiment. The code culminates in experimentation, and our research confirms that this is predicted by all eight preceding skill sets (three in Get Set, three in Get Safe and two in Get Strong). You first share mental models about your tasks at hand, including agreeing on the explicit norms that support experimentation and ensuring skin in the game for experimentation. Then, ensure your team acquires reasonably high levels of psychological safety to enable mistakes to be made and to be learned from. The science then tells us that your team members will then take risks, execute without having every box ticked first, and apply lateral thinking to their problem solving, all features of the experimenting team.

To really experiment, team members also have to productively engage in conflict and learn to improvise with whatever emerges.[18-23] When they do this, as Edmondson has advocated, they are learning by "doing," and are "organized to learn."

So how do we do get the team to experiment? Easy—recruit the team with an experimentation mind-set and skillset and then follow the code. Encourage them to experiment and celebrate it when it happens. That's not just my opinion. That's what the science tells us.

TAKEAWAYS

1. Don't wait for the team to be Strong—encourage it from the outset, but recognize that being "accountable," operating with "constructive tension," and "experimenting" are all built on the foundations of the two previous stages, Getting Set and Getting Strong.

2. Build accountability by:

   + Empowering sub-team accountability as well as individual accountability.

   + Building and practicing humble leadership and influencing.

   + Encouraging X by Y commitment making.

3. Create constructive tension by:

   + Embracing facts and feelings and engaging in descriptive feedback.

   + Avoiding enemifiction.

   + Promoting and modeling calmness and composure.

4. Foster experimentation by:

   + Hiring the talent who are able and prepared to experiment.

   + Building up competence in the Get Set and especially the Get Safe phase.

   + Encouraging experimentation and celebrating it when you see it, regardless of the outcomes created.

PART 5

Teaming and The Future

Chapter 11

The Third Rail

It's much easier to row with the tide than against it. Working in an organisation that supported team working was one of Hackman's three key foundations for better team working. The other two, he said, were ensuring that a team was a necessary entity in the first instance and that selection was done well. He estimated that organizational support and selection into the team alone explained about 60 percent of a team's performance.[1] Other researchers have also found that team-friendly cultures tend to produce more effective teams but have questioned exactly how much the culture actually matters.[2-5] One thing is for sure: teams will work better if they exist in a team-oriented culture.

If we are going to turn around a dodgy track record of team working, then we have to challenge and reframe several deep-seated outdated assumptions into new and more team orientated assumptions such as ensuring there's skin in the team game, measuring leadership effectiveness using team diagnostics rather than individual diagnostics and making teams rather than individuals our heroes. Trusting in the world's first simple but scientific code to guide team development will also help. To enable all of these shifts in thinking to take place, though, there are two additional and highly influential reframes to be made by leaders.

From "Psychometrics Are the Answer" to "Psychometrics Are a Small Part of the Answer"

When I was trained to use my first of many psychometric tools over 20 years ago, the facilitator shared an unforgettable story. On another course where he was training users on the same tool, he went to the restroom during a coffee break and found himself standing at a urinal next to one of his delegates. Looking silently straight ahead, as men awkwardly do when standing next to someone they know, the silence was broken with the words, "Great course, really enjoying it—and a hell of a tool you've got there."

Despite the magnificence of whatever psychometric tool you use in your organization, there is not one shred of evidence, anywhere, that your team will be more effective if it were to employ another "green color," "plant," or "ENTJ." Evidence just doesn't exist. Why is it, then, that for decades, so many companies have been using psychometric profiles as the go-to approach to help their teams perform better, especially the more senior teams?

I have used psychometrics and will probably use them again. They can help team members open up a bit and learn about each other's natural tendencies. They can facilitate discussion. They can especially be very helpful in selection decisions, so you know who you're bringing into the team. However, do I use them, like so many organizations and consultants as a go-to approach to team development? Absolutely not.

Most teams I work with have bigger fish to fry than discussing personality profiles. Nor do they need a psychometric, and all the time it takes to understand them and to tell each other what is important to reveal about themselves. Are we really going to remember all that information, anyway? In a team of twelve, it requires a team member to have to remember 11 different profiles, not to mention working out and remembering how they are going to mesh their own profile with each of them. Is this really going to happen? Seriously?

Let's be honest, these "reports" are individual development reports, not really team development reports at all. Amalgamating twelve individual reports into a team report is simply that—an amalgamation of component parts, not a report on the team system. There is a profound difference. It's crazy to think that in a team, with its complex system of inter-dependencies and feedback loops, you can add up all the individual reports and then predict how the whole team will behave. Team member personalities are not like segments of an orange that add up to make one big orange personality. If only it were that simple!

If we are to improve the way our teams work, we have to be more discerning and challenge our over-reliance on psychometrics. To do that, we have to understand their lure. Maybe we use them because we trust them, and this is because those flogging them have an "ology" and a tool that they know more about than we do. Maybe it's because they are super colorful and that means they are interesting. Maybe it's because they tell me about me, and there's no more fascinating subject out there. Maybe because the team coach doesn't have much else to offer the team other than the tool they've been trained in. Maybe they do have a lot to offer, but as working in the moment with a team can be so stressful for a team coach, they seek refuge in them. Or maybe it's because those buying them are too gullible or not discerning enough. I suspect all have played their part over the years. The benefits they bring to help break down barriers and enable the team to relax into itself before then working on how it will become a high performing team is actually misguided. We build more trust more quickly these days when we start to get on the same page about why we exist, what we are going to achieve, and how we intend to work together. Let's get that team moving forward to *help* us feel more comfortable about each other. These days, time is so scarce, so let's get to know each other *as* we make progress. That's why in the code, the Get Safe phase follows the Get Set phase.

We now need less fizz and more substance in the way we develop our teams. It's time we all relied less on psychometrics. They are a niche aid only, and with all the money that we've spent on them, too many of our teams still don't work that well.

From Transformational back to Transactional

Be authentic. Lead with purpose. Be vulnerable. Show humility. Connect with others' emotions. Be a servant to your team. Influence with charisma. Lead through your values. Coach and develop the potential around you. Create the learning team. Empower. Foster creativity. Be inspirational.

These are all part of being a transformational leader and have, for a while now, been dominating leadership books, articles, and development programs the world over. It was the late, great Bernard Bass who introduced the term "transformational leadership" back in the early '80s. Together with his friend and colleague Bruce Avolio, he discovered that transformational leadership raises the "discretionary effort" of followers, beyond that required to simply achieve a goal. Bass wanted to explain why some of us run through walls, work extra hours, or make personal sacrifices simply because of the way we relate to our leaders.[6;7]

Transformational leadership was part of what Bass termed, The Full Range of Leadership (FRL), a spectrum of leadership behaviors.[8;9] He found that leadership was like a piano, we all play all the notes, but some of them more than others. The FRL was composed of three elements, "non-leadership behaviors," "transactional leadership," and "transformational leadership." The model was based on the relationship between leader and follower. Bass proved that when playing the non-leadership range such as laissez-faire leadership, we are not that present, and unsurprisingly, we produce poor leadership outcomes. When we move up a notch and play in the transactional leadership range, we produce good but unspectacular results. Here the transaction is between the leader and each member of the team to ensure a fair exchange is made for the work done. Typically, this means the leader providing information and resources in the form of role clarity, feedback, encouragement, support, knowledge, and clarity of what's expected. It's the basics. It's what managers get taught in their first ABC management development courses. Notice the transaction is not with the team, though. It's between the leader and the individual. Moving up another notch, when we play the chords in the "higher leadership range," we exhibit transformational leadership, and we demonstrate the types of behaviors listed in the opening paragraph to create outstanding results. Since its inception, The Full Range of Leadership has become the most validated leadership model that exists today.[10]

I've met both Bruce and Bernard. In 1998, I flew out to Monterey, California to present my own research into the adoption of transformational leadership in the financial industry at a conference they had organized and to be trained in their tool. They were two of the most unassuming, lovely, and authentic academics you could ever meet. Charisma is great, they pointed out, but there has to be more than charisma to leadership; after all, Hitler had loads of it. To their credit, they weren't too bothered about building a massive shiny leadership 360 brand and business. They just wanted to get the truth about leadership out there. As a result, their model used language and headings that weren't the most user-friendly. Sure enough, their somewhat clunky phrases like "Full Range of Leadership," "Active Management by Exception," "Contingent Reward Behavior," and "Transactional Leadership" became less talked about in favor of the big new shiny toy, transformational leadership. It is quite remarkable that there has been very little advancement in the leadership field since they produced their FRL over forty years ago. Pick up any book on leadership and you will find its content matter will slip somewhere in the Full Range of Leadership, and especially these days, in the transformational leadership range. Literally nothing I've seen has really added to their model, only brought a bit more depth.

The problem is that the transformational leadership approach was never intended to exist on its own. Bass and Avolio's research culminated in a very important caveat, that *without* sufficient transactional leadership in place to support it, transformational failed to produce outstanding results. In fact, transformational leadership *without* transactional leadership can be downright dangerous.

Nowadays, there's little mention of transactional leadership in business. It's as if it's the embarrassing cousin some people don't want their relatives to meet. And yet through all the years I've worked with teams, I have seen much more dysfunction as a direct consequence of shortfalls in transactional leadership than from any lack of transformational leadership. So many teams are just not on the same team page when it comes to clarity of shared goals, roles, and decision making, and there is often a distinct lack of feedback. Part of the reason might be that Bass and Avolio focused solely on the transaction between leader and follower. Quite right too, but effective *teams* also require a transaction between the leader and the team as a whole and between the team members. I may understand my role, but do I understand the role of my virtual team mate over in Shanghai? I'm clear on the team purpose, but I'm not convinced others are. I may feel empowered by my boss to perform my role, but I also share another goal with two other members of the team, are we, as a sub-team also empowered? To team well, teams require transactions between the leader and the *whole* team, and between shared goal owners of *sub teams*. And as emphasized in the Get Set phase, where we set them up, and in the Get Strong phase, where we execute this agreement, it is these transactions that are the most pivotal and the ones so many teams need to be making.

Transactional Leadership at the Team Level

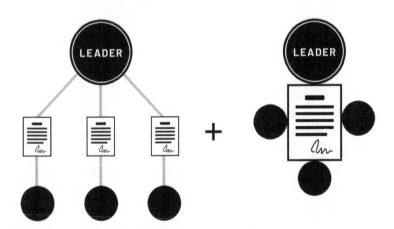

The Get Set phase also contains some transformational elements such as firing the team up to believe in the team vision, mission, and purpose and then in Get Safe, inspiring confidence that they can all be achieved. Optimism, self-belief, and charisma can help grab the teams' emotions and get it fizzing with the belief and energy it can succeed, but the bread and butter for your team is to know what is collectively doing, who's doing it and how they are going to do it.

So it's time we talked less of "transformational leadership" as a solitary endeavor and reignited the importance of its quieter, more introverted unassuming sibling—good ol' fashioned transactional leadership—at the team level as well as at the individual level. Without the transactional basics in place, you will have no foundation from which to build a great team.

TEAM INSIGHT: *UNDERESTIMATE TRANSACTIONAL LEADERSHIP AT YOUR PERIL*

Not so long ago, I coached a C Suite leader and his team at one of the UK's largest Institutions. He was blessed with absolutely buckets of transformational leadership but very little on the transactional side. He was an unbelievably charismatic leader, a visionary who empowered and commanded tremendous loyalty, someone who possessed almost cult like status in the organization. When I first met his leadership team, though, it was chaotic, dysfunctional, and fractured. Roles were ambiguous, conflict wasn't addressed, priorities were unclear, and meetings were tense. An unbelievable transformational leader he may have been, but without a reasonable dose of transactional leadership, it meant his team were neither cohesive, aligned, nor effective. He ended up putting a deputy in place to effectively take care of the more transactional stuff and principally as a result of this, his team began to grow into a far more cohesive and adaptable unit. Ultimately though, it was his bread-and-butter transactional leadership which led to his downfall—he ended up being removed from his post due to unforeseen spiraling costs and a perception that he wasn't across what he needed to be.

TAKEAWAYS

1. Team-orientated cultures support better team working.

2. If the code in this book is to reap the greatest rewards, then
    several assumptions about how to team require reframing
    at the highest levels in our organisations.

3. It's time we valued more transactional leadership,
    especially at the team level.

4. It's time we jumped off the psychometric gravy train and
    applied more science and discernment to how we build
    our teams.

Chapter 12

It's Our Destiny

"Devastated, humiliated, I felt like walking away from the sport."

—KATE WALSH[1]

These were the sentiments of player Kate Walsh after GB women's hockey team had embarrassingly lost 2–0 to Korea in the Olympic qualifiers in 2004. It was a shattering experience. Years later, players still get upset talking about it, as they recall the heartache of knowing, after four years of training, competing, and dreaming, that they were not going to the Athens 2004 Olympics. Now though, the same players recognize this low point was also the turning point for Team GB Hockey.

Twelve years later, Kate captained Team GB to a spectacular and dramatic penalty shoot win in the 2016 Rio Olympics Hockey final. Team GB become the first ever GB women team to win a Hockey gold medal. Nine million British viewers watched the spellbinding final. Holland, who they beat in the final, were the number one ranked team in the world, blessed with more technical ability. Team GB scored an equalizing goal ten minutes before the final whistle then won a penalty shoot-out. It was the stuff of dreams—a true fairy-tale ending. From the depths of despair, they had picked themselves up to become Olympic champions.

It was Ed and Cho all over again, against all the odds, conquering the Amazon on the heels of failure. Their story represents the cycles so many great teams go through, the pain, the sweat, and the tears, and ultimately, when the team gets it right, and with a bit of luck along the way, a happy ending. Like Ed and Cho, it's a story of resetting, building trust, staying strong under duress, and ultimately coming out as winners. More than anything though, it's a story about deep feelings of togetherness, lifelong friendship, and love. It's another story that so perfectly illustrates why I love working with teams.

On closer examination we see once again the code being applied to great effect. The resetting took place back in 2004, immediately after Team GB crashed out of the Olympic qualifiers. The England team immediately lost 60 to 70 percent of its funding. According to their new CEO Philip Kimberley, it was already in a financial mess:

> "It was very, very bad. There was a very shell-shocked team. We had a completely new governance structure and a completely new board. We owed £500,000, we had no strategy, and we had no financial control. We couldn't even afford a sandwich for a volunteer."

Kimberley developed the concept of the Great Britain Framework, and after months of negotiation, managed to convince all three home nations: England, Scotland, and Wales to agree to sign a game changing legally binding document. Game changing because it established Great Britain Primacy, meaning that all three nations committed to putting the ultimate goal of Team GB above national interests. Sally Munday, the current chief executive officer for England Hockey and chief operating officer of Great Britain Hockey, agreed:

> "I cannot stress enough the significance of that framework agreement and what it has allowed us to do."

So the resetting really started with the creation of clear shared purpose that put Team GB first. They went further with their purpose, though; they talked about "creating history" and "inspiring a generation." They made these their mantras. From this repurposing, we see the rest of Get Set being played out to perfection, shared vision to win Olympic gold, shared performance goals including tournament wins, ranking places, agreed plans, including recruiting coaches much earlier in the Olympic cycle to give the team extra practice time, agreed roles including a wider coaching support group and deep seated, crystal clear playing responsibilities, and agreed values and norms revolving around making marginal gains, team comes first thinking, and finding ways to win against the odds.

Meanwhile, as all this resetting took place with new coaches, the team worked on building psychological safety by rebuilding trust, togetherness, and a learning team. All of this was led by coaches, specifically recruited for their learning mind-sets, as Kimberley states:

> "I was pretty clear that I wanted coaches with brains who could work up a learning curve."

Over time, the coaching, training, and learning together enabled them to set high standards from which they held each other to account. Players had to be dropped, experiments were taken with different players trying out different things to help the team to perform better. People spoke up in meetings. The tension was constructive, both supportive and challenging:

> "So in the Rio Olympics we walked onto the field as one team, we jogged off as one team. We were united in everything. We all contribute to meetings, we all have a say. It created a sense of ownership in the team."

Ownership and accountability blossomed, and the team became characterized by exceptional coordination rather than brilliant individualism. This gave them an edge over their more technically gifted opponents. Ultimately, as the code would have predicted, with all boxes ticked, they were in a position to win:

> "We won Olympic gold because we were a team, there were no superstars...we were such a team... We did our jobs."

—ALEX DANSON[2]

Like the story of Ed and Cho, it's a lovely, heart-warming, feel-good story. And because of the journey from despair to success, it proves that teaming is not so easy to get right. Both stories can give our teams working in organizations hope. By teaming well and following a code that statistically raises our chances of success, we can enjoy our journeys a little bit more, safe in the knowledge that the prize of high performance is there to be gained. We may not always have the chance to win gold medals or break world records but we're going to bloody well do our best to achieve our best.

The Amazon and GB Women's Hockey stories give me goosebumps. I frequently get them when I work with teams. It's one of the reasons I love working with them. But it wasn't always this way for me.

In my younger days, I was not interested in teams at all. I was wrapped up in my own world. Although I played team sports like cricket and rugby at school, I was more comfortable and better at playing individual sports such as tennis. The concept of team working was alien to me, and part of the reason I didn't value teams was that I didn't trust them. My sister Rachel had serious brain damage following a whooping cough vaccination that went drastically wrong around the time I was born. We were only eighteen months apart, and so I was born into a family that was in shock and trauma trying to come to terms with this. My father, a busy eye surgeon with an unbelievably caring disposition, threw all of his energy into his work and in looking after Rachel, both at which he excelled. He became one of the top eye surgeons in Wales and was awarded an OBE at Buckingham Palace by the Queen for his services to the Greek community in Cardiff, whose eyesight he looked after largely without charge. However, there was a consequence of having his caring energy depleted. Hugely loving, he was also often angry, short-tempered, and intolerant. He was also very dogmatic and single-minded. He had to be to assert himself and to overcome the prejudice he received as a working-class Greek immigrant in the more Anglo-Saxon middle-class world of medicine. My late mother, also very loving and caring, was very young but not so well equipped to cope with Rachel. When my younger brother, Hugh, came along four years after I was born, by all accounts she sought refuge in him, leaving me a little bit in no-man's land. My identity and a sense of security within this unpredictable set-up were probably missing as I grew up without the secure early attachments in place to equip me with the self-confidence, trust, and skillset to cope so well in team environments.

Although likeable and good fun to be around, I failed to acquire several important key skills that are important for effective team working: self-belief, assertiveness, and influence. I was brought up mainly being told what to do by my father who, shall we say, didn't lack any confidence in how he saw the world, including deciding on all my school subjects at school. I didn't have a sense of my own purpose, goals, plans, and values. They were largely my father's. Consequently, I always felt a bit of an outsider, suspicious of the intentions of others and without a voice that was worth listening to. I inherited a strong work ethic and encouraged to channel my energy only really into individual pursuits such as academia and tennis. Not feeling too proud of who I was, I became depressed but without knowing it. Talented at tennis, I tried to make it as a pro, but without the necessary physical and mental skills, I was never going to make it. And I failed academically, too, dramatically underperforming in all my school exams. Both failures only fueled my depression. So when I left home, I had no sense of who I really was, and opted to go to a very average polytechnic, one I didn't even bother to visit beforehand. Throughout my time there, I was profoundly unhappy in and with myself and didn't know what a team was or how to behave in one.

My love for teams started when I took on my first job as a medical representative. Days were spent driving to doctors' surgeries alone, sitting in doctors' surgeries alone, seeing doctors alone, and returning home, alone. Even though I hated it, with much better mental health thanks to discovering anti-depressants, I started to discover I could relate very well to others, I had a voice, and I started to develop my confidence. I also had the most important things a young man could ever want, loads of stickie pads, pens, atlases, flashlights, and staplers. I was also beginning to relish the team events, the quarterly sales meetings, and the conferences. Something was happening. Being an active and influential part of the most successful sales team in the UK was the most amazing part of a very lonely job. Feeling I was onto something, I took the travel vouchers I won from a

sales competition, handed in my notice, and went travelling with my friend
Jona, to "find myself." It was then, in my late twenties that I started to learn
more about myself. By traveling as a team with Jona through deepest New
Guinea, where, just like Ed, we visited the remotest of tribal communities,
I started to discover much more about the value of communities and
teams. We returned home after four months, and I decided to take up a
career in psychology. No longer was my head down all alone in my books. I
surrounded myself with other learners and a team of friends and advisors
who challenged me, supported me, and helped me keep sane. I was now
realizing that learning was not just an acquirable skill, it was also much
more of a team endeavor than I had ever realized. I also engaged in some
therapy, and with a clearer head, and with lessons learned from previous
academic experiences, I knuckled down and in three months graduated
with GBR, the equivalent of a degree in psychology before going on twelve
months later to complete a Masters in Occupational Psychology which
I attained with a Distinction. Something significant was happening. I'd
gone from a serial academic underperformer to what I believe to be a UK
academic record in psychology. A few years later, I then also became the
only psychologist in the UK who was chartered as both an occupational
and sports psychologist. I credit this transformation largely to discovering
a team of people outside my immediate family who helped me to get the
best out of me.

It was no surprise that at the age of twenty-nine, I started a career as a
sport psychologist and business psychologist with a company specializing
in team building called Sporting BodyMind. Under the tutelage of two
amazing psychologists, John Syer and Christopher Connolly, I immediately
became drawn to the joy of working in a team and in helping other teams
work well. John and Christopher were two humanistic psychologists who
were way head of their time. They trained emotional intelligence and
systems thinking in professional sports and business teams years before
Daniel Goleman and Senge wrote their books. They were developing the
equivalent of psychological safety decades before Amy Edmondson really
brought the term to the fore in team building. Their love for team working,
with all of its wonderful systems complexity, was infectious. More than
anything, they taught me about what was required to feel safe and sound

inside a team, and to their eternal credit, how it also felt to be in one. I learned all about vulnerability and empathy from them.

My full immersion into teams occurred after I left Sporting BodyMind to join KPMG Consulting. I was employed in the Change function, and I became the go-to person when it came to any consulting requiring team working. KPMG helped me to appreciate the importance of building commercially successful teams, as well as building safe teams. The experience gave me a bit more edge. It was here that I learned to understand about culture, stakeholder management, accountability, and assertiveness. In 2005, after getting increasingly frustrated at having to shoe-horn what I felt were crucial team development interventions into pre-sold large programs of change, I decided to leave and start my own consultancy to bring all of my education and experience to bear. I suppose I also wanted to have the freedom to express myself, too, something, unsurprisingly, I hold very dear. Running my own business has since taught me the importance of emotional self-control, experimenting, and risk taking. Now I'm very much part of several teams and loving all the experiences I have with them. In all of them, I now have what I couldn't find when I was much younger, the joy from achieving something, or at the very least, from trying to achieve something special, in highly functional, safe, and driven teams. I also have redefined and created a very special relationship with my father. Together, we've been able to reset.

My story illustrates a transition from team working uncertainty, insecurity, and failure to one of confidence, security, and modest success. It mirrors what is possible for all of us. Some of us may not be so competent at it. But as I have proved, that's more to do with not being enabled to team rather than a lack of talent to team.

It's in all of our destinies to team well because biologically, and through evolution, we've been programmed to team well. We have survived and we will continue to survive because we are essentially tribal, communal animals. Before we had conscious thought and speech, which happened 70,000 years ago, we were already well accustomed to teaming. It is believed that for about two million years, our Homo forefathers and mothers, were connected by our five senses, especially sight and sound, and it was through these connections that we were better able to survive against those that threatened us. Over the more recent hundreds and thousands of years, we have learned, in teams, to hunt game, fight for survival, protect ourselves and our families from animal and human attacks, cultivate our land, invent tools, make homes, migrate to new territories, and assemble IKEA furniture.

There are parts of our brains that process threat and activate reactions before we even recognize it in order to warn ourselves and others to take care. We have other parts of brain that contain mirror neurons that fire off electrical responses without conscious control, that naturally allow us to empathize with others. We've had to empathize to survive. How else would we warn our tribe that there's a dangerous animal on the loose or to know how many grapes to pick to feed the family? This genetic disposition to relate and to empathize isn't going away anytime soon, even with all the extra screen time. Our history is one of survival and reinvention. Just look at Madonna.

So we can be optimistic about teaming. As we progress further into the digital age with all its impending machine learning, we can take heart from our biological disposition to team. And we can take heart from the accrued knowledge we've acquired about how to team. We're going to need it. We want more societal compassion, and we want more equality. We have to shift from being "me-focused" to being more "other centric" as the gap between the societal have's and the have-not's keeps on increasing. Most importantly of all, we also want to cultivate "team earth" when it comes to saving our planet from deforestation, global warming, and species extinction.

These changes sit ostensibly with our nations' governments, but they don't end there. We are now seeing an upsurge in corporate responsibility fueled by a more purposeful agenda emanating from our younger generation, in particular. Good on them. We want to see more collaborations and partnerships between our organizations and our societies. But if we want to see more macro-level team working like this, then don't you think we have to improve the micro-level team working first? If we can get our teams inside our organizations working well, it will then help our organizations collaborate better with their external stakeholders. In team working, charity really does start at home.

And I, for one, see absolutely no reason why we can't do this and take our teaming to a whole new level.

Happy Teaming.

Acknowledgments

There are a number of teams behind this book I'd like to thank here. Firstly, my family, and especially my loving wife Caro who encouraged me, supported me, and patiently tolerated the time we lost as a family and my countless emotional ups and downs throughout this project. I couldn't have done this unless you had held the fort so magnificently. I love you, and I thank you. To my wonderful children: Emily, Sophie, and Alexander who were always interested in how the book was coming along and even helped with a little research—you provided me with my ultimate purpose to write. To my late mother, unwavering in her loyalty and unconditional love, you ultimately set me up to write this book. To my giving, selfless, and indescribably inspirational father, who passed away the same day I was due to submit my final manuscript: You shaped my writing in the most profound of ways, showed me what caring for others looked like, and taught me that the team around us is literally everyone we come into contact with. To my darling sister Rachel, who won't be able to comprehend these words but who I thank for her powerful influence on me, without which, this book would never have been written. Thank you so much Marilia Angove—you gave me the self-awareness and self-confidence to work it all out and to find myself.

To Suzanne Davis, my rock throughout, I couldn't have done this without you. Not only was the quality of your research and all the work related to the book quite remarkable, but I felt you and your huge heart close by my side throughout even though we were working from separate offices. I also want to thank Olivia Solomon who was instrumental in researching the early advancement of the code and to Jack Aaron for his contribution to Chapters One, Six, and Seven. Both of your work was outstanding.

To my editor at Mango, Yaddyra Peralta, a huge thank you for your calm and confident support and for giving me the confidence to express myself fully. To Jackie Sousa for additional editing support and for help with the images. And big thanks to Shawn Hoult who commissioned my work, believed in me and this project from the outset, and whose presence gave me good reason to want to team up with Mango.

To all those who read and gave me feedback on my early texts, including Rob Green, Jane Hull, Carrie Sabin, Paul Blair, Kevin Turner—your feedback and encouragement meant the world to me at times when I really did need it. To the talented and utterly delightful Gillie Turner; we weren't able to use your cartoons, but I was so glad for the time we spent together.

To Christopher Connolly, John Syer, Ed Schein, and Amy Edmondson, a huge thank you. Your work has inspired me like no others. Christopher and John, you both shaped me and taught me—more than anybody else in my professional career. I carry with me your voices and your intentions with every team I work with. To Ed Schein, you kindly accepted my request for an endorsement, and you made some additional suggestions on the text; your writing has influenced me ever since I sat in a lecture room in 1989 and first heard of the words "organizational culture." To Amy Edmondson, like Ed, you will receive countless invitations for book endorsements each week, and I was so thrilled you agreed to write one for this book. Just like Ed Schein, your writing has taught me the importance of substance, humanity, and kindness. And just like Ed, your humility in your expertise and fame is truly inspirational.

To all those who kindly give me so many wonderful and gracious endorsements, I thank you all and am touched by your investment of time in me. I'm sorry we couldn't feature all of them here, but everyone is visible on a well-known website named after that long river in South America.

I'd like to express my gratitude and awe to Dee Cafferi, Andy Cotton, Greg Hill, Andy Denton, Ewen Denning, and Charlie Pitcher for volunteering for the TeamUp YouTube Extreme interview series, excerpts of which feature in this book. What you do is extraordinary. How you each have kept your feet on the ground is even more so.

To all my clients, past and present, some of whom are featured in this book, thank you for giving me the subject matter to write about. I've found joy, meaning, and purpose in working with you and your teams. Big thanks especially to Karen Geary, formerly Chief People officer at Sage and Helen Deeble CBE, formerly CEO of P&O Ferries, who gave me my first ever consulting gigs when I ventured out alone back in 2005. You set me on my way, and I shall be forever grateful. Also, I'm indebted to Adrian Grace formerly at AEGON UK, Jayne Archbold at Iptor, Donald Kerr and Cambridge and Counties Bank, and Adrian Walker at Lloyds Banking Group who have been with me for all or major parts of my journey. Working with each of you has been an honor, a pleasure, and a great deal of fun.

Thanks to all the academics and authors referenced in this book. Ideas create ideas which create ideas. I'm pleased to join you all in one big idea team.

Finally, I want to thank Ed Stafford for agreeing to foreword this book, and to be scrutinized in the public domain. An extraordinary man with an extraordinary story. Most of all, though, an extraordinary willingness to humbly look at himself in the mirror and to fearlessly share his mistakes and his learnings for the benefit of others. Now that's what I call a proper team player.

About the Author

George Karseras MSc is a Chartered Occupational and Chartered Sports Psychologist and the Founder of www.Team-Up.company, a UK-based digital training and management consultancy firm, and author of *Teams: Systems Within Systems* and *Business Psychology in Practice*. In addition to his work as an executive coach and consultant, George is a sought-after speaker. Prior to founding Team-Up, George worked as a Principal Consultant at KPMG Consulting. He now works globally with hundreds of teams and CEOs all wishing to harness their potential in a variety of industries—including Banking, Asset Management, Travel, Education, Manufacturing, Property, Building, Insurance, Oil and Gas, Publishing, Retail, Software Development, Professional Sports, and Media. George has a passion for discovering what makes extreme teams work under pressure, and you can view his interviews with leaders of extreme teams on the *TeamUp* YouTube channel.

George lives with his family in North Somerset where he loves cycling, running, surfing, and generally pretending to be an extreme sportsman. You can reach him at the Team Up's website, www.team-up.company or at george@team-up.company.

References

Introduction

Teams that Walk the Amazon

1. This telling of Ed Stafford's expedition of walking the length of the Amazon River is based on details told to the author by Stafford.

2. EdStafford.org (2020). *Walking the Amazon.* Ed Stafford. https://www. edstafford.org/walking-the-amazon

3. National Geographic (2010). *The Explorer: Ed Stafford.* National Geographic. https://www.nationalgeographic.com/adventure/article/ed-stafford-2010

4. Adventurer of the Year (2011). *Adventure Articles.* Adventurer of the Year. http://www.adventureroftheyear.com/adventure-articles.html

Chapter 1

Extreme Times for Extreme Teams

1. Wiles, J. (2018). *Mobilize Every Function in the Organization for Digitalization.* Gartner. https://www.gartner.com/smarterwithgartner/ mobilize-every-function-in-the-organization-for-digitalization/

2. Bailey, S. (2013, March). *How To Beat the Five Killers of Virtual Working.* Forbes. https://www.forbes.com/sites/sebastianbailey/2013/03/05/ how-to-overcome-the-five-major-disadvantages-of-virtual-working/#798588912734

3. Daspit, J., Tillman, C. J., Boyd, N. G., & McKee, V. (2013). Cross-functional team effectiveness: An examination of internal team environment, shared leadership, and cohesion influences.

Team Performance Management, 19(1/2), 34–56. https://doi.
org/10.1108/13527591311312088

4. Dulebohn, J. H., & Hoch, J. E. (2017). Virtual teams in organizations.
    Human Resource Management Review, 27(4), 569–574. https://doi.
    org/10.1016/j.hrmr.2016.12.004

5. Paul, S., He, F., & Dennis, A. R. (2018). Group Atmosphere, Shared
    Understanding, and Team Conflict in Short Duration Virtual Teams.
    *Proceedings of the 51st Hawaii International Conference on System
    Sciences, Hawaii,* 361-370 http://hdl.handle.net/10125/49935

6. Türkmen, A. (2013) *Cognitive Diversity and innovation: Does cognitive
    diversity in multinational corporations influence workgroup innovation?*
    (UMI No. 3566296) [Doctoral dissertation, Fielding Graduate University]
    ProQuest Dissertations & Theses Global database.

7. Harvey Nash / KPMG (2020). *Harvey Nash / KPMG CIO Survey 2020:
    Everything changed. Or did it?* KPMG. https://home.kpmg/xx/en/home/
    insights/2020/09/harvey-nash-kpmg-cio-survey-2020-everything-
    changed-or-did-it.html

8. Deloitte (2014). *The Deloitte Millennial Survey 2014.* Deloitte. https://
    www2.deloitte.com/content/dam/Deloitte/global/Documents/About-
    Deloitte/gx-dttl-2014-millennial-survey-report.pdf

9. Burton, C.M., Mayhall, C., Cross, J. and Patterson, P. (2019). Critical
    elements for multigenerational teams: a systematic review. *Team
    Performance Management, 25*(7/8), 369-401. https://doi.org/10.1108/
    TPM-12-2018-0075

10. Hillman, D. R. (2014). Understanding multigenerational work-value conflict
    resolution. *Journal of Workplace Behavioral Health, 29*(3), 240–257.
    https://doi.org/10.1080/15555240.2014.933961

11. Haynes, B. (2011). The impact of generational differences on the
    workplace. *Journal of Corporate Real Estate, 13*(2), 98–108. https://doi.
    org/10.1108/14630011111136812

12. Hillman, D. R. (2014). Understanding Multigenerational Work-Value
    Conflict Resolution. *Journal of Workplace Behavioral Health, 29*(3),
    240–257. https://doi.org/10.1080/15555240.2014.933961

13. Woodward, I. C., Vongswasdi, P., & More, E. A. (2015). Generational
    Diversity at Work: A Systematic Review of the Research. *SSRN Electronic
    Journal,* INSEAD Working Paper No. 2015/48/OB. https://doi.org/10.2139/
    ssrn.2630650

14. Fry, R., Igielnik, R., & Patten, E. (2018, March 16). How Millennials today compare with their grandparents 50 years ago [Pew Research Center]. http://www.pewresearch.org/fact-tank/2018/03/16/how-millennials-compare-with-their-grandparents/

15. Becton, J. B., Walker, H. J., & Jones-Farmer, A. (2014). Generational differences in workplace behavior: Generational differences in behavior. *Journal of Applied Social Psychology, 44*(3), 175–189. https://doi.org/10.1111/jasp.12208

16. Mencl, J., & Lester, S. W. (2014). More alike than different what generations value and how the values affect employee workplace perceptions. *Journal of Leadership & Organizational Studies, 21*(3), 257-272. https://doi.org/10.1177/1548051814529825

17. Doyle, A. (2019). *How Long Should an Employee Stay at a Job?* The Balance Careers. https://www.thebalancecareers.com/how-long-should-an-employee-stay-at-a-job-2059796

18. da Costa, P. N. (2017). *More Americans need a 2nd job to make ends meet — and it's sending a troubling message about the economy.* Business Insider. https://www.businessinsider.com/more-americans-working-more-than-one-job-to-make-ends-meet-2017-8?r=US&IR=T

19. De Stefano, V. (2015). The Rise of the 'Just-in-Time Workforce': On-Demand Work, Crowd Work and Labour Protection in the 'Gig-Economy.' *Comparative Labor Law & Policy Journal, Forthcoming,* Bocconi Legal Studies Research Paper No. 2682602. Available at SSRN: https://ssrn.com/abstract=2682602 or http://dx.doi.org/10.2139/ssrn.2682602

20. Partington, R. (2019, June). *Gig economy in Britain doubles, accounting for 4.7 million workers.* The Guardian. https://www.theguardian.com/business/2019/jun/28/gig-economy-in-britain-doubles-accounting-for-47-million-workers

21. Office for National Statistics (2020, June). *Labour Market Overview, UK: June 2020.* Office for National Statistics. https://www.ons.gov.uk/employmentandlabourmarket/peopleinwork/employmentandemployeetypes/bulletins/uklabourmarket/june2020

22. Grant Thornton (2018). *Women in business: beyond policy to progress.* Grant Thornton. https://www.grantthornton.global/globalassets/1.-member-firms/global/insights/women-in-business/grant-thornton-women-in-business-2018-report.pdf

23. Pew Research Center (2015, January). *Women and Leadership: Public Says Women are Equally Qualified, but Barriers Persist.* Pew Research

Center. https://www.pewresearch.org/social-trends/wp-content/uploads/
sites/3/2015/01/2015-01-14_women-and-leadership.pdf

24. Schmitt, D. P, Realo, a., Voracek, M. & Allik, J. (2008). Why Can't a Man
Be More Like a Woman? Sex Differences in Big Five Personality Traits
Across 55 Cultures. *Journal of Personality and Social Psychology, 94*(1),
168–182. https://doi.org/10.1037/0022-3514.94.1.168

25. Costa, P. T., Jr., Terracciano, A., & McCrae, R. R. (2001). Gender
differences in personality traits across cultures: Robust and surprising
findings. *Journal of Personality and Social Psychology, 81*(2), 322–331.
https://doi.org/10.1037/0022-3514.81.2.322

26. The Parker Review (2017). *A Report into the Ethnic Diversity of UK
Boards.* Diversity UK. https://diversityuk.org/wp-content/uploads/2017/10/
EY-Parker-Review-2017.pdf

27. The McGregor Smith Review (2017). *Race in the workplace.*
The McGregor-Smith Review. Assets Publishing Service. https://
assets.publishing.service.gov.uk/government/uploads/system/
uploads/attachment_data/file/594336/race-in-workplace-mcgregor-
smith-review.pdf

28. Laurence, J., Schmid, K., & Hewstone, M. (2019). Ethnic diversity, ethnic
threat, and social cohesion: (re)-evaluating the role of perceived out-group
threat and prejudice in the relationship between community ethnic diversity
and intra-community cohesion. *Journal of Ethnic and Migration Studies,
45*(3), 395-418. https://doi.org/10.1080/1369183X.2018.1490638

29. Martin, A., & Bal, V. (2015). *The State of Teams.* Centre for Creative
Leadership. http://cclinnovation.org/wp-content/uploads/2020/03/
stateofteams.pdf

30. Cross, R., Rebele, R., & Grant, A. (2016, January-February). *Collaboration
Overload.* Harvard Business Review. https://hbr.org/2016/01/
collaborative-overload

31. Santos, H. C., Varnum, M. E. W., & Grossmann, I. (2017). Global
increases in individualism. *Psychological Science, 28*(9), 1228–1239.
https://doi.org/10.1177/0956797617700622

32. Uhls, Y. T., & Greenfield, P. M. (2012). The value of fame: Preadolescent
perceptions of popular media and their relationship to future
aspirations. *Developmental Psychology, 48*(2), 315–326. https://doi.
org/10.1037/a0026369

33. Twenge, J. M., Dawson, L., & Campbell, W. K. (2016). Still standing out:
children's names in the United States during the Great Recession and

correlations with economic indicators: Names and economic conditions. *Journal of Applied Social Psychology, 46*(11), 663–670. https://doi. org/10.1111/jasp.12409

34. Grainger, K. (2018). *Traditional Baby Names People Aren't Using Anymore Updated 15/10/20.* The List. https://www.thelist.com/111605/ traditional-baby-names-uncommon/

35. Hampson, L. (2019, July). *The names Craig, Kirsty and Lee could soon be extinct in the UK.* Evening Standard. https://www.standard.co.uk/lifestyle/ london-life/extinct-baby-names-2019-a4184526.html

36. Ogihara, Y., Fujita, H., Tominaga, H., Ishigaki, S., Kashimoto, T., Takahashi, A., Toyohara, K., & Uchida, Y. (2015). Are common names becoming less common? The rise in uniqueness and individualism in Japan. *Fronters in Psychology.* https://doi.org/10.3389/fpsyg.2015.01490

37. Office for National Statistics (ONS) (2020). *Gross domestic product (Average) per head, CVM market prices: SA.* Office for National Statistics. https://www.ons.gov.uk/economy/grossdomesticproductgdp/ timeseries/ihxw/pn2

38. Roser, M., & Ortiz-Ospina, E. (2016). *"Global Education."* OurWorldInData. org. https://ourworldindata.org/global-education

39. Bianchi, E. (2016). American Individualism Rises and Falls with the Economy: Cross-Temporal Evidence that Individualism Declines when the Economy Falters. *Journal of Personality and Social Psychology, 111*(4), 567–584. https://doi.org/10.1037/pspp0000114

40. Ogihari, Y. (2018). Economic shifts and cultural changes in individualism: A cross-temporal perspective. In A. Uskul & S. Oishi (Eds.), *Socioeconomic environment and human psychology: Social, ecological, and cultural perspectives* (pp. 247-270). Oxford: Oxford University Press. https://www.researchgate.net/profile/ Yuji_Ogihara/publication/322951921_Economic_shifts_and_ cultural_changes_in_individualism_A_cross-temporal_perspective/ links/5b072c3fa6fdcc8c25298b1a/Economic-shifts-and-cultural-changes- in-individualism-A-cross-temporal-perspective.pdf

41. Yu, F., Peng, T., Peng, K., Tang, S., Shi Chen, C., Pei Sun, X. Q., Han, T., & Chai, F. (2016). Cultural Value Shifting in Pronoun Use. *Journal of Cross-Cultural Psychology, 42*(2), 310-316. https://doi. org/10.1177/0022022115619230

42. Twenge, J. M., Foster, J. D. (2010). Birth cohort increases in narcissistic personality traits among American college students, 1982-2009. *Social*

Psychological and Personality Science, 1(1), 99–106. https://doi. org/10.1177/1948550609355719

43. Twenge, J. M., Konrath, S., Foster, J. D., Campbell, W. K., Bushman, B. J. (2008). Egos inflating over time: A cross-temporal meta-analysis of the Narcissistic Personality Inventory. *Journal of Personality, 76*(1), 875–901. https://doi.org/10.1111/j.1467-6494.2008.00507.x

44. Twenge, J. M. (2013). The Evidence for Generation Me and Against Generation We. *Emerging Adulthood, 1*(1), 11–16. https://doi. org/10.1177/2167696812466548

45. Twenge, J. M. (2013). Overwhelming Evidence for Generation Me: A Reply to Arnett. *Emerging Adulthood, 1*(1) 21–26. https://doi. org/10.1177/2167696812468112

46. Simić, I., Matović, I. M., & Stojković, N. (2015). Analysis of Machiavellian Behavior of Students in The Republic of Serbia. *Facta Universitatis: Economics & Organisation, 12*(3), 199-208. Retrieved from: http:// casopisi.junis.ni.ac.rs/index.php/FUEconOrg/article/view/1272

47. Webster, R. L., & Harmon, H. A. (2002). Comparing levels of Machiavellianism of today's college students with college students of the 1960s. *Teaching Business Ethics, 6*(4), 435–445. https://doi. org/10.1023/A:1021149204098

48. Barlett, C. P., & Barlett, N. D. (2015). The young and the restless: Examining the relationships between age, emerging adulthood variables, and the Dark Triad. *Personality and Individual Differences, 86*(1), 20–24. https://doi.org/10.1016/j.paid.2015.05.024

49. Götz, F. M., Bleidorn, W., & Rentfrow, P. J. (2020). Age differences in Machiavellianism across the life span: Evidence from a large-scale cross-sectional study. *Journal of Personality, 88*(5), 978-992. https://doi. org/10.1111/jopy.12545

50. Ruegger, D., & King, E. W. (1992). A study of the effect of age and gender upon student business ethics. *Journal of Business Ethics, 11*(3), 179–186. https://doi.org/10.1007/BF00871965

51. Babiak, P., Neumann, C., & Hare, R. (2010). Corporate psychopathy: Talking the walk. *Behavioral Sciences & The Law, 28*(2), 174-193 https:// doi.org/10.1002/bsl.925

52. Werner, K. B., Few, L. R., & Bucholz, K. K. (2015). Epidemiology, Comorbidity, and Behavioral Genetics of Antisocial Personality Disorder and Psychopathy. *Psychiatric annals, 45*(4), 195–199. https://doi. org/10.3928/00485713-20150401-08

53. Babiak, P., & Hare, R. D. (2007). Snakes in Suits: When Psychopaths Go to Work. New York, NY: Harper Business

54. Ragatz, L (2011). *A Comparison of White-Collar Offenders and Non-White-Collar Offenders on the Psychological Variables of Personality, Criminal Thinking, and Psychopathy.* (No. 4770) [Graduate Theses, Eberly College of Arts and Sciences] Research Repository. https:// researchrepository.wvu.edu/etd/4770

55. Saft, J. (2017, June). *A psychopath CEOs destroy value, nice ones create it.* Reuters. https://www.reuters.com/article/us-markets-saft/ as-psychopath-ceos-destroy-value-nice-ones-create-it-james-saft-idUSKBN19C2Y0

56. Brooks, N., & Fritzon, K. (2016). RETRACTED ARTICLE: Psychopathic personality characteristics amongst high functioning populations. *Crime Psychology Review, 2*(1), 22–44. https://doi.org/10.1080/23744006. 2016.1232537

57. Tokarev, A., Phillips, A. R., Hughes, D. J., & Irwing, P. (2017). Leader dark traits, workplace bullying, and employee depression: Exploring mediation and the role of the dark core. *Journal of Abnormal Psychology, 126*(7), 911–920. https://doi-org.ezproxy.derby.ac.uk/10.1037/abn0000299.supp

58. Twenge, J., Joiner, T., Duffy, M., Cooper, B., and Binau, S. (2019). Age, Period, and Cohort Trends in Mood Disorder and Suicide-Related Outcomes in a Nationally Representative Dataset, 2005-2017. *Journal of Abnormal Psychology, 128*(3), 185–199. http://dx.doi.org/10.1037/ abn0000410

59. Weinberger, A., Gbedemah, M., Martinez, A., Nash, D., Galea, S., & Goodwin, R. (2018). Trends in depression prevalence in the USA from 2005 to 2015: Widening disparities in vulnerable groups. *Psychological Medicine, 48*(8), 1308-1315. doi:10.1017/S0033291717002781

60. CIPD (2020, *March*). *Health And Well-Being at Work. Survey Report, 2020.* Chartered Institute of Personnel and Development. https://www. cipd.co.uk/Images/health-and-well-being-2020-report_tcm18-73967.pdf

61. Stewart, C. (2020, July). *Stress in the UK—statistics & facts.* Statista. https://www.statista.com/topics/6735/stress-in-the-uk/

62. Marshall, L., Bibby, J., & Abbs, I. (2020, June). *Emerging evidence on COVID-19's impact on mental health and health inequalities.* The Health Foundation. https://www.health.org.uk/news-and-comment/blogs/ emerging-evidence-on-covid-19s-impact-on-mental-health-and-health

63. Butler, T., North, P., & Palmer, J. (2018, March). *A New Paradigm for Regulatory Change and Compliance. A Whitepaper by the RegTech Council.* BNY Mellon. https://www.bnymellon.com/content/dam/bnymellon/documents/pdf/emea/regtech-council-weighs-in.pdf.coredownload.pdf

64. Crews, C. W. (2014, March). *New Data: Code of Federal Regulations Expanding, Faster Pace under Obama.* Competitive Enterprise Institute. https://cei.org/blog/new-data-code-of-federal-regulations-expanding-faster-pace-under-obama/

Chapter 2
In Search of the Holy Grail

1. Wageman, R., Nunes, D. A., Burruss, J. A., & Hackman, J. R. (2008). *Senior leadership teams: What it takes to make them great.* Harvard Business Review Press.

2. Parisi-Carew, E. (2011). *Why teams fail—And what to do about it.* Human Resource Executive Online. http://www.hreonline.com/HRE/view/story.jhtml?id=533342576

3. Nilsen, D., & Curphy, G. J. (2018). Organizations That Get Teamwork Right. *People & Strategy, 41*(2), 42–46. https://tinyurl.com/ycgjgpau

4. Tabrizi, B. (2015, June 23). *75% of Cross-Functional Teams Are Dysfunctional.* Harvard Business Review. https://hbr.org/2015/06/75-of-cross-functional-teams-are-dysfunctional

5. Nink, M. (2019). *Cooperation Is Key to an Agile Workplace.* Gallup. https://www.gallup.com/workplace/246908/cooperation-key-agile-workplace.aspx

6. Sinek, S. (2011). *Start with Why: How Great Leaders Inspire Everyone to Take Action.* Penguin Portfolio, London.

7. Schein, E.H. and Bennis, W. (1965). *Personal and Organizational Change Through Group Methods.* New York: Wiley.

8. Edmondson, A. (1999). Psychological Safety and Learning Behavior in Work Teams. *Administrative Science Quarterly, 44*(1), 350-383. https://journals.sagepub.com/doi/pdf/10.2307/2666999

9. Brown, B. (2018). *Dare to Lead: Brave Work. Tough Conversations.* London: Vermillion

10. Kahane, A. (2017). *Collaborating with the Enemy: How to Work with People You Don't Agree with*. Oakland, CA: Berrett-Koehler Publishers Inc.

11. Goleman, D. (1996). *Emotional Intelligence*. London: Bloomsbury Publishing Plc

12. Syer, J. and Connolly, C. (1996). *How Teamworking Works: The Dynamics of Effective Team Development*. McGraw-Hill.

13. Fisher, R., and Ury, W. L. (1981). *Getting to Yes: Negotiating Agreement Without Giving In*. London: Penguin.

14. Schein, E. H. (1992). *Organizational Culture and Leadership*. San Francisco, CA: Jossey-Bass Publishers.

15. Schein, E. H. and Schein, P. A. (2018). *Humble Leadership: The Power of Relationships, Openness, and Trust*. Oakland, CA: Berrett-Koehler Publishers.

16. Taleb, N. N. (2018). *Skin in the Game: Hidden Asymmetries in Daily Life*. New York: Random House.

17. Kofman, F., & Senge, P. M. (1993). Communities of commitment: The heart of learning organizations. *Organizational Dynamics, 22*(2), 5–23. https://doi.org/10.1016/0090-2616(93)90050-B

18. Senge, P. M. (1990). *The Fifth Discipline – The Art & Practice of the Learning Organisation*. London: Random House Business Books.

19. Katzenbach, J. R., & Smith, D. K. (1993). *Organizational Culture: The Discipline of Teams*. Harvard Business Review, March-April 1993. https://hbr.org/1993/03/the-discipline-of-teams-2

20. Hawkins, P. (2011). *Leadership Team Coaching: Developing Collective Transformational Leadership*. London: Kogan Page Limited.

21. Meyerson, D., Weick, K., & Kramer, R. (1996). Swift trust and temporary groups. In R. Kramer, & T. Tyler *Trust in organizations: Frontiers of theory and research* (pp. 166-195). SAGE Publications, Inc. https://www.doi.org/10.4135/9781452243610.n9

22. Shaw, R. B. (2017). *Extreme Teams: Why Pixar, Netflix, Airbnb, and Other Cutting-Edge Companies Succeed Where Most Fail*. New York City: American Management Association

23. Gibb Dyer Jr., W., Dyer, J. H., and Dyer, W. G. (2013). *Building Proven Strategies for Improving Team Performance*. San Francisco, CA: Jossey-Bass

24. Bion, W. R. (1959). Attacks on linking. *The International Journal of Psychoanalysis, 40(1)*, 308–315. https://doi.org/10.1002/j.2167-4086.2013.00029.x

25. Tuckman, B. W. (1965). Developmental sequence in small groups. *Psychological Bulletin, 63*(6), 384–399. https://doi.org/10.1037/h0022100

26. Lencioni, P. M. (2002). *The Five Dysfunctions of a Team: A Leadership Fable (J–B Lencioni Series)*. Jossey-Bass Inc.

27. Clutterbuck, D. (2019). Towards a pragmatic model of team function and dysfunction. In. D. Clutterbuck, J. Gannon, S. Hayes, I. Iordanou, K. Lowe, and D. MacKie (Eds.), *The Practitioner's Handbook of Team Coaching* (Chapter 10). London: Routledge Available at: https://www.cityandguilds.com/~/media/AEC77F130CD54B2CA8A1AE02246E8811.ashx

28. Hackman, J.R., & Wageman, R. (1995). Total quality management: empirical, conceptual, and practical issues. *Administrative Science Quarterly, 40*(2), 309-342. https://doi.org/10.2307/2393640

29. Morecambe, E. (1971). Ammonds, J. (Producer). (1971, Christmas). *The Morecambe & Wise Show – 1971 Christmas Show* [Television broadcast]. British Broadcasting Corporation (BBC)

Chapter 3

Building Swift Trust

1. Akgün, A. E., Lynn, G. S., Keskin, H., & Dogan, D. (2014a). *Trust measure* [Database record]. Retrieved from PsycTESTS. https://doi.org/10.1037/t33431-000

2. Akgün, A. E., Lynn, G. S., Keskin, H., & Dogan, D. (2014b). Team learning in IT implementation projects: Antecedents and consequences. *International Journal of Information Management, 34*(1), 37–47. https://doi.org/10.1016/j.ijinfomgt.2013.09.007

3. Erdem, F., Ozen, J., & Atsan, N. (2003). The relationship between trust and team performance. *Work Study, 52*(7), 337–340. https://doi.org/10.1108/00438020310502633

4. Edmondson, A. (1999). Psychological safety and learning behavior in work teams. *Administrative Science Quarterly, 44*(2), 350–383. https://doi.org/10.2307/2666999

5. Kramer, R. M., & Messick, D. M. (1998). Getting by with a little help from our enemies: Collective paranoia and its role in intergroup relations. In

C. Sedikides (Ed.). *Intergroup cognition and intergroup behavior* (pp. 233–255). Mahwah, NJ: Lawrence Erlbaum Associates.

6. Mayer, R. C., Davis, J. H., & Schoorman, F. D. (1995). An integrative model of organizational trust. *The Academy of Management Review, 20*(3), 709–734. https://doi.org/10.2307/258792

7. Chowdry, S. (2005). The Role of Affect- and Cognition-based Trust in Complex Knowledge Sharing. *Journal of Managerial Issues, 17*(3), pp. 310-326. https://www.jstor.org/stable/40604504

8. Chua, R. Y. J., Ingram, P. and Morris, M. W. (2008). From the Head and the Heart: Locating Cognition- and Affect-Based Trust in Managers' Professional Networks. *Academy of Management Journal,* 51(3), 436–452. https://doi.org/10.5465/amj.2008.32625956

9. Kauffman, D., and Golan, C. (2017). The Mediating Effect of Interpersonal Trust on Virtual Team's Collaboration. *International Journal of Knowledge Management, 13*(3), 20–37. https://doi.org/10.4018/IJKM.2017070102

10. Lu, S. C. Kong, D. J., Ferrin, D. L., and Dirks, K. T. (2017). What are the determinants of interpersonal trust in dyadic negotiations? Meta-analytic evidence and implications for future research. *Journal of Trust Research, 7*(1), 22–50. Available at: https://ink.library.smu.edu.sg/lkcsb_research/5295

11. McAllistair, D. J. (1995). Affect- and Cognition-Based Trust as Foundations for Interpersonal Cooperation in Organizations. *The Academy of Management Journal, 38*(1), pp. 24–59. https://doi.org/10.2307/256727

12. Rotter, J. B. (1971). Generalized expectancies for interpersonal trust. *American Psychologist, 26*(5), 443–452. https://doi.org/10.1037/h0031464

13. Breuer, C., Hüffmeier, J., Hibben, F., & Hertel, G. (2020). Trust in teams: A taxonomy of perceived trustworthiness factors and risk-taking behaviors in face-to-face and virtual teams. *Human Relations, 73*(1) 3–34. https://doi.org/10.1177/0018726718818721

14. Savolainen, T., Ivakko, E. & Ikonen, M. (2017) Trust development in workplace relations during change: A multi-level analysis of narratives from leaders and followers. *In: Proceedings of the 5th International Conference on Management, Leadership and Governance, ICMLG 2017, Wits Business School, University of Witwatersrand Johannesburg, South Africa, 16–17 March.* Zanele, N. Mokoteli, T. (Eds.). Academic Conferences and Publishing International Limited (ACPI Ltd.). Reading, UK. pp. 393-400.

15. Barsade, S. G., Coutifaris, C. G., & Pillemer, J. (2018). Emotional contagion in organizational life. *Research in Organizational Behavior, 38*(1), 137-151. https://doi.org/10.1016/j.riob.2018.11.005

16. Yagil, D. (2015). Display rules for kindness: Outcomes of suppressing benevolent emotions. *Motivation and Emotion, 39*(1), 156–166. https://doi.org/10.1007/s11031-014-9418-1

17. Zaccaro, S. J., Rittman, A. L. and Marks, M. A. (2001). Team Leadership. *The Leadership Quarterly, 12*(1), 451 – 483. http://www.qub.ac.uk/elearning/media/Media,264498,en.pdf

18. Lencioni, P. M. (2002). *The Five Dysfunctions of a Team: A Leadership Fable (J–B Lencioni Series)*. Jossey-Bass Inc.

19. Crisp, C. B. & Jarvenpaa, S.L., (2013). Swift trust in global virtual teams trusting beliefs and normative actions. *Journal of Personnel Psychology, 12* (1), 45–56. https://doi.org/10.1027/1866-5888/a000075

20. Yang, I. (2019). What makes an effective team? The role of trust (dis)confirmation in team development. *European Management Journal, 32*(6), 858–869. https://doi.org/10.1016/j.emj.2014.04.001

21. Zakaria, N., & Yusof, S. A. M (2020). Crossing Cultural Boundaries Using the Internet: Toward Building a Model of Swift Trust Formation in Global Virtual Teams. *Journal of International Management, 26*(1), *100654*. https://doi.org/10.1016/j.intman.2018.10.004

22. Fahy, M. J. (2012). *Understanding Swift Trust to Improve Interagency Collaboration in New York City*. Naval Postgraduate School, Monterey CA Dept of National Security. Retrieved from: https://calhoun.nps.edu/handle/10945/17362

23. Triplett, S.M., & Loh, J.M.I. (2018). The moderating role of trust in the relationship between work locus of control and psychological safety in organizational work teams. *Australian Journal of Psychology, 70*(1), 76–84. https://doi.org/10.1111/ajpy.12168

24. Erdem, F., Ozen, J., & Atsan, N. (2003). The relationship between trust and team performance. *Work Study, 52*(7), 337–340. https://doi.org/10.1108/00438020310502633

25. Ghiringhelli, C., & Lazazzara, A. (2016). Blended learning for developing effective virtual teams: a proposed intervention format. *European Alliance for Innovation, 3*(12). https://doi.org/10.4108/eai.2-12-2016.151718

26. Meyerson, D., Weick, K., & Kramer, R. (1996). Swift trust and temporary groups. In R. Kramer, & T. Tyler *Trust in organizations: Frontiers of theory*

and research (pp. 166-195). SAGE Publications, Inc., https://www.doi.
org/10.4135/9781452243610.n9

27. Adler, T.R. (2007). Swift trust and distrust in strategic partnering
    relationships: key considerations of team-based designs. *Journal of
    Business Strategies, 24* (2), 105–121. https://www.semanticscholar.org/
    paper/Swift-Trust-and-Distrust-in-Strategic-Partnering-of-Adler/31b06da1
    56f1d1b93b65bd975cb7e91d44772caf

28. Greenberg, P.S., Greenberg, R.H., & Antonucci, Y.L. (2007). Creating
    and sustaining trust in virtual teams. *Business Horizons, 50*(4), 325–333.
    https://doi.org/10.1016/j.bushor.2007.02.005.

29. Kim, Y.Y. (2015). Achieving synchrony: a foundational dimension
    of intercultural communication competence. *International Journal
    of Intercultural Relations, 48*(1), 27–37. https://doi.org/10.1016/j.
    ijintrel.2015.03.016

30. de Laat, P.B. (2005). Trusting Virtual Trust. *Ethics & Information
    Technology, 7*(3), 167–180. https://doi.org/10.1007/s10676-006-0002-6

31. Remidez, H., Stam, A., & Laffey, J.M. (2007). Web-based, template-driven
    communication support systems: using shadow network space to support
    trust development in virtual teams. *International Journal of e-Collaboration,
    3*(1), 65–73. https://doi.org/10.4018/978-1-59904-648-8.ch018

32. Edmondson, A. C. & Harvey, J-F. (2017). *Extreme Teaming: Lessons in
    Complex, Cross-Sector Leadership.* Bingley, UK: Emerald Publishing Ltd.

33. Dulebohn, J. H., & Hoch, J. E. (2017). Virtual teams in organizations.
    Human Resource Management Review, 27(4), 569–574. https://doi.
    org/10.1016/j.hrmr.2016.12.004

34. Mohammed, S., & Dumville, B. C. (2001) Team mental models in a team
    knowledge framework: expanding theory and measurement across
    disciplinary boundaries. *Journal of Organizational Behavior, 22*(2),
    89–106. https://doi.org/10.1002/job.86

35. Paul, S., He, F., & Dennis, A. R. (2018). Group Atmosphere, Shared
    Understanding, and Team Conflict in Short Duration Virtual Teams.
    *Proceedings of the 51st Hawaii International Conference on System
    Sciences, Hawaii,* 361-370 http://hdl.handle.net/10125/49935

36. Mayfield, C. O., Tombaugh, J. R., and Lee, M. (2016). Psychological
    Collectivism and Team Effectiveness: Moderating Effects of Trust
    and Psychological Safety. *Journal of Organizational Culture,
    Communications and Conflict, 20*(1), 78–94. Available at: https://www.
    researchgate.net/profile/Issam-Ghazzawi/publication/303370032_

Faith_and_Job_Satisfaction_Is_Religion_a_Missing_Link/
links/58f8e591aca272e9fac79274/Faith-and-Job-Satisfaction-Is-Religion-a-Missing-Link.pdf#page=83

37. Walter, F., & Bruch, H. (2008). The positive group affect spiral: A dynamic model of the emergence of positive affective similarity in work groups. *Journal of Organizational Behavior, 29*(2), 239–261. https://doi.org/10.1002/job.505

38. Bailey, S. (2013, March). *How To Beat the Five Killers of Virtual Working.* Forbes. https://www.forbes.com/sites/sebastianbailey/2013/03/05/how-to-overcome-the-five-major-disadvantages-of-virtual-working/#798588912734

39. Daspit, J., Tillman, C. J., Boyd, N. G., & McKee, V. (2013). Cross-functional team effectiveness: An examination of internal team environment, shared leadership, and cohesion influences. *Team Performance Management, 19*(1/2), 34–56. https://doi.org/10.1108/13527591311312088

40. Hinds, P. J. and Mortensen, M. (2005). Understanding Conflict in Geographically Distributed Teams: The Moderating Effects of Shared Identity, Shared Context, and Spontaneous Communication. *Organization Science, 16*(3), 203-325. https://doi.org/10.1287/orsc.1050.0122

41. Mortensen, M. and Neeley, T. B. (2012). Reflected Knowledge and Trust in Global Collaboration. *Management Science, 58*(12), iv–2308. https://doi.org/10.1287/mnsc.1120.1546

42. Santos, C. M., & Passos, A. M. (2013). Team Mental Models, Relationship Conflict and Effectiveness over Time. *Team Performance Management 19*(7/8), 363 – 385. https://doi.org/10.1108/TPM-01-2013-0003

43. Cave, D., Pearson, H., Whitehead, P., and Rahim-Jamal, S. (2016). CENTRE: creating psychological safety in groups. *The Clinical Teacher, 13*(1), 1–5. https://doi.org/10.1111/tct.12465

Chapter 4

The Code

1. van der Haar, S., Li, J., Segers, M., Jehn, K. A., & Van den Bosschen, P. (2015). Evolving team cognition: The impact of team situation models on team effectiveness. *European Journal of Work and Organizational Psychology, 24*(4), 596-610. https://doi.org/10.1080/135943 2X.2014.942731

2.   Tabrizi, B. (2015, June 23). *75% of Cross-Functional Teams Are Dysfunctional.* Harvard Business Review. https://hbr.org/2015/06/75-of-cross-functional-teams-are-dysfunctional

3.   Breuer, C., Hüffmeier, J., Hibben, F., & Hertel, G. (2020). Trust in teams: A taxonomy of perceived trustworthiness factors and risk-taking behaviors in face-to-face and virtual teams. *Human Relations, 73*(1) 3–34. https://doi.org/10.1177/0018726718818721

4.   Bailey, S. (2013, March). *How To Beat the Five Killers of Virtual Working.* Forbes. https://www.forbes.com/sites/sebastianbailey/2013/03/05/how-to-overcome-the-five-major-disadvantages-of-virtual-working/#798588912734

5.   Haas, M., and Mortensen, M. (2016, June). *The Secrets of Great Teamwork.* Harvard Business Review. https://hbr.org/2016/06/the-secrets-of-great-teamwork

6.   Daspit, J., Tillman, C. J., Boyd, N. G., & McKee, V. (2013). Cross-functional team effectiveness: An examination of internal team environment, shared leadership, and cohesion influences. *Team Performance Management, 19*(1/2), 34–56. https://doi.org/10.1108/13527591311312088

7.   Chen, G., & Tjosvold, D. (2012). Shared rewards and goal interdependence for psychological safety among departments in China. *Asia Pacific Journal of Management, 29*(1), 433–452. https://doi.org/10.1007/s10490-010-9201-0

8.   Cave, D., Pearson, H., Whitehead, P., & Rahim-Jamal, S. (2016). CENTRE: creating psychological safety in groups. *The Clinical Teacher, 13*(1), 1–5. https://doi.org/10.1111/tct.12465

9.   Gibson, C. B., Dunlop, P. D., & Raghav, S. (2020). Navigating identities in global work: Antecedents and consequences of intrapersonal identity conflict. *Human Relations, 74*(4), 556–586. https://doi.org/10.1177/0018726719895314

10. Wilkinson. D.J. (2019, December). *Group decision-making. What the latest research says.* Oxford Review Special Report. The Oxford Review, www.oxford-review.com

11. Edmondson, A. (1999). Psychological safety and learning behavior in work teams. *Administrative Science Quarterly, 44*(2), 350–383. https://doi.org/10.2307/2666999

12. Wilkinson. D.J. (2019, February). *High-Performance Teams: What the research says.* Oxford Review Special Report. The Oxford Review, www. oxford-review.com

13. Duhigg, C. (2016, February). *What Google learned from its quest to build the perfect team.* The New York Times Magazine, 26. https://www. nytimes.com/2016/02/28/magazine/what-google-learned-from-its-quest-to-build-the-perfect-team.html

14. Rozovsky, J. (2015, November). *The five keys to a successful Google team.* https://rework.withgoogle.com/blog/five-keys-to-a-successful-google-team/

15. Brouwer, R. (2016). When Competition is the Loser: The Indirect Effect of Intra-team Competition on Team Performance through Task Complexity, Team Conflict and Psychological Safety. 49th Hawaii International Conference on System Sciences (HICSS), Koloa, HI, 1348-1357. https://doi.org/10.1109/HICSS.2016.170

16. Cauwelier, P., Ribiere, V. M., & Bennet, A. (2019). The influence of team psychological safety on team knowledge creation: a study with French and American engineering teams. Journal of Knowledge Management, 23(6), 1157-1175. https://doi.org/10.1108/JKM-07-2018-0420

17. Erkutlu, H. & Chafra, J. (2015). The mediating roles of psychological safety and employee voice on the relationship between conflict management styles and organizational identification. Am*erican Journal of Business*, 30(1), 72–91. https://doi.org/10.1108/AJB-06-2013-0040

18. Feng, X-D., Cao, B-L., Li, N-B., Che, H-S., Yu, W. (2015). Influence Factors and Construction Strategy of R & D Team Psychological Safety. *Proceedings of the 2015 International Conference on Management Science and Management Innovation (MSMI 2015), Guilin, China, Atlantis Press, 167-170.* https://doi.org/10.2991/msmi-15.2015.31

19. Harvey, J.-F., Johnson, K. J., Roloff, K. S., & Edmondson, A. C. (2019). From orientation to behavior: The interplay between learning orientation, open-mindedness, and psychological safety in team learning. *Human Relations, 72*(11), 1726–1751. https://doi.org/10.1177/0018726718817812

20. Edmondson, A.C. (2003). Speaking Up in the Operating Room: How Team Leaders Promote Learning in Interdisciplinary Action Teams. *Journal of Management Studies, 40*(6), 1419-1452. https://doi.org/10.1111/1467-6486.00386

21. Edmondson, A. C. (2004). Learning from failure in health care: frequent opportunities, pervasive barriers. *Quality & Safety in Health Care, 13(Suppl 2)*, ii3–ii9. https://doi.org/10.1136/qhc.13.suppl_2.ii3

22. Edmondson, A. (2018). *The importance of psychological safety.* HR Magazine. https://www.hrmagazine.co.uk/content/features/the-importance-of-psychological-safety

23. Carmeli, A. and Gittell, J.H. (2009). High-quality relationships, psychological safety, and learning from failures in work organizations. *Journal of Organizational Behavior, 30*(6), 709-729. https://doi.org/10.1002/job.565

24. Kark, R. and Carmeli, A. (2009). Alive and creating: the mediating role of vitality and aliveness in the relationship between psychological safety and creative work involvement. *Journal of Organizational Behavior, 30*(6), 785-804. https://doi.org/10.1002/job.571

25. Mitra, R. K. (2019). *Visionary Leadership and Role Ambiguity: Impact of Psychological Safety in Clinical Work Teams* (Publication No. 27547801) [Doctoral dissertation, University of South Alabama]. ProQuest Dissertations & Theses Global.

26. O'Neill, T. A., & McLarnon, M. J. W. (2018). Optimizing team conflict dynamics for high performance teamwork. *Human Resource Management Review, 28*(4), 378–394. https://doi.org/10.1016/j.hrmr.2017.06.002

27. Osborne, S., Brandsen, T., Mele, V., Nemec, J., van Genugten, M., & Flemig, S. (2020). Risking innovation. Understanding risk and public service innovation— evidence from a four-nation study. *Public Money & Management, 40*(1), 52–62. https://doi.org/10.1080/09540962.2019.1621051

Chapter 6

Digitalization and The Code

1. Brynjolfsson, E., & McAfee, A. (2014). *The second machine age: Work, progress, and prosperity in a time of brilliant technologies.* W. W. Norton & Co.

2. Wiles, J. (2018, December). *Mobilize Every Function in the Organization for Digitalization.* Gartner. https://www.gartner.com/smarterwithgartner/mobilize-every-function-in-the-organization-for-digitalization/

3. Reddy, S. (2020, October). *Companies now face an urgent choice: go digital, or go bust.* World Economic Form. https://www.weforum.org/agenda/2020/10/digital-transformation-or-bust/

4. KPMG (2020). *Harvey Nash / KPMG CIO Survey 2020: Everything changed. Or did it?* KPMG. https://home.kpmg/xx/en/home/insights/2020/09/harvey-nash-kpmg-cio-survey-2020-everything-changed-or-did-it.html

5. Bulao, J. (2021, March). *How Much Data Is Created Every Day in 2020?* Tech Jury. https://techjury.net/blog/how-much-data-is-created-every-day/#gref

6. Statista (2021, January). *Big data market size revenue forecast worldwide from 2011 to 2027.* Statista. https://www.statista.com/statistics/254266/global-big-data-market-forecast/

7. McCarthy, N. (2020, September). *Rise Of the Machines: The Countries with The Highest Density of Robot Workers.* Forbes. https://www.forbes.com/sites/niallmccarthy/2020/09/28/rise-of-the-machines-the-countries-with-the-highest-density-of-robot-workers-infographic/?sh=2b7098a31308

8. Statista (2021, March). *Global robotics market revenue 2018-2025.* Statista. https://www.statista.com/statistics/760190/worldwide-robotics-market-revenue/

9. Armstrong, J., Green, K., & Graefe, A. (2015). Golden Rule of Forecasting: Be Conservative. *Journal of Business Research 68*(8), 1717-1731. https://doi.org/10.1016/j.jbusres.2015.03.031

10. Galeon, D., & Reedy, C. (2017, March). *Ray Kurzweil claims singularity will happen by 2045.* Futurism. https://www.kurzweilai.net/futurism-ray-kurzweil-claims-singularity-will-happen-by-2045

11. Grace, K., Salvatier, J., Dafoe, A., Zhang, B., & Evans, O. (2017). Viewpoint: When Will AI Exceed Human Performance? Evidence from AI Experts. *Journal Of Artificial Intelligence Research, 62*(1), 729-754. https://doi.org/10.1613/jair.1.11222

12. Smith, A., and Anderson, J. (2014). *AI, Robotics, and the Future of Jobs.* PEW Research Centre. https://www.pewresearch.org/internet/2014/08/06/future-of-jobs/

13. Andersen, P., & Ross, J. W. (2016). Transforming the LEGO Group for the Digital Economy. *Proceedings of the 30 Seventh International Conference on Information Systems (ICIS), Dublin, Ireland,* 1-13, https://core.ac.uk/download/pdf/301370224.pdf

14. Berg, A., Buffie, E., & Zanna, L. (2017). Should we fear the robot
     revolution? (The correct answer is yes). *Journal Of Monetary Economics,
     97*(1), 117-148. https://doi.org/10.1016/j.jmoneco.2018.05.014

15. Haughton, J. (2015, May). *Five Reasons Why Leaderless Organizations
     Are Leading the Way.* Chartered Management Institute. https://www.
     managers.org.uk/knowledge-and-insights/article/why-leaderless-
     organisations-are-leading-the-way/

16. Sarkar-Basu, P. (2019, July). *Five Predictions: The Impacts of AI and
     Automation on The Future of Work.* Forbes Communication Council.
     https://www.forbes.com/sites/forbescommunicationscouncil/2019/07/01/
     five-predictions-the-impacts-of-ai-and-automation-on-the-future-of-
     work/?sh=5389563e3838

17. Ramarajan, L., & Reid, E. (2013). Shattering the myth of separate worlds:
     Negotiating nonwork identities at work. *The Academy of Management
     Review, 38*(4), 621–644. https://doi.org/10.5465/amr.2011.0314.

18. Jackson, T., Dawson, R., & Wilson, D. (2001). The cost of email
     interruption. *Journal Of Systems and Information Technology, 5*(1), 8192.
     https://doi.org/10.1108/13287260180000760.

19. Reyt, J-N., & Wiesenfeld, B. M. (2015). Seeing the Forest for the Trees:
     Exploratory Learning, Mobile Technology, and Knowledge Workers' Role
     Integration Behaviors. *Academy of Management Journal, 58*(3), 739–762.
     https://doi.org/10.5465/amj.2013.0991

20. Consultancy.uk (2018, May). *Agile working is booming. Five trends
     in Agile to look out for.* Consultancy UK. https://www.consultancy.uk/
     news/17043/agile-working-is-booming-five-trends-in-agile-to-look-out-for

21. Fischer, K., Jensen, L., Kirstein, F., Stabinger, S., Erkent, Ö., Shukla,
     D., & Piater, J. (2015). The Effects of Social Gaze in Human-Robot
     Collaborative Assembly. In: Tapus A., André E., Martin JC., Ferland F.,
     Ammi M. (eds) *Social Robotics. ICSR 2015. Lecture Notes in Computer
     Science, 9388*(1), 204-213. Springer, Cham. https://doi.org/10.1007/978-
     3-319-25554-5_21

22. Turkle, S. (2011). Alone Together: *Why We Expect More from Technology
     and Less from Each other.* New York: Basic Books

23. Goldie, J. G. S. (2016). Connectivism: A knowledge learning theory for the
     digital age? *Medical Teacher, 38*(10), 1064–1069. https://doi.org/10.3109/
     0142159X.2016.1173661

24. Villani, V., Sabattini, L., Czerniak, J., Mertens, A., & Fantuzzi, C. (2018).
     MATE Robots Simplifying My Work: The Benefits and Socioethical

Implications. *IEEE Robotics & Automation Magazine, 25*(1), 37-45. https://doi.org/10.1109/MRA.2017.2781308

25. Johnson, A., Dey, S., and Nguyen, H., Groth, M., Joyce, S., Tan, L., Glozier, N., and Harvey, S. B. (2020). A review and agenda for examining how technology-driven changes at work will impact workplace mental health and employee well-being. *Australian Journal of Management 45*(3), 402–424. https://doi.org/10.1177/0312896220922292

26. Greenleaf, R. K. (1998). *The Power of Servant Leadership.* San Francisco: Berrett-Koehler Publishers

27. Dinić, B. M., & Vujić, A. (2018). Five-Factor Model Best Describes Narcissistic Personality Inventory Across Different Item Response Formats. *Psychological Reports, 122*(5), 1946-1966. https://doi.org/10.1177/0033294118794404

28. Sy, T., Horton, C., & Riggio, R. (2018). Charismatic leadership: Eliciting and channelling follower emotions. *The Leadership Quarterly, 29*(1), 58–69. https://doi.org/10.1016/j.leaqua.2017.12.008

29. Rigby, D. K., Sutherland, J., & Takeuchi, H. (2016, MY). Embracing agile. *Harvard Business Review, 94*(5), 40–50. Available at: https://hbr.org/2016/05/embracing-agile

30. Denning, S. (2018). *The Age of Agile: How Smart Companies Are Transforming the Way Work Gets Done* (pp.19). New York: American Management Association AMA

31. Blindenbach-Driessen, F. (2015). The (In)Effectiveness of Cross-Functional Innovation Teams: The Moderating Role of Organizational Context. *IEEE Transactions on Engineering Management, 62*(1), 29-38. https://doi.org/10.1109/TEM.2014.2361623

32. McChrystal, S. General, Silverman, D., Collins, T., & Fussell, C. (2015). *Team of Teams: New Rules of Engagement for a Complex World.* Manhattan, NY: Penguin Random House

33. Colbert, A., Yee, N., & George, G. (2016). The Digital Workforce and the Workplace of the Future. *Academy of Management Journal, 59*(3), 731–739. https://doi.org/10.5465/amj.2016.4003

34. Yee, N. (2014). *The Proteus Paradox.* New Haven & London: Yale University Press

35. Ambrosini, V.,Bowman, C., and Burton-Taylor, S. (2007). Inter-team coordination activities as a source of customer satisfaction. *Human Relations, 60*(1), 59–98. https://doi.org/10.1177%2F0018726707075283

36. Presbitero, A., Roxas, B., & Chadee, D. (2017). Effects of intra- and inter-team dynamics on organizational learning: role of knowledge-sharing capability. *Knowledge Management Research & Practice, 15*(1), 146-154. https://doi.org/10.1057/kmrp.2015.15

37. Haas, M., Criscuolo, P., & George, G. (2015). Which Problems to Solve? Online Knowledge Sharing and Attention Allocation in Organizations. *Academy Of Management Journal, 58*(3), 680-711. http://dx.doi.org/10.5465/amj.2013.0263

38. Daspit, J., Tillman, C. J., Boyd, N. G., & McKee, V. (2013). Cross-functional team effectiveness: An examination of internal team environment, shared leadership, and cohesion influences. *Team Performance Management, 19*(1/2), 34-56. https://doi.org/10.1108/13527591311312088

39. Bungay, S. (2010). *The Art of Action: How Leaders Close the Gaps Between Plans, Actions and Results.* London: Nicholas Brealey Publishing

40. US Army Heritage and Education Center (2019, May). *Who first originated the term VUCA (Volatility, Uncertainty, Complexity and Ambiguity)?* Available at: https://usawc.libanswers.com/faq/84869

41. Angelo, R., & McCarthy, R. (2020). A Pedagogy to Develop Effective Virtual Teams. *Journal of Computer Information Systems,* 1-8. https://doi.org/10.1080/08874417.2020.1717396

42. Karriker, J. H., Madden, L. T., & Katell, L. A. (2017). Team Composition, Distributed Leadership, and Performance: It's Good to Share. *Journal of Leadership & Organizational Studies, 24*(2), 507-518. http://dx.doi.org/10.1177/1548051817709006

43. Scott-Young, C. M., Georgy, M., & Grisinger, A. (2019). Shared leadership in project teams: An integrative multi-level conceptual model and research agenda. *International Journal of Project Management, 37*(4), 565-581. http://dx.doi.org/10.1016/j.ijproman.2019.02.002

44. Ambrose, S. C., Matthews, L. M., & Rutherford, R. N. (2018) Cross-functional teams and social identity theory: A study of sales and operations planning (S&OP). *Journal of Business Research, 92*(1), 270-278. https://doi.org/10.1016/j.jbusres.2018.07.052

45. Gibson, C. B., Dunlop, P. D., & Raghav, S. (2020). Navigating identities in global work: Antecedents and consequences of intrapersonal identity conflict. *Human Relations, 74*(4), 556–586. https://doi.org/10.1177/0018726719895314

46. Henttonen, K., Johanson, J.-E. and Janhonen, M. (2014). Work-team bonding and bridging social networks, team identity and performance effectiveness. *Personnel Review, 43*(3), 330-349. https://doi.org/10.1108/PR-12-2011-0187

47. Pignata, S., Boyd, C. M., Winefield, A. H., & Provis, C. (2017). Interventions: Employees' Perceptions of What Reduces Stress. *BioMed Research International, 2017*, 3919080 https://doi.org/10.1155/2017/3919080

48. Edmondson, A. (2018). *The importance of psychological safety.* HR Magazine. https://www.hrmagazine.co.uk/content/features/the-importance-of-psychological-safety

49. Bartel, C.A., and Saavedra, R. (2000). The collective construction of work group moods. *Administrative Science Quarterly, 45*(2), 197-231. http://www.jstor.org/stable/2667070?origin=JSTOR-pdf

50. Farahnak, L. R., Ehrhart, M. G., Torres, E. M., & Aarons, G. A. (2020). The influence of transformational leadership and leader attitudes on subordinate attitudes and implementation success. *Journal of Leadership & Organizational Studies, 27*(1), 98-111. https://doi.org/10.1177/1548051818824529

51. McEwen, K., & Boyd, C. M. (2018). Measure of Team Resilience Developing the Resilience at Work Team Scale. *Journal of Occupational and Environmental Medicine, 60*(3), 258-272. http://dx.doi.org/10.1097/JOM.0000000000001223

52. Parker, S. K., Wang, Y., & Liao, J. (2019). When is proactivity wise? A review of factors that influence the individual outcomes of proactive behavior. *Annual Review of Organizational Psychology and Organizational Behavior, 6*(1), 221-248. https://doi.org/10.1146/annurev-orgpsych-012218-015302

53. van Kleef, G. A., Heerdink, M. W., & Homan, A. C. (2017). Emotional influence in groups: the dynamic nexus of affect, cognition, and behavior. *Current Opinion in Psychology, 17*(1), 156-161. https://doi.org/10.1016/j.copsyc.2017.07.017

54. Zhong, J., Zhang, L., Li, P., & Zhang, D. Z. (2019). Can leader humility enhance employee wellbeing? The mediating role of employee humility. *Leadership & Organization Development Journal, 41*(1), 19-36. http://dx.doi.org/10.1108/LODJ-03-2019-0124

55. Fredrickson B. L. (2004). The broaden-and-build theory of positive emotions. *Philosophical transactions of the Royal Society of London.*

Series B, Biological sciences, 359(1449), 1367–1378. https://doi.org/10.1098/rstb.2004.1512

56. Goleman, D. (1996). *Emotional Intelligence.* London: Bloomsbury Publishing Plc

57. James, C., Davis, K., Charmaraman, L., Konrath, S., Slovak, P., Weinstein, E., and Yarosh, L. (2017). Digital Life and Youth Well-being, Social Connectedness, Empathy, and Narcissism. *Pediatrics, 140*(Supplement 2), S71-S75. https://doi.org/10.1542/peds.2016-1758F

58. Reiss, H. (2019). *The Empathy Effect: 7 Neuroscience-Based Keys for Transforming the Way We Live, Love, Work, and Connect Across Differences.* Boulder, Colorado: Sounds True Inc.

59. Common Sense Media (2019). *The New Normal: Parents, Teens, Screens, and Sleep in the United States.* Common Sense Media. https://www.commonsensemedia.org/sites/default/files/uploads/research/2019-new-normal-parents-teens-screens-and-sleep-united-states.pdf

60. Common Sense Media (2019). *The Common Sense Census: Media Use by Tweens and Teens, 2019.* Common Sense Media. https://www.commonsensemedia.org/sites/default/files/uploads/research/2019-census-8-to-18-full-report-updated.pdf

61. Salked, A. (2019). *US Screentime & Smartphone Usage Stats for 2019.* Simple Texting. https://simpletexting.com/screentime-smartphone-usage-statistics/

62. Asurion (2019, November). *Americans Check Their Phones 96 Times a Day.* Azurion. https://www.asurion.com/about/press-releases/americans-check-their-phones-96-times-a-day/

63. Kick, A. L., Contacos-Sawyer, J., & Thomas, B. (2015). How Generation Z's reliance on digital communication can affect future workplace relationships. *Competition Forum, 13*(1), 214-223. Available from: http://iblog.iup.edu/americansocietyforcompetitiveness/journal-archives-jcs-and-cf-2019/

64. Edmondson, A. (2012). *Teaming How organizations learn, innovate, and compete in the Knowledge economy.* San Francisco, CA: Jossey Bass.

65. Morikawa, M. (2016). Firms' Expectations About the Impact of AI and Robotics: Evidence from A Survey. *Economic Inquiry, 55*(2), 1054-1063. https://doi.org/10.1111/ecin.12412

66. Kettley, P., and Hirsh, W. (2000). *Learning from Cross Functional Teamwork.* Brighton: The Institute for Employment Studies.

67. Khalid, A., Lee, O., Choi, M., & Ahn, J. (2018). The effects of customer satisfaction with e-commerce system. *Journal of Theoretical and Applied Information Technology, 96*(2), 481-491. https://www.researchgate.net/ publication/323111412_The_effects_of_customer_satisfaction_with_e-commerce_system

68. Ungureanu, P., Cochis, C., Bertolotti, F., Mattarelli, E., & Scapolan, A. C. (2020). Multiplex boundary work in innovation projects: the role of collaborative spaces for cross-functional and open innovation. *European Journal of Innovation Management, Ahead-of-print*(Ahead-of-print). http:// dx.doi.org/10.1108/EJIM-11-2019-0338

69. Furumo, K., De Pillis, E., Buxton, M., 2012. The impact of leadership on participation and trust in virtual teams. *Proceedings of the 50th annual conference on Computers and People Research* (SIGMIS-CPR '12), *New York, USA,* 123–126. https://doi.org/10.1145/2214091.2214125

70. Gajendran, R. S., & Joshi, A. (2012). Innovation in globally distributed teams: The role of LMX, communication frequency, and member influence on team decisions. *Journal of Applied Psychology, 97*(6), 1252–1261. https://doi.org/10.1037/a0028958

71. Hoogeboom, M. A. M. G., & Wilderom, C. P. M. (2020). A Complex Adaptive Systems Approach to Real-Life Team Interaction Patterns, Task Context, Information Sharing, and Effectiveness. *Group & Organization Management, 45*(1), 3–42. https://doi.org/10.1177/1059601119854927

72. Roubal, J., Francesetti, G., & Gecele, M. (2017). Aesthetic Diagnosis in Gestalt Therapy. *Behavioral Sciences, 7*(4), 70-83. https://doi. org/10.3390/bs7040070

73. Ury, W. (1993). *Getting Past No: Negotiating in Difficult Situations.* London: Random House Business Books

74. Ury, W. (2015). *Getting to Yes with Yourself: (and Other Worthy Opponents).* London : HarperThorsons

75. Fisher, R., and Ury, W. (1991). *Getting To Yes: Negotiating agreement without giving in.* London: Random House Business Books

76. Stoverink, A. C., Kirkman, B. L., Mistry, S., & Rosen, B. (2020). Bouncing back together: Toward a theoretical model of work team resilience. *Academy of Management Review, 45*(2), 395-422. https://doi.org/10.5465/ amr.2017.0005

77. Kašpárková, L., Vaculík, M., Procházka, J., & Schaufeli, W. B. (2018). Why resilient workers perform better: The roles of job satisfaction and

work engagement. *Journal of Workplace Behavioral Health, 33*(1), 43-62. https://doi.org/10.1080/15555240.2018.1441719

78. Kuntz, J., Connell, P., & Näswall, K. (2017). Workplace resources and employee resilience: The role of regulatory profiles. *Career Development International, 22*(4), 419-435. https://doi.org/10.1108/CDI-11-2016-0208

79. Malik, P., & Garg, P. (2020). Learning organization and work engagement: The mediating role of employee resilience. *The International Journal of Human Resource Management, 31*(8), 1071-1094. https://doi.org/10.1080 /09585192.2017.1396549

80. Gucciardi, D.F., Crane, M., Ntoumanis, N., Parker, S.K., Thøgersen-Ntoumani, C., Ducker, K.J., Peeling, P., Chapman, M.T., Quested, E. and Temby, P. (2018). The emergence of team resilience: A multilevel conceptual model of facilitating factors. *Journal of Occupational and Organizational Psychology, 91*(1), 729-768. https://doi.org/10.1111/ joop.12237

81. Paul, S., He, F., & Dennis, A. R. (2018). Group Atmosphere, Shared Understanding, and Team Conflict in Short Duration Virtual Teams. *Proceedings of the 51st Hawaii International Conference on System Sciences, Hawaii,* 361-370 http://hdl.handle.net/10125/49935

82. Degbey, W.Y. & Einola, K. (2019). Resilience in Virtual Teams: Developing the Capacity to Bounce Back. *Applied Psychology, 69*(4), 1301-1337. http://dx.doi.org/10.1111/apps.12220

83. Meneghel, I., Martínez, I. M., & Salanova, M. (2016). Job-related antecedents of team resilience and improved team performance. *Personnel Review, 45*(3), 505–522. https://doi.org/10.1108/PR-04-2014-0094

84. Borek, A.J., Abraham, C., Greaves, C.J., & Tarrant, M. (2018). Group-Based Diet and Physical Activity Weight-Loss Interventions: A Systematic Review and Meta-Analysis of Randomised Controlled Trials. *Applied Psychology: Health & Well Being, 10*(1), 62-86. https://doi.org/10.1111/ aphw.12121

85. Butler, L. D., Koopman, C., Neri, E., Giese-Davis, J., Palesh, O., Thorne-Yocam, K. A., Dimiceli, S., Chen, X.-H., Fobair, P., Kraemer, H. C., & Spiegel, D. (2009). Effects of supportive-expressive group therapy on pain in women with metastatic breast cancer. *Health Psychology, 28*(5), 579–587. https://doi.org/10.1037/a0016124

86. Classen, C.C., Kraemer, H.C., Blasey, C., Giese-Davis, J., Koopman, C., Palesh, O.G., Atkinson, A., DiMiceli, S., Stonisch-Riggs, G., Westendorp, J., Morrow, G.R. and Spiegel, D. (2008), Supportive–expressive group

therapy for primary breast cancer patients: a randomized prospective multicenter trial. *Psycho-Oncology, 17*(5), 438-447. https://doi.org/10.1002/pon.1280

87. Karfopoulou, E., Anastasiou, C.A., Avgeraki, E., Kosmidis, M. H., and Yannakoulia, M. (2016). The role of social support in weight loss maintenance: results from the MedWeight study. *Journal of Behavioural Medicine, 39*(1), 511–518 (2016). https://doi.org/10.1007/s10865-016-9717-y

88. Kissane, D. W., Grabsch, B., Clarke, D. M., Smith, G. C., Love, A. W., Bloch, S., Snyder, R. D., & Li, Y. (2007). Supportive-expressive group therapy for women with metastatic breast cancer: survival and psychosocial outcome from a randomized controlled trial. *Psychooncology, 16*(4), 277–286. https://doi.org/10.1002/pon.1185

89. Song, X., Jin, J., Liu, Y-.H, and Yan, X et al., 2020; Lose your weight with online buddies: behavioral contagion in an online weight-loss community. *Information Technology & People, 33*(1), 22-36. https://doi.org/10.1108/ITP-11-2018-0525

90. Stead, L.F., Carroll, A.J., and Lancaster, T. (2017). Group behavior therapy programmes for smoking cessation. *Cochrane Database of Systematic Reviews, Issue 3*. Art. No.: CD001007. https://doi.org/10.1002/14651858.CD001007.pub3

91. Wing, R. R., & Jeffery, R. W. (1999). Benefits of recruiting participants with friends and increasing social support for weight loss and maintenance. *Journal of Consulting and Clinical Psychology, 67*(1), 132–138. https://doi.org/10.1037/0022-006X.67.1.132

92. Yorks, D. M., Frothingham, C. A., & Schuenke, M. D. (2017). Effects of Group Fitness Classes on Stress and Quality of Life of Medical Students. *The Journal of the American Osteopathic Association, 117*(11), e17–e25. https://doi.org/10.7556/jaoa.2017.140

93. Clarkson, B. G., Wagstaff, C. R. D., Arthur, C. A. A., & Thelwell, R. C. (2020). Leadership and the contagion of affective phenomena: A systematic review and mini meta-analysis. *European Journal of Social Psychology, 50*(1), 61–80. https://doi.org/10.1002/ejsp.2615

94. Keltner, D., van Kleef, G.A., Chen, S., & Kraus, M.W. (2008). A reciprocal influence model of social power: emerging principles and lines of inquiry. *Advances in Experimental Social Psychology, 40*(1), 151-192. https://doi.org/10.1016/S0065-2601(07)00003-2

95. Kao, R-H. (2017). The relationship between work characteristics and change-oriented organizational citizenship behavior. *Personnel Review, 46*(8), 1890-1914. https://doi.org/10.1108/PR-01-2016-0012

96. Parker, S. K., Wang, Y., & Liao, J. (2019). When is proactivity wise? A review of factors that influence the individual outcomes of proactive behavior. *Annual Review of Organizational Psychology and Organizational Behavior, 6*(1), 221-248. https://doi.org/10.1146/annurev-orgpsych-012218-015302

97. Sinaga, H. G., Asmawi, M., Madhakomala, R., & Suratman, A. (2018). Effect of Change in Management, Organizational Culture and Transformational Leadership on Employee Performance PT. *International Review of Management and Marketing, 8*(6), 15-23. https://ideas.repec.org/a/eco/journ3/2018-06-3.html

98. van Kleef, G.A., Homan, A.C., Beersma, B., Van Knippenberg, D., Van Knippenberg, B., & Damen, F. (2009). Searing sentiment or cold calculation? The effects of leader emotional displays on team performance depend on follower epistemic motivation. *Academy of Management Journal, 52*(3),562-580. https://doi.org/10.5465/amj.2009.41331253

99. van Kleef, G. A., Heerdink, M. W., & Homan, A. C. (2017). Emotional influence in groups: the dynamic nexus of affect, cognition, and behavior. *Current Opinion in Psychology, 17*(1), 156-161. https://doi.org/10.1016/j.copsyc.2017.07.017

100. Wang, H-J., Demerouti, E., & Le Blanc, P. (2017). Transformational leadership, adaptability, and job crafting: The moderating role of organizational identification. *Journal of Vocational Behavior, 100*(1), 185-195. https://doi.org/10.1016/j.jvb.2017.03.009

101. Canning, E. A., Murphy, M. C., Emerson, K. T. U., Chatman, J. A., Dweck, C. S., & Kray, L. J. (2020). Cultures of Genius at Work: Organizational Mindsets Predict Cultural Norms, Trust, and Commitment. *Personality and Social Psychology Bulletin, 46*(4), 626–642. https://doi.org/10.1177/0146167219872473

102. King, R. B. (2020). Mindsets are contagious: The social contagion of implicit theories of intelligence among classmates. *Annals of Behavioural Medicine, 52*(12), 1046-1059. https://doi.org/10.1093/abm/kay008

103. Degbey, W.Y. & Einola, K. (2019). Resilience in Virtual Teams: Developing the Capacity to Bounce Back. *Applied Psychology, 69*(4), 1301-1337. http://dx.doi.org/10.1111/apps.12220

Chapter 7

Virtual Teaming and the Code

1. Grenny, J., & Maxfield, D. (2017, November). *A study of 1,100 employees found that remote workers feel shunned and left out.* Harvard Business Review. https://hbr.org/2017/11/a-study-of-1100-employees-found-that-remote-workers-feel-shunned-and-left-out

2. Cascio, W. F. (2000). Managing a Virtual Workplace. *Academy of Management Executive, 14*(3), 81-90. https://doi.org/10.5465/AME.2000.4468068

3. Marshall, L. & Bibby, J. (2020). *Emerging evidence on COVID-19's impact on mental health and health inequalities. How is mental health being affected by the pandemic?* The Health Foundation. Available at: https://www.health.org.uk/news-and-comment/blogs/emerging-evidence-on-covid-19s-impact-on-mental-health-and-health

4. Bakken, R. (2018). *Challenges to Managing Virtual Teams and How to Overcome Them.* Harvard Professional Development https://blog.dce.harvard.edu/professional-development/challenges-managing-virtual-teams-and-how-overcome-them

5. Watkins, S. (2018, June). *Challenges of virtual teams and how to solve them.* Cirkus. https://cirkus.com/blog/9-challenges-of-virtual-teams/

6. Badrinarayanan, V., & Arnett, D.B., (2008). Effective virtual new product development teams: an integrated framework. *Journal of Business and Industrial Marketing, 23*(4), 242-248. https://doi.org/10.1108/08858620810865816

7. Hossain, L., & Wigand, R.T. (2004) ICT Enabled Virtual Collaboration through Trust. *Journal of Computer-Mediated Communication, 10*(1), 00-00. https://doi.org/10.1111/j.1083-6101.2004.tb00233.x

8. Rice, D.J., Davidson, B.D., Dannenhoffer, J.F. & Gay, G.K. (2007). Improving the Effectiveness of Virtual Teams by Adapting Team Processes. *Computer Supported Cooperative Work, 16*(1), 567-594. https://doi.org/10.1007/s10606-007-9070-3

9. Martínez-Sánchez, A., Pérez-Pérez, M., de-Luis-Carnicer, P., & José Vela-Jiménez, M. (2006). Teleworking and new product development. *European Journal of Innovation Management, 9*(2), 202-214. https://doi.org/10.1108/14601060610663578

10. Wong, S.S., & Burton, R.M., (2000) Virtual Teams: What are their Characteristics, and Impact on Team Performance? *Computational*

and Mathematical Organization Theory, 6(4), 339-360. https://doi. org/10.1023/A:1009654229352

11. Stowell, F., & Cooray, S. (2016). Addressing Team Dynamics in Virtual Teams: The Role of Soft Systems. *International Journal of Information Technologies and Systems Approach, (IJITSA), 9*(1), 32-53. https://doi. org/10.4018/IJITSA.2016010103

12. Furumo, K., de Pillis, E., & Green, D. (2009). Personality influences trust differently in virtual and face-to-face teams. *International Journal of Human Resources Development & Management, 9*(1), 36–58. https://doi. org/10.1504/IJHRDM.2009.021554

13. Lira, E. M., Ripoll, P., Peiró, J. M., & Orengo, V. (2008). How do different types of intragroup conflict affect group potency in virtual compared with face-to-face teams? A longitudinal study. *Behavior & Information Technology, 27*(2), 107–114. https://doi.org/10.1080/01449290600875151

14. O'Leary, M. B., & Mortensen, M. (2010). Go (con)figure: Subgroups, imbalance, and isolates in geographically dispersed teams. *Organisation Science, 21*(1), 115-131. https://doi.org/10.1287/orsc.1090.0434

15. Sarkar, S., & Valacich, J. S. (2010). An Alternative to Methodological Individualism: A Non-Reductionist Approach to Studying Technology Adoption by Groups. *MIS Quarterly, 34*(4), 779-808. https://www.jstor.org/ stable/25750705

16. Kankanhalli, A., Tan, B., & Wei, K. (2006). Conflict and Performance in Global Virtual Teams. *Journal of Management Information Systems, 23*(3), 237-274. https://doi.org/10.2753/MIS0742-1222230309

17. Solomon, C. (2016, April). *Trends in Global Virtual Teams: Virtual Teams Survey Report—2016.* RW3 CultureWizard. http://cdn.culturewizard.com/ PDF/Trends_in_VT_Report_4-17-2016.pdf

18. Eubanks, D. L., Palanski, M., Olabisi, J., Joinson, A., & Dove, J. (2016). Team dynamics in virtual, partially distributed teams: Optimal role fulfillment. *Computers in Human Behavior, 61*(1), 556–568. https://doi. org/10.1016/j.chb.2016.03.035

19. Bailey, S. (2013, March). *How To Beat the Five Killers of Virtual Working.* Forbes. https://www.forbes.com/sites/sebastianbailey/2013/03/05/ how-to-overcome-the-five-major-disadvantages-of-virtual- working/#798588912734

20. Hinds, P. J. and Mortensen, M. (2005). Understanding Conflict in Geographically Distributed Teams: The Moderating Effects of Shared

Identity, Shared Context, and Spontaneous Communication. *Organization Science, 16*(3), 203-325. https://doi.org/10.1287/orsc.1050.0122

21. Chun, J. S., & Choi, J. N. (2014). Members' needs, intragroup conflict, and group performance. *Journal of Applied Psychology, 99*(3), 437–450. https://doi.org/10.1037/a0036363

22. Gould, R. V. (2003). *Collision of wills: How ambiguity about social rank breeds conflict.* Chicago, IL: University of Chicago Press.

23. Jehn, K. A., & Mannix, E. A. (2001). The dynamic nature of conflict: A longitudinal study of intragroup conflict and group performance. *Academy of Management Journal, 44*(2), 238–251. https://doi.org/10.5465/3069453

24. Lee, H. W., Choi, J. N, & Seongsu, K. (2018). Does gender diversity help teams constructively manage status conflict? An evolutionary perspective of status conflict, team psychological safety, and team creativity. *Organizational Behavior and Human Decision Processes, 144*(1), 187–199. https://doi.org/10.1016/j.obhdp.2017.09.005

25. Simons, T., & Peterson, R. (2000). Task conflict and relationship conflict in top management teams: The pivotal role of intragroup trust. *Journal Of Applied Psychology, 85*(1), 102-111. https://doi.org/10.1037/0021-9010.85.1.102

26. Berry, G. R. (2011). Enhancing Effectiveness on Virtual Teams: Understanding Why Traditional Team Skills Are Insufficient. *Journal of Business Communication, 48*(2), 186-206. https://doi.org/10.1177/0021943610397270

27. Mortensen, M. and Neeley, T. B. (2012). Reflected Knowledge and Trust in Global Collaboration. *Management Science, 58*(12), iv-2308. https://doi.org/10.1287/mnsc.1120.1546

28. Zakaria, N., & Yusof, S. A. M (2020). Crossing Cultural Boundaries Using the Internet: Toward Building a Model of Swift Trust Formation in Global Virtual Teams. *Journal of International Management, 26*(1), *100654.* https://doi.org/10.1016/j.intman.2018.10.004

29. International Workplace Group (2018)— *The IWG Flexible Working Survey.* International Workplace Group. http://contact.regus.com/GBS18_Report_Download_Request

30. Lister, K. (2018). *Telecommuting Statistics. Global Workplace Analytics* https://globalworkplaceanalytics.com/telecommuting-statistics

31. Bloom, N., Liang, J., Roberts, J., & Ying, Z.J. (2015). Does Working from Home Work? Evidence from a Chinese Experiment *. The Quarterly Journal of Economics, 130*(1), 165–218. https://doi.org/10.1093/qje/qju032

32. Citrix (2020, April). *Remote Work: The New Normal?* Citrix. https://www.
    citrix.com/en-gb/news/announcements/apr-2020/remote-work-the-new-
    normal.html

33. Upwork (2019, March). *Third Annual "Future Workforce Report" Sheds
    Light on How Younger Generations are Reshaping the Future of Work.*
    Upwork. https://www.upwork.com/press/releases/third-annual-future-
    workforce-report

34. Meunier, J. (2021, February). *Remote Working Statistics.* https://www.
    alliancevirtualoffices.com/virtual-office-blog/remote-working-statistics/

35. Hoch, J., & Dulebohn, J. (2017). Team personality composition,
    emergent leadership and shared leadership in virtual teams: A theoretical
    framework. *Human Resource Management Review, 27*(4), 678–693.
    https://doi.org/10.1016/j.hrmr.2016.12.012

36. Crisp, C. B. & Jarvenpaa, S.L., (2013). Swift trust in global virtual teams
    trusting beliefs and normative actions. *Journal of Personnel Psychology,
    12*(1), 45-56. https://doi.org/10.1027/1866-5888/a000075

37. Zakaria, N., & Yusof, S. A. M (2020). Crossing Cultural Boundaries Using
    the Internet: Toward Building a Model of Swift Trust Formation in Global
    Virtual Teams. *Journal of International Management, 26*(1), *100654.*
    https://doi.org/10.1016/j.intman.2018.10.004

38. Eubanks, D. L., Palanski, M., Olabisi, J., Joinson, A., & Dove, J. (2016).
    Team dynamics in virtual, partially distributed teams: Optimal role
    fulfillment. *Computers in Human Behavior, 61*(1), 556–568. https://doi.
    org/10.1016/j.chb.2016.03.035

39. Gundlach, M., Zivnuska, S., & Stoner, J. (2006). Understanding the
    relationship between individualism-collectivism and team performance
    through an integration of social identity theory and the social
    relations model. *Human Relations, 59*(12), 1603–1632. https://doi.
    org/10.1177%2F0018726706073193

40. Erhart, J. (2018). *The relationship between the amount of FtF-interaction
    and conflict in virtual teams: The moderating role of a shared identity.*
    [Doctoral Thesis, Catholic University of Portugal, Lisbon, Portugal]. http://
    hdl.handle.net/10400.14/25434

41. Gibson, C. B., Dunlop, P. D., & Raghav, S. (2020). Navigating identities
    in global work: Antecedents and consequences of intrapersonal
    identity conflict. *Human Relations, 74*(4), 556–586. https://doi.
    org/10.1177/0018726719895314

42. Bal, J., & Foster P. (2000). Managing the virtual team and controlling effectiveness. *International Journal of Production Research, 38*(17), 4019-4032. https://doi.org/10.1080/00207540050204885

43. Bourgault, M., Drouin, N., & Hamel, E. (2008). Decision making within distributed project teams: An exploration of formalization and autonomy as determinants of success. *Project Management Journal, 39*(1), S97-S110. https://doi.org/10.1002/pmj.20063

44. Horwitz, F.M., Bravington, D., & Silvas U. (2006) The promise of virtual teams: identifying key factors in effectiveness and failure. *Journal of European Industrial Training, 30*(6), 472-494. https://doi.org/10.1108/03090590610688843

45. Rework.withgoogle.com (2012). *Understand team effectiveness.* Re:work. https://rework.withgoogle.com/print/guides/5721312655835136/

46. Duhigg, C. (2016, February. *What Google Learned from Its Quest to Build the Perfect Team.* The New York Times. https://www.nytimes.com/2016/02/28/magazine/what-google-learned-from-its-quest-to-build-the-perfect-team.html?smid=pl-share

47. Rozovsky, J. (2015). *The five keys to a successful Google team.* rework.withgoogle.com. https://rework.withgoogle.com/blog/five-keys-to-a-successful-google-team/

48. Maynard, M. T., Mathieu, J. E., Gilson, L. L., R. Sanchez, D., & Dean, M. D. (2019). Do I Really Know You and Does It Matter? Unpacking the Relationship Between Familiarity and Information Elaboration in Global Virtual Teams. *Group & Organization Management, 44*(1), 3-37. https://doi.org/10.1177%2F1059601118785842

49. Eldor, L. (2019). How Collective Engagement Creates Competitive Advantage for Organizations: A Business Level Model of Shared Vision, Competitive Intensity, and Service Performance. *Journal of Management Studies, 57*(2), 177-209. https://doi.org/10.1111/joms.12438

50. Yang, I. (2019). What makes an effective team? The role of trust (dis)confirmation in team development. *European Management Journal, 32*(6), 858-869. https://doi.org/10.1016/j.emj.2014.04.001

51. Kirkman, B. L., Rosen, B., Tesluk, P. E., & Gibson, C. B. (2004). The impact of team empowerment on virtual team performance: The moderating role of face-to-face interaction. *Academy of Management Journal, 47*(2), 175–192. https://doi.org/10.2307/20159571

52. Hoegl, M., & Muethel, M. (2016). Enabling shared leadership in virtual project teams: A practitioners' guide. *Project Management Journal, 47*(1), 7–12. https://doi.org/10.1002%2Fpmj.21564

53. Carter, S. M., & West, M. A. (1998). Reflexivity, Effectiveness, and Mental Health in BBC-TV Production Teams. *Small Group Research, 29*(5), 583-601. https://doi.org/10.1177/1046496498295003

54. Hoch, J. E., & Kozlowski, S. W. J. (2014). Leading virtual teams: Hierarchical leadership, structural supports, and shared leadership. *Journal of Applied Psychology, 99*(3), 390–403. https://doi.org/10.1037/a0030264

55. Degbey, W.Y. & Einola, K. (2019). Resilience in Virtual Teams: Developing the Capacity to Bounce Back. *Applied Psychology, 69*(4), 1301-1337. http://dx.doi.org/10.1111/apps.12220

56. Hoegl, M., & Muethel, M. (2016). Enabling Shared Leadership in Virtual Project Teams: A Practitioners' Guide. *Project Management Journal, 47*(1), 7–12. https://doi.org/10.1002/pmj.21564

57. Furumo, K., De Pillis, E., Buxton, M., 2012. *The impact of leadership on participation and trust in virtual teams. Proceedings of the 50th annual conference on Computers and People Research (SIGMIS-CPR '12). Association for Computing Machinery, New York, USA,* 123–126. https://doi.org/10.1145/2214091.2214125

58. Gajendran, R. S., & Joshi, A. (2012). Innovation in globally distributed teams: The role of LMX, communication frequency, and member influence on team decisions. *Journal of Applied Psychology, 97*(6), 1252–1261. https://doi.org/10.1037/a0028958

59. Breuer, C., Hüffmeier, J., Hibben, F., & Hertel, G. (2020). Trust in teams: A taxonomy of perceived trustworthiness factors and risk-taking behaviors in face-to-face and virtual teams. *Human Relations, 73*(1), 3–34. https://doi.org/10.1177/0018726718818721

60. Henttonen, K. & Blomqvist, K. (2005). Managing distance in a global virtual team: The evolution of trust through technology-mediated relational communication. *Strategic Change 14*(2), 107–119. https://doi.org/10.1002/jsc.714

61. De Smet, A., Rubenstein, K., Schrah, G., Vierow, M., & Edmondson, A. C. (2021, February). *Psychological safety and the critical role of leadership development.* McKinsey & Company. https://www.mckinsey.com/business-functions/organization/our-insights/psychological-safety-and-the-critical-role-of-leadership-development

62. Ayoko, O. B., Konrad, A. M., & Boyle, M. V. (2012). Online work: Managing conflict and emotions for performance in virtual teams. *European Management Journal, 30*(2), 156-174. https://doi.org/10.1016/j. emj.2011.10.001

63. Edmondson, A. (1999). Psychological Safety and Learning Behavior in Work Teams. *Administrative Science Quarterly, 44*(1), 350-383. https:// journals.sagepub.com/doi/pdf/10.2307/2666999

64. Liu, X. Y., & Liu, J. (2012). The Influence Mechanism of Team Emotional Atmosphere on Team Innovation Performance. *Acta Psychologica Sinica, 44*(1), 546-557. (In Chinese) https://doi.org/10.3724/ SP.J.1041.2012.00546

65. Peñarroja, V., Orengo, V., Zornoza, A., Sánchez, J., & Ripoll, P. (2015). How team feedback and team trust influence information processing and learning in virtual teams: A moderated mediation model. *Computers in Human Behavior, 48*(1), 9–16. https://doi.org/10.1016/j.chb.2015.01.034

66. Schaubroeck, J. M., & Yu, A. (2017). When does virtuality help or hinder teams? Core team characteristics as contingency factors. *Human Resource Management Review, 27*(4), 635–647. https://doi.org/10.1016/j. hrmr.2016.12.009

67. Peñarroja, V., González-Anta, B., Orengo, V., Zornoza, A., & Gamero, N. (2020). Reducing Relationship Conflict in Virtual Teams with Diversity Faultlines: The Effect of an Online Affect Management Intervention on the Rate of Growth of Team Resilience. *Social Science Computer Review.* https://doi.org/10.1177%2F0894439320907575

68. Holtz, K., Orengo Castella, V., Zornoza Abad, A., & González-Anta, B. (2020). Virtual team functioning: Modeling the affective and cognitive effects of an emotional management intervention. *Group Dynamics: Theory, Research, and Practice, 24*(3), 153-167. https://doi.org/10.1037/ gdn0000141

69. Paul, S., He, F., & Dennis, A. R. (2018). *Group Atmosphere, Shared Understanding, and Team Conflict in Short Duration Virtual Teams.* Proceedings of the 51st Hawaii International Conference on System Sciences. http://hdl.handle.net/10125/49935

70. Facchin, S., Tschan, F., Gurtner, A., Cohen, D., & Dupuis, A. (2006). Validation de la version française de l'échelle de réflexivité en groupe de Carter et West, 1998 [Validation of the French version of the team reflexivity scale of Carter and West, 1998]. *Psychologie du Travail et des Organizations, 12*(4), 291–306. https://doi.org/10.1016/j.pto.2006.09.003

71. Hoegl, M. & Parboteeah, K. P. (2006). Team reflexivity in innovative projects. *R&D Management, 36*(2), 113–125. https://doi.org/10.1111/j.1467-9310.2006.00420.x

72. Konradt, U., Otte, K-P., Schippers, M., & Steenfatt, C. (2015). Reflexivity in Teams: A Review and New Perspectives. *The Journal of Psychology: Interdisciplinary and Applied, 150*(2), 1-34. https://doi.org/10.1080/002239 80.2015.1050977

73. Schippers, M. C., den Hartog, D. N., Koopman, P. L., & van Knippenberg, D. (2008). The role of transformational leadership in enhancing team reflexivity. *Human Relations, 61*(11), 1593–1616. http://dx.doi.org/10.1177/0018726708096639

74. Schippers, M. C., Homan, A. C., & van Knippenberg, D. (2013). To reflect or not to reflect: Prior team performance as a boundary condition of the effects of reflexivity on learning and final team performance. *Journal of Organizational Behavior, 34*(1), 6–23. http://dx.doi.org/10.1002/job.1784

75. Schippers, M. C., West, M. A., & Dawson, J. F. (2015). Team reflexivity and innovation: The moderating role of team context. *Journal of Management, 41*(3), 769–788. http://dx.doi.org/10.1177/0149206312441210

76. Zhang, H. (2015). The Project Team Reflexivity's Effects on Team Performance. *Proceedings of the 3d International Conference on Applied Social Science Research* (ICASSR 2015). Atlantis Press. https://doi.org/10.2991/icassr-15.2016.13

77. Nemiro, J. E. (2016). Connection in creative virtual teams. *Journal of Behavioral and Applied Management, 2*(2), 814. https://jbam.scholasticahq.com/article/814-connection-in-creative-virtual-teams

78. Meyer, E. (2010, August). *The Four Keys to Success with Virtual Teams.* Forbes. https://www.forbes.com/2010/08/19/virtual-teams-meetings-leadership-managing-cooperation.html#4c78067430cc

79. Angelo, R., and McCarthy, R. (2020). A Pedagogy to Develop Effective Virtual Teams. *Journal of Computer Information Systems,* 1-8. https://doi.org/10.1080/08874417.2020.1717396

80. Goh, S., and Wasko, M. (2012). The effects of leader-member exchange on member performance in virtual world teams. *Journal of the Association for Information Systems, 13*(10), 861-885. https://doi.org/10.17705/1jais.00308

81. Pentland, A. (2012, April). *The New Science of Building Great Teams.* Harvard Business Review. https://hbr.org/2012/04/the-new-science-of-building-great-teams

82. Peters, S. (2012). *The Chimp Paradox.* Vermillion: London

83. Breuer, C., Hüffmeier, J., & Hertel, G. (2016). Does trust matter more in virtual teams? A meta-analysis of trust and team effectiveness considering virtuality and documentation as moderators. *Journal of Applied Psychology, 101*(8), 1151 –1177. https://doi.org/10.1037/apl0000113

Chapter 8

How to Get Set

1. Hastings, R. (2009, August). *Netflix Culture: Freedom & Responsibility.* Slideshare. https://www.slideshare.net/reed2001/culture-1798664/23-Unlike_many_companieswe_practiceadequate_performance

2. Ramachandran, S., and Flint, J. (2018, October, 25). *At Netflix, Radical Transparency and Blunt Firings Unsettle the Ranks.* Wall Street Journal. https://www.wsj.com/articles/at-netflix-radical-transparency-and-blunt-firings-unsettle-the-ranks-1540497174

3. Comparably (2018, October). *Happiest Employees 2018.* Comparably. https://www.comparably.com/blog/happiest-companies-2018/

4. Booz, M. (2018, March). *These 3 Industries Have the Highest Talent Turnover Rates.* LinkedIn. https://business.linkedin.com/talent-solutions/blog/trends-and-research/2018/the-3-industries-with-the-highest-turnover-rates

5. Hackman, J. R. (2002). *Leading teams: Setting the stage for great performances.* Boston: Harvard Business School Press.

6. Choi, E. U., & Hogg, M. A. (2020). Self-uncertainty and group identification: A meta-analysis. *Group Processes & Intergroup Relations, 23*(4), 483-501. https://doi.org/10.1177/1368430219846990

7. Daspit, J., Tillman, C. J., Boyd, N. G., & McKee, V. (2013). Cross-functional team effectiveness: An examination of internal team environment, shared leadership, and cohesion influences. *Team Performance Management, 19*(1/2), 34-56. https://doi.org/10.1108/13527591311312088

8. Santos, V., Goldman, A., & de Souza, C.R.B. (2017). Fostering effective inter-team knowledge sharing in agile software development. *Empirical*

Software Engineering, 20(4), 1006-1051. https://doi.org/10.1007/
s10664-014-9307-y

9. Wilkinson. D.J. (2019, December). *Group decision-making. What the latest research says.* Oxford Review Special Report. The Oxford Review, www.oxford-review.com

10. Sinek, S. (2011). *Start with Why: How Great Leaders Inspire Everyone to Take Action.* Penguin Portfolio, London.

11. Gibb Dyer Jr., W., Dyer, J. H., and Dyer, W. G. (2013). *Building Proven Strategies for Improving Team Performance.* San Francisco, CA: Jossey-Bass

12. Aubé, C., & Rousseau, V. (2005). Team Goal Commitment and Team Effectiveness: The Role of Task Interdependence and Supportive Behaviors. *Group Dynamics: Theory, Research, and Practice, 9*(3), 189–204. https://doi.org/10.1037/1089-2699.9.3.189

13. Gilson, T., Heller, E., & Stults-Kolehmainen, M. (2013). The Relationship Between an Effort Goal and Self-Regulatory Efficacy Beliefs for Division I Football Players. *Journal of Strength and Conditioning Research, 27*(10), 2806-2815. https://doi.org/10.1519/jsc.0b013e31828151ca

14. Pedersen, M. (2015). A 'Heart of Goal' and the will to succeed: Goal Commitment and Task Performance Among Teachers in Public Schools. *Public Administration, 94*(1), 75-88. https://doi.org/10.1111/Padm.12201;

15. Seville, E., Brunsdon, D., Dantas, A., Masurier, J.L., Wilkinson, S., & Vargo, J. (2008). Building Organizational Resilience: A New Zealand Approach. *Journal of Business Continuity & Emergency Planning 2*(2), 258-66. https://www.researchgate.net/publication/29488232_Organisational_Resilience_in_New_Zealand

16. Katzenbach, J. R., & Smith, D. K. (1993). The discipline of teams. *Harvard Business Review, 71*(2), 111–120. https://pubmed.ncbi.nlm.nih.gov/10124632/

17. Nieto-Rodriguez, A. (2014, October). *Organizational ambidexterity.* London School of Business. https://www.london.edu/think/organisational-ambidexterity

18. Sinha, S. (2015). The Exploration–Exploitation Dilemma: A Review in the Context of Managing Growth of New Ventures. *Vikalpa, 40*(3), 313–323. https://doi.org/10.1177/0256090915599709

19. Snowden, D. J., & Boone, M. (2007). *A Leader's Framework for Decision Making.* Harvard Business Review. https://hbr.org/2007/11/a-leaders-framework-for-decision-making

20. Taleb, N. N. (2018). *Skin in the Game: Hidden Asymmetries in Daily Life.*
     London: Penguin Books

Chapter 9
How to Get Safe

1.   Kim, B.S.K., and Hong, S. (2004). A psychometric revision of the Asian
     Values Scale using the Rasch model. *Measurement and Evaluation in
     Counseling and Development, 37*(1), 15–27. https://doi.org/10.1080/0748
     1756.2004.11909747

2.   Kim, B.S.K., Atkinson, D.R., & Yang, P.H. (1999). The Asian Values
     Scale: Development, factor analysis, validation, and reliability. *Journal of
     Counseling Psychology, 46*(3), 342–352. https://doi.org/10.1037/0022-
     0167.46.3.342

3.   Kramer, E. J., Kwong, K., Lee, E., & Chung, H. (2002). Cultural factors
     influencing the mental health of Asian Americans. *The Western Journal
     of Medicine, 176*(4), 227–231. https://www.ncbi.nlm.nih.gov/pmc/articles/
     PMC1071736/

4.   Tabrizi, B. (2015, June 23). *75% of Cross-Functional Teams Are
     Dysfunctional.* Harvard Business Review. https://hbr.org/2015/06/75-of-
     cross-functional-teams-are-dysfunctional

5.   Edmondson, A. (1999). Psychological Safety and Learning Behavior in
     Work Teams. *Administrative Science Quarterly, 44*(1), 350-383. https://
     journals.sagepub.com/doi/pdf/10.2307/2666999

6.   Brown, B. (2012). *Daring Greatly: How the Courage to Be Vulnerable
     Transforms the Way We Live, Love, Parent, and Lead.* London: Vermillion.

7.   Elberse, A. (2013, October). *Ferguson's Formula.* Harvard Business
     Review. https://hbr.org/2013/10/fergusons-formula

8.   Ayoko, A. B. (2015). Workplace conflict and willingness to cooperate.
     The importance of apology and Forgiveness. *International Journal
     of Conflict Management, 27*(2), 172-198. https://doi.org/10.1108/
     IJCMA-12-2014-0092

9.   Basford, T.E., Offermann, L.R. & Behrend, T.S. (2014). Please Accept My
     Sincerest Apologies: Examining Follower Reactions to Leader Apology.
     Journal of Business Ethics, 119(1), 99–117. https://doi.org/10.1007/
     s10551-012-1613-y

10. Tucker, S., Turner, N., Barling, J., Reid, E. M., & Elving, C. (2006). Apologies and Transformational Leadership. *Journal of Business Ethics,* 63(1), Article No. 195. https://doi.org/10.1007/s10551-005-3571-0

11. Frederickson, B. (2009). *Positivity.* New York: Three Rivers Press.

12. Losada, M., & Heaphy, E. (2004). The Role of Positivity and Connectivity in the Performance of Business Teams: A Nonlinear Dynamics Model. *American Behavioral Scientist, 47*(6), 740–765. https://doi.org/10.1177/0002764203260208

13. Peters, S. (2012). *The Chimp Paradox.* Vermillion: London.

14. Carl Rogers (2015). *Carl R. Rogers.* Carl Rogers. http://carlrrogers.org/

15. Arghode, V. (2012). Role of Empathy in Instruction. *Global Education Journal, 2012*(3), p128-143.

16. Corlett, S., Ruane, M., & Mavin, S. (2021). Learning (not) to be different: The value of vulnerability in trusted and safe identity work spaces. *Management Learning,* 1-18. https://doi.org/10.1177/1350507621995816

17. Kutlu, A., & Coskun, L. (2014). The Role of Empathy in the Learning Process and Its Fruitful Outcomes: A Comparative Study. *Journal of Educational and Social Research, 4*(2), 203. Retrieved from https://www.richtmann.org/journal/index.php/jesr/article/view/2818

18. Lutz, A (2018, September). *The Importance of Being Vulnerable in the Classroom.* EdgeNuity. https://blog.edgenuity.com/the-importance-of-being-vulnerable-in-the-classroom/

19. Ratka A. (2018). Empathy and the Development of Affective Skills. *American Journal of Pharmaceutical Education, 82*(10), 7192. https://doi.org/10.5688/ajpe7192

20. Toiviainen, H., Kersh, N., & Hyytiä, J. (2019). Understanding vulnerability and encouraging young adults to become active citizens through education: the role of adult education professionals. *Journal of Adult and Continuing Education, 25*(1), 45–64. https://doi.org/10.1177/1477971419826116

21. Edmondson, A. (2010). *Teaming: How Organizations Learn, Innovate, and Compete in the Knowledge Economy.* Jossey Bass: San Francisco, CA.

22. Schein, E. H. (1999). *Process Consultation Revisited: Building the Helping Relationship.* New York: Addison-Wesley Publishing Company, Inc.

23. Goodman, N. (2012, November). *James Dyson on Using Failure to Drive Success.* Entrepreneur Europe. https://www.entrepreneur.com/article/224855

Chapter 10
How to Get Strong

1. Elberse, A. & Ferguson, A. (Sir) (2013, October). Ferguson's Formula. *Harvard Business Review, 91*(10), 116–125. https://www.hbs.edu/faculty/Pages/item.aspx?num=45601

2. Love, D. (2011, October). *16 Examples Of Steve Jobs Being A Huge Jerk.* Business Insider. https://www.businessinsider.com/steve-jobs-jerk-2011-10?r=US&IR=T

3. Kantor, J., and Streitfeld, D. (2018, August). *Inside Amazon: Wrestling Big Ideas in a Bruising Workplace.* New York Times. https://www.nytimes.com/2015/08/16/technology/inside-amazon-wrestling-big-ideas-in-a-bruising-workplace.html

4. Adkin, D. (2019). *The Evolution of Elon Musk: The Good, The Bad, and the Ugly.* Adalo. https://www.adalo.com/posts/the-evolution-of-elon-musk-the-good-the-bad-and-the-ugly

5. Walker, S. (2018). *The Captain Class: The Hidden Force Behind the World's Greatest Teams.* Ebury Press.

6. Janis, I. L. 1972. *Victims of Groupthink.* Houghton Mifflin, Boston.

7. Janis, I. L. 1982. *Groupthink.* Houghton-Mifflin, Boston.

8. Barsade, S. G., Coutifaris, C. G., & Pillemer, J. (2018). Emotional contagion in organizational life. *Research in Organizational Behavior, 38*(1), 137-151. https://doi.org/10.1016/j.riob.2018.11.005

9. Dasborough, M. T., Ashkanasy, N. M., Tee, E. Y., & Herman, H. M. (2009). What goes around comes around: How meso-level negative emotional contagion can ultimately determine organizational attitudes toward leaders. *The Leadership Quarterly, 20*(4), 571-585. https://doi.org/10.1016/j.leaqua.2009.04.009

10. Demerouti, E., Xanthopoulou, D., & Bakker, A. B. (2018). How do cynical employees serve their customers? A multi-method study. *European Journal of Work and Organizational Psychology, 27*(1), 16-27. https://doi.org/10.1080/1359432X.2017.1358165

11. Farahnak, L. R., Ehrhart, M. G., Torres, E. M., & Aarons, G. A. (2020). The influence of transformational leadership and leader attitudes on subordinate attitudes and implementation success. *Journal of Leadership & Organizational Studies, 27*(1), 98-111. https://doi.org/10.1177/1548051818824529

12. Oreg, S., Bartunek, J. M., Lee, G., & Do, B. (2018). An affect-based model of recipients' responses to organizational change events. *Academy of Management Review, 43*(1), 65-86. https://doi.org/10.5465/amr.2014.0335

13. Riddell, R. V., & Røisland, M. T. (2017). *Change Readiness Factors influencing employees' readiness for change within an organization: A systematic review* [Master's thesis, University of Agder]. http://hdl.handle.net/11250/2452955

14. Sharma, D., & Pareek, S. (2019). Organizational Commitment, Job Embeddedness and Turnover Intention: A Comparative Study on Bank Employees. *Journal of the Gujarat Research Society, 21*(16), 430-440. Available at: http://gujaratresearchsociety.in/index.php/JGRS/article/view/1937

15. van Dam, K. (2018). Feelings about change: The role of emotions and emotion regulation for employee adaptation to organizational change. In M. Vakola and P. Petrou (Eds.), *Organizational change: Psychological effects and strategies for coping* (pp. 67-77). London: Routledge.

16. van Kleef, G. A., Heerdink, M. W., & Homan, A. C. (2017). Emotional influence in groups: the dynamic nexus of affect, cognition, and behavior. Current Opinion in Psychology, 17(1), 156-161. https://doi.org/10.1016/j.copsyc.2017.07.017

17. Zhong, J., Zhang, L., Li, P., & Zhang, D. Z. (2019). Can leader humility enhance employee wellbeing? The mediating role of employee humility. Leadership & Organization Development Journal, 41(1), 19–36. https://doi.org/10.1108/LODJ-03-2019-0124

18. Baron, R.A. and Tang, J. (2011). The role of entrepreneurs in firm-level innovation: joint effects of positive affect, creativity, and environmental dynamism. *Journal of Business Venturing, 26*(1), 49-60 http://dx.doi.org/10.1016/j.jbusvent.2009.06.002

19. Bradley, B. H., Anderson, H. J., Baur, J. E., & Klotz, A. C. (2015). When conflict helps: Integrating evidence for beneficial conflict in groups and teams under three perspectives. *Group Dynamics: Theory, Research, and Practice, 19*(4), 243–272. https://doi.org/10.1037/gdn0000033

20. Breuer, C., Hüffmeier, J., Hibben, F., & Hertel, G. (2020). Trust in teams: A taxonomy of perceived trustworthiness factors and risk-taking behaviors in face-to-face and virtual teams. *Human Relations, 73*(1) 3–34. https://doi.org/10.1177/0018726718818721

21. O'Neill, T. A., Hoffart, G. C., McLarnon, M. M. J. W., Woodley, H. J., Eggermont, M., Rosehart, W., & Brennan, R. (2017). Constructive

Controversy and Reflexivity Training Promotes Effective Conflict Profiles and Team Functioning in Student Learning Teams. *Academy of Management Learning & Education, 16*(2), 257–276. https://doi. org/10.5465/amle.2015.0183

22. Schepers, J. J., Nijssen, E. J., & van der Heijden, G. A. (2016). Innovation in the frontline: Exploring the relationship between role conflict, ideas for improvement, and employee service performance. *International Journal of Research in Marketing, 33*(4), 797-817. https://doi.org/10.1016/j. ijresmar.2016.01.004

23. Stojčić, N., Hashi, I., & Orlić, E. (2018). Creativity, innovation effectiveness and productive efficiency in the UK. *European Journal of Innovation Management, 21*(4), 564-580. https://doi.org/10.1108/EJIM-11-2017-0166

Chapter 11

The Third Rail

1. Hackman, J.R., & Wageman, R. (2004). When And How Team Leaders Matter. *Research in Organizational Behavior, 26*(1), 37-74. https://doi. org/10.1016/S0191-3085(04)26002-6

2. Breuer, C., Hüffmeier, J., Hibben, F., & Hertel, G. (2020).Trust in teams: A taxonomy of perceived trustworthiness factors and risk-taking behaviors in face-to-face and virtual teams. *Human Relations, 73*(1) 3–34. https://doi. org/10.1177/0018726718818721

3. Doz, Y. (2020). Fostering strategic agility: How individual executives and human resource practices contribute. *Human Resource Management Review, 30*(1), Article No. 100693 https://doi.org/10.1016/j. hrmr.2019.100693

4. Serrat O. (2017) *Building Trust in the Workplace.* In: Knowledge Solutions. Springer, Singapore. https://doi.org/10.1007/978-981-10-0983-9_69

5. van Bunderen, L., Greer, L. L., & van Knippenberg, D. (2018). When Inter-team Conflict Spirals into Intra-team Power Struggles: The Pivotal Role of Team Power Structures. *Academy of Management Journal, 61*(3), 1100–1130. https://doi.org/10.5465/amj.2016.0182

6. Bass, B., & Avolio, B. (1993). Transformational Leadership and Organizational Culture. *International Journal of Public Administration, 17*(3-4), 112-121. https://doi.org/10.1080/01900699408524907

7.   Bass, B.M, and Avolio, B.J. (1997) *Full Range leadership development: Manual for the Multifactor Leadership Questionnaire*. Palo Alto, USA: Mind Garden Inc

8.   Bass, B.M. (1985). *Leadership and performance beyond expectation*. New York: Free Press

9.   Bass, B.M. (1990). From transactional to transformational leadership: Learning to share the vision. *Organizational Dynamics, 18*(3), 19-31. https://doi.org/10.1016/0090-2616(90)90061-S

10.   Avolio, B. J. (2011). Full range leadership development. SAGE Publications, Inc., https://www.doi.org/10.4135/9781483349107

Chapter 12

It's Our Destiny

1.   Juggins, S. & Stainthorpe, R. (2017). *The History Makers—How Team GB Stormed to a First Ever Gold in Women's Hockey*. Worthing, Sussex: Pitch Publishing Ltd.

2.   McRae, D. (2016, November) *Alex Danson: 'We won Olympic gold because we were a team, there were no superstars.'* Guardian Online. https://www.theguardian.com/sport/2016/nov/28/alex-danson-team-gb-hockey-olympic-gold-rio-2016

Mango Publishing, established in 2014, publishes an eclectic list of books by diverse authors—both new and established voices—on topics ranging from business, personal growth, women's empowerment, LGBTQ studies, health, and spirituality to history, popular culture, time management, decluttering, lifestyle, mental wellness, aging, and sustainable living. We were recently named 2019 *and* 2020's #1 fastest-growing independent publisher by *Publishers Weekly*. Our success is driven by our main goal, which is to publish high-quality books that will entertain readers as well as make a positive difference in their lives.

Our readers are our most important resource; we value your input, suggestions, and ideas. We'd love to hear from you—after all, we are publishing books for you!

Please stay in touch with us and follow us at:
Facebook: Mango Publishing
Twitter: @MangoPublishing
Instagram: @MangoPublishing
LinkedIn: Mango Publishing
Pinterest: Mango Publishing
Newsletter: mangopublishinggroup.com/newsletter

Join us on Mango's journey to reinvent publishing, one book at a time.